THE

SANKHYA KARIKA

OR

MEMORIAL VERSES ON THE SANKHYA PHILOSOPHY

THE

SANKHYA KARIKA

OR

MEMORIAL VERSES ON THE SANKHYA PHILOSOPHY,

BY

ISWARA KRISHNA;

TRANSLATED FROM THE SANSCRIT

BY

HENRY THOMAS COLEBROOKE, ESQ.

ALSO

THE BHASHYA OR COMMENTARY OF

GAURAPADA;

TRANSLATED BY

HORACE HAYMAN WILSON, M.A. F.R.S.

GYAN

Published by

Gyan Publishing House
5, Ansari Road
Daryaganj, New Delhi-110002
Phone: 011-47034999, 9811692060
E-mail: books@gyanbooks.com

Distribution Network
gyanbooks.com
India, USA, Canada, UK, Australia

ISBN: 978-81-212-7075-5 (PB)
First Published, 1837

2nd Impression 2024

Printed at: Gyan Press, Delhi.

THE SANKHYA KARIKA OR MEMORIAL VERSES ON THE SANKHYA PHILOSOPHY

Author: ISWARA KRISHNA, Translators: HENRY THOMAS COLEBROOKE, HORACE HAYMAN WILSON

THE

SÁNKHYA KÁRIKÁ,

OR

MEMORIAL VERSES ON THE SÁNKHYA PHILOSOPHY,

BY

ÍSWARA KRISHNA;

TRANSLATED FROM THE SANSCRIT

BY

HENRY THOMAS COLEBROOKE, ESQ.

ALSO

THE BHÁSHYA OR COMMENTARY OF GAURAPÁDA;

TRANSLATED BY AN ORIGINAL COMMENT,

BY

HORACE HAYMAN WILSON, M.A. F.R.S.

MEMBER OF THE ROYAL ASIATIC SOCIETY, AND OF THE ASIATIC SOCIETIES OF PARIS AND CALCUTTA, &c. &c.;

AND BODEN PROFESSOR OF SANSCRIT IN THE UNIVERSITY OF OXFORD.

OXFORD,

PRINTED FOR THE ORIENTAL TRANSLATION FUND OF GREAT BRITAIN AND IRELAND,

BY S. COLLINGWOOD, PRINTER TO THE UNIVERSITY.

PUBLISHED AND SOLD BY A. J. VALPY, A. M., LONDON.

1837.

TO

SIR GRAVES CHAMNEY HAUGHTON, M.A. F.R.S.

AS TO ONE

WHO WAS THE FRIEND AND ADMIRER

OF THE LATE

HENRY THOMAS COLEBROOKE;

WHO IS QUALIFIED,

BY HIS CONVERSANCY WITH THE SANSCRIT LANGUAGE

AND METAPHYSICAL INQUIRIES,

TO APPRECIATE THE CORRECTNESS WITH WHICH

THE PHILOSOPHY OF THE HINDUS

IS REPRESENTED IN THE FOLLOWING PAGES;

AND

WHO HAS FOR MANY YEARS BEEN UNITED WITH THEIR AUTHOR

IN STUDIES, SENTIMENTS, AND FRIENDSHIP;

THE PRESENT WORK IS INSCRIBED,

AS A PUBLIC TESTIMONY OF ESTEEM AND REGARD,

BY

HORACE HAYMAN WILSON.

PREFACE.

ONE of the works earliest announced for publication by the Oriental Translation Fund Committee was the *Sánkhya Káriká*, a text book of that system of Hindu philosophy to which the term *Sánkhya* is applied, and which had been translated from Sanscrit into English by that eminent Sanscrit scholar the late Henry Thomas Colebrooke. The accession of the lingering illness which finally terminated in his decease prevented Mr. Colebrooke from conducting his work through the press, and from adding to the translation those explanations and illustrations which the text required, and which he was most competent to supply. Upon my return to England from India, therefore, in the beginning of 1833, I found that no progress had been made in the publication, and that the Translation of the text alone was in the possession of the Committee.

Being desirous of redeeming the pledge which they had publicly given, and of accomplishing the purpose which they had announced, the Committee thought it desirable that the Translation, in its then existing form, should be printed; and conceived that, as its extent was insufficient to constitute a separate work, it would be advisable to print it in the Transactions of the Royal Asiatic Society. With this view the manuscript was placed in my hands, that I should render such assistance as I might be able to afford in the correction of the press.

Conceiving that the appearance of the Translation in the pages of the Transactions would be equally incompatible with the views of the Translator and the original intention of the Committee, I ventured to recommend that their purpose should be adhered to, and that the Translation should be printed, as at first designed, as a separate work; offering at the same time to supply such annotations as the text might seem to require, to be rendered sufficiently intelligible and explicit. The Committee approved of the suggestion, and Mr. Colebrooke's concurrence was readily obtained.

In the meantime, in the interval that had elapsed since the work was announced, other translations of the *Sánkhya Káriká* had appeared. The Sanscrit text, and a version of it in Latin by Professor Lassen, had been printed at Bonn *; and the text in Roman characters, with a French translation, had been published at Paris by Mons. Pauthier †. Many of the verses of the translation had been also embodied in Mr. Colebrooke's general view of the Sánkhya philosophy; and it appeared to me expedient, therefore, to make some such addition to the work as should give it at least more novelty than it was otherwise likely to possess. It seemed also to be a favourable occasion for offering to Sanscrit students an exemplification of the mode in which philosophical works are illustrated by native commentators; and I accordingly procured the consent of the Translation Committee to print, not only the text and translation of the *Sánkhya Káriká*, but the text and a translation of the oldest, and perhaps the best, commentary upon the *Káriká*, the *Bháshya* of Gaurapáda. In order likewise to fulfil the object of attempting to render the doctrines of both text and comment as clear and explicit as it was in my power to represent them, I further added to the translation of the *Bháshya* a comment of my own, deriving my elucidations however, to a very great extent, from the works of native scholiasts, and giving the original passages at the foot of the page.

The scholia which have been used for this purpose are the

* Gymnosophista: sive Indicæ Philosophiæ documenta. Vol. I. Iswara Crishnæ Sankhya-Caricam tenens. Bonnæ ad Rhenum, 1832.

† Essais sur la Philosophie des Hindous, traduits de l'Anglais, et augmentés de textes Sanskrits, &c.; par G. Pauthier. Paris, 1833.

Sánkhya Tatwa Kaumudí of VÁCHESPATI MISRA, and the *Sánkhya Chandriká* of NÁRÁYÁNA TÍRTHA. The *Sánkhya Kaumudí* of RÁMA KRISHNA has been also consulted, but it is almost word for word the same as the *S. Chandriká*, and is therefore in most instances superfluous. I have occasionally referred to the *Sánkhya Sára*, a separate tract on the doctrines of this school by VIJNÁNA BHIKSHU; but another work by the same scholiast, the *Sánkhya Pravachana Bháshya*, a commentary on the *Sútras* or aphorisms of KAPILA, the first teacher of the Sánkhya, according to tradition, has been of particular service, and will be found often cited. Copies of these different commentaries, as well as of the text, exist in the library of the East India Company, and the *Sánkhya Pravachana Bháshya* was printed at Serampore in 1821. I have, however, followed a manuscript copy, as I did not obtain a copy of the printed work until my translation was finished.

There was little need of the labour of collation, after the very accurate text of Professor Lassen. I have not failed, however, to compare the reading of the different copies, and have noticed a few of the variations: none of them are of any great importance. Where collation was most wanted, it was unfortunately not practicable, there being but a single copy of the *Bháshya* of GAURAPÁDA in my possession. The manuscript was luckily tolerably correct, but it was doubtful in some places, and clearly faulty in others; and I may not have always succeeded in rightly correcting, or in accurately interpreting it. With regard to typographical errors in the present edition of text and comment, I trust they will not be found very inexcusable, especially when it is known that the work was for the greater part necessarily carried on at a distance from me, during my absence in London, and that it is the first publication in Sanscrit printed at the Press of the University of Oxford.

Not having made the Sánkhya philosophy a subject of study in India, I have executed my task without the advantage of previous preparation. The subject indeed is but little cultivated by the Pandits, and during the whole of my intercourse with learned natives I met with but one Brahman who professed to be acquainted with the writings of this school. Opportunity was wanting to benefit by his instructions, and I cannot therefore venture to claim exemption from those liabilities to error to which the unassisted study of Sanscrit literature in Europe is exposed, especially when directed to topics sufficiently obscure and difficult in themselves, and rendered still more so by the sententious and elliptical style in which they are treated. It is the fashion with some of the most distinguished Sanscrit scholars on the continent to speak slightingly of native scholiasts and Pandits, but this is the consequence of measuring their merits by a wrong scale, and censuring them for venial inaccuracies which often proceed from too entire a familiarity with their subject. In all studies which native scholars professedly pursue, they have the advantage of traditional tuition, of a course of instruction, coming down, through successive generations, from the founder of a system, or the author of a book, to the individual who explains the one or illustrates the other, and from whose interpretation we may therefore reasonably expect to learn what it was originally meant to teach. There are also in all philosophical works, especially, brief hints and conventional allusions, which without such aid it is not possible to decipher, and for the proper understanding of which a native explanation is indispensable. Without therefore in the least degree undervaluing European industry and ability, I cannot consent to hold in less esteem the attainments of my former masters and friends, the Sanscrit learning of learned Brahmans.

The translations to which I have above referred are highly creditable to the translators. That of Professor Lassen in particular is of great merit and accuracy, and is illustrated by annotations, in which he has successfully cleared up many of the obscurities of the original text. I have taken the plan of his notes as in some degree the model of my comment; and although I do not always concur in his interpretations or explanations, I have found them always entitled to attention and respect. In one or two instances, and especially in regard to the first stanza, where I have most widely differed from him, I have sought rather to vindicate the accuracy of Mr. Colebrooke, than to impugn that of Professor Lassen. Variety of interpretation in such a case as that of a difficult work, on an abstruse subject, is no more than may be expected from different interpreters; and occasional misapprehension implies no want of either competency or care.

In the course of my attempts to elucidate the text, I have in a few instances pointed out what seemed to me to offer remarkable coincidences with the doctrines of classical philosophers. That an intimate connection exists between the metaphysical systems of the Hindus and those of the Greeks is generally admitted, although its extent has not yet been fully made out. We are scarcely yet indeed in possession of the means of instituting an accurate comparison, as the text books of the Hindus have not been printed or translated, and general dissertations, however comprehensive or profound, are insufficient for the purpose. The present publication will go some way, perhaps, towards supplying the deficiency, and may afford, as far as it extends, authentic materials for the use of those better qualified classical scholars who may be curious to ascertain in what degree the speculations of Plato and Aristotle correspond with those of Kapila and Gautama, or how far the teachers of one school may have been indebted to those of another. That the Hindus derived any of their philosophical ideas from the Greeks seems very improbable; and if there is any borrowing in the case, the latter were most probably indebted to the former. It has been objected to this conjecture, that the total want of chronology in Hindu writings renders it impossible to pronounce upon their date, and that it is probable that many works regarded as ancient are really very modern, as they may have been composed long after the æra of Christianity; the notions which they inculcate being in fact acquired from the Greeks of Alexandria, through the intercourse between India and Egypt. That this intercourse may have exercised a mutual influence upon some parts of the philosophy of both countries in the first ages of Christianity—that resemblances, respectively interchanged, may be detected in the notions of the new Platonists or Platonic Christians and of the more modern Védantis, or in the eclectic pantheism of the Pauraniks—is not impossible; but the Greek philosophy of that period can scarcely have suggested the severer abstractions of the Sánkhya, and we must go back to a remoter age for the origin of the dogmas of Kapila. In truth, the more remote the period, the closer the affinity that seems to prevail; and as far as we are acquainted with the tenets of the Ionic and Italic schools, it is with them that Hindu philosophy, unalloyed with pantheism, seems to claim kindred, rather than with the mysticism of Plato, or the subtleties of Aristotle. The metempsychosis itself is an important feature in this similitude: for this belief is not to be looked upon as a mere popular superstition; it is the main principle of all Hindu metaphysics; it is the foundation of all Hindu philosophy. The great object of their philosophical research in every system, Brahmanical or Buddhist, is the discovery of the means of putting a stop to further transmigration; the discontinuance of corporeal being; the liberation of soul from body. That such was the leading principle of the philosophy of Pythagoras we learn from ancient testimony, and it essentially influences the speculations of Plato. Concurrence in this principle involves agreement in all the most important deductions from it, and establishes, if not a mutual interchange, at least a common origin, for much of the oldest philosophy of the Greeks and the Hindus. This is a subject, however, to which I can here but thus briefly allude, and to which I would rather invite the attention of some of the eminent scholars of whom the University of Oxford has reason to be proud, than impair its interest by my own less competent attempts at its elucidation.

The whole scope and leading tenets of the Sánkhya philosophy have been most accurately described by the late Mr. Colebrooke, in the Transactions of the Royal Asiatic Society, from various original authorities, including that now published, the *Káriká*, or rather *Kárikás*, of the Sánkhya system; the term designating a collection of memorial verses, of apothegmatical stanzas, in which the chief tenets of the school are textually and dogmatically stated. The Sánkhya philosophy is so termed, as Mr. Colebrooke has mentioned, because it observes precision of reckoning in the enumeration of its principles, *Sánkhya* being understood to signify 'numeral,' agreeably to the usual acceptation of *Sankhyá*, 'number;' "and hence its analogy to the Pythagorean philosophy has been presumed." The term is also explained, however, as Mr. Colebrooke proceeds to mention, to denote the result of deliberation or judgment, such being one sense of the word *Sankhyá*, from which *Sánkhya* is derived.

Agreeably to the purport of the word *Káriká*, 'a technical or memorial verse,' the following work consists of a series of stanzas systematically arranged, though not always obviously connected; and asserting principles, rather than discussing arguments. The tract opens with an explanation of the object of this and of all philosophy, ascertainment of the means by which the pain of corporeal existence may be finally and absolutely remedied, and the soul freed for ever from body: this is declared alone to be philosophy, or the knowledge of the real nature of all that is, agreeably to the *Sánkhya* enumeration of things. These things, in number twenty-five, are briefly indicated with reference to their relative character, as producing or produced; and the work then pauses to explain the means by which they may be known, or perception, inference, and authority. Reverting then to such of the twenty-five things or principles as are imperceptible, especially to the first material cause, and to soul, logical proofs of their actual existence are adduced, and the points in which they agree or differ with other things, and with each other, are described. We have then an explanation of the three essential qualities of things; purity or goodness; imperfection, foulness, or passion; and indifference, stupidity, or darkness. The existence of a general, imperceptible, unseparated, universal cause, the substance of which all is made, the eternal matter of the Greek cosmogonies, is then argued; and, as a consequence of its existence, that also of a spiritual nature, or soul, is asserted. The properties of soul are then detailed. We have next the twenty-five *Tatwas*, 'categories or principles,' of the Sánkhya philosophy severally described. These all resolve themselves, as may be inferred from what has preceded, into but two, matter and spirit, nature and soul; the rest are all the progeny or products of nature, evolved spontaneously through the necessity of nature's providing for the two purposes of soul, fruition and liberation. These products are, intelligence; egotism or individuality; eleven senses, ten external and one internal, or mind; five rudimental elements, or elements of elements; and five gross or perceptible elements, ether, air, water, fire or light, and earth. The description of these different categories, of their mode and objects of acting, of their modifications, and of their effects, occupies a considerable number of *Kárikás*. We have then a general account of bodily condition of two kinds, subtile and gross; the latter perishing at death, the former accompanying and investing soul through all the migrations to which the various conditions of the intellectual faculty, or virtue and vice, subject it. Those conditions are then detailed at length, and in all their modifications, constituting what is called intellectual creation, or life, consequent upon conduct, originating with the intellect. But, to give effect to these modifications, form, as well as life, is said to be necessary; and hence results personal or bodily creation of various descriptions. Bodily existence, however, is described as confinement and pain, from which soul is anxious to be exempted. Nature is said to labour also for soul's liberation, and to supply the means, in the display which it makes of its products, until soul, fully possessed of their real character and tendency, is represented as casting away all notions of individuality and self, and is no more condemned to bodily incarceration. The work closes with stating that these truths were taught originally by KAPILA to ÁSURI, and by him to PANCHASIKHA, from whom it descended, through repeated generations of disciples, to ÍSWARA KRISHNA, the author of the *Kárikás*. The date of this writer is not known, but Mr. Colebrooke considers GAURAPÁDA, the scholiast on the *Káriká*, to be the same as the preceptor of the celebrated teacher SANKARA ÁCHÁRYA, whom there is reason to place in the eighth century. How long anterior to this the *Kárikás* existed in their present form, we have no means of knowing, but they were avowedly subsequent to other standard compositions of the school, and evidently represent doctrines of high antiquity, doctrines exhibiting profound reflection and subtle reasoning; although, like all the efforts of human intellect to penetrate unaided the mysteries of existence, wholly unavailing, and too often ending, as Cicero complains, in doubt and impiety: "Cogimur dissensione sapientum Dominum nostrum ignorare."

Some excuse is perhaps necessary for having delayed to publish the present work so long after the Committee of the Oriental Translation Fund had sanctioned its publication. The work, as it is now offered to the public, was ready for press in the course of the year following that in which it was undertaken. Being desirous, however, of printing it at Oxford, where the University had liberally resolved to provide its Press with two new founts of Devanagari letters, I was under the necessity of awaiting the completion of the types. As soon as one fount was supplied, the text was printed. It was my wish to have employed the other and smaller fount for the citations which accompany my Comment; but that fount being not yet cast,

I have thought it preferable to incur no further delay. It is scarcely doing justice to types of the size here employed to place them in juxtaposition with characters so much smaller as those of the English alphabet; but looking at them by themselves, in the pages of the text, I think they will be found to wear a more genuinely Oriental aspect than any that have yet been fabricated in Europe.

OXFORD,
July 1, 1837.

SÁNKHYA KÁRIKÁ.

I.

THE inquiry is into the means of precluding the three sorts of pain; for pain is embarrassment: nor is the inquiry superfluous because obvious means of alleviation exist, for absolute and final relief is not thereby accomplished.

BHÁSHYA.

Salutation to that KAPILA by whom the Sánkhya philosophy was compassionately imparted, to serve as a boat for the purpose of crossing the ocean of ignorance in which the world was immersed.

I will declare compendiously the doctrine, for the benefit of students; a short easy work, resting on authority, and establishing certain results.

Three sorts of pain.—The explanation of this *Árya* stanza is as follows;

The divine KAPILA, the son of BRAHMÁ indeed: as it is said, "SANAKA, SANANDANA, and SANÁTANA the third; ÁSURI, KAPILA, BORHU, and PANCHASIKHA: these seven sons of Brahmá were termed great sages." Together with KAPILA were born Virtue, Knowledge, Dispassion, and Power: for he being born, and observing the world plunged in profound darkness by the succeeding series of worldly revolutions, was filled with compassion; and to his kinsman, the Brahman ÁSURI, he communicated a knowledge of the TWENTY-FIVE PRINCIPLES; from which knowledge the destruction of pain proceeds. As it is said; "He who knows the twenty-"five principles, whatever order of life he may have entered, and whether "he wear braided hair, a top-knot only, or be shaven, he is liberated "(from existence): of this there is no doubt."

The inquiry is in consequence of the *embarrassment* of the three sorts of pain. In this place the three sorts of pain are, 1. (*ádhyátmika*) natural and inseparable; 2. (*ádhibhautika*) natural and extrinsic; and 3. (*ádhidaivika*) non-natural or superhuman. The first is of two kinds, corporeal and mental: corporeal is flux, fever, or the like, arising from disorder of the wind, bile, or phlegm: mental is privation of what is liked, approximation of what is disliked. Extrinsic but natural pain is fourfold, according to the aggregation of elementary matter whence it originates; that is, it is produced by any created beings, whether viviparous, oviparous, generated by heat and moisture, or springing from the soil; or in short, by men, beasts, tame or wild birds, reptiles, gnats, musquitoes, lice, bugs, fish, alligators, sharks, trees, stones, &c. The third kind of pain may be called superhuman, *daivika* meaning either divine or atmospheric: in the latter case it means pain which proceeds from cold, heat, wind, rain, thunderbolts, and the like.

Where then, or into what, is inquiry, in consequence of the embarrassment of the three kinds of pain, to be made? *Into the means of precluding them.* This is the inquiry. *Nor is the inquiry superfluous.* That is; if this inquiry be (regarded as) superfluous, the means of precluding the three sorts of pain being obvious (seen); as for example; the internal means of alleviating the two inseparable kinds of pain are obvious, through the application of medical science, as by pungent, bitter, and astringent decoctions, or through the removal of those objects that are disliked, and accession of those that are liked; so the obvious obstruction of pain from natural causes is protection and the like; and these means being obvious, any (farther) inquiry is superfluous: if you think in this manner, it is not so; for *absolute*, certain, *final*, permanent, obstruction (of pain) is not (to be effected) by obvious means. Therefore inquiry is to be made by the wise elsewhere, or into means of prevention which are absolute and final.

COMMENT.

The first verse of the *Káriká* proposes the subject of the work, and not only of that, but of the system to which it belongs, and of every philosophical system studied by the Hindus; the common end of which is, ascertainment of the means by which perpetual exemption from the metempsychosis, or from the necessity of repeated births, may be attained: for life is uniformly regarded by the Hindus as a condition of pain and suffering, as a state of bondage and evil; escape from which finally and for ever is a consummation devoutly to be wished.

The liberation thus proposed as the object of rational existence cannot be attained as long as man is subject to the ordinary infirmities of his nature, and the accidents of his condition: and the primary object of philosophical inquiry therefore is, the means by which the imperfections flesh is heir to may be obviated or removed. As preparatory then to their right determination, it is first shewn in the text what means are not conducive to this end; such, namely, as obvious but temporary expedients, whether physical or moral.

Of this introductory stanza Professor Lassen, in the first number of his *Gymnosophista*, containing the translation of the *Káriká*, has given a version differing in some respects from Mr. Colebrooke's. He thus renders it: "E tergeminorum dolorum impetu oritur desiderium cognoscendæ rationis, qua ii depellantur. Quod cognoscendi desiderium licet in visibilibus rebus infructuose versetur, non est (infructuosum) propter absentiam absoluti, et omni ævo superstitis remedii."

In the first member of this sentence, the translation of *abhighára* by 'impetus' is irreconcilable with the context. The sense required by the doctrine laid down is 'impediment, embarrassment, the prevention of liberation by worldly cares and sufferings.' So the same word *abhighátaka* is immediately used to mean 'preventing, removing,' 'depellens.' Professor Lassen's text, it is true, reads *apaghátaka*, but this is not the reading followed by Mr. Colebrooke, nor that of the citation of the text given in the *S. Bháshya* or *S. Kaumudí*; it is that of the *S. Tatwa Kaumudí* and *S. Chandriká*, and although in itself unobjectionable, yet is not a necessary nor preferable variation. At any rate there can be no question that the word *abhighάta* may be used in the sense of 'depellere,' and that sense therefore equally attaches to it in the prior member of the hemistich. So in the *Bháshya* of Gaurapáda we have *ádhibhautikasya rakshádina abhighátah;* 'The prevention of extrinsic pain is by protection and the like.' It would not be possible here to render *abhigháta* by 'impetus.' By VÁCHESPATI the term *abhigháta* is defined 'the confinement of the sentient faculty (explained to mean here 'life'), through the impediment opposed by threefold distress abiding in spirit*.' NÁRÁYANA interprets it more concisely *asahya sambandha*†, 'intolerable restraint.' 'Embarrassment' therefore sufficiently well expresses the purport of these definitions, or the obstructions offered by worldly sufferings to the spirit anxious to be free.

This variation, however, is of no great consequence: the more important difference is in the second portion of the stanza; and as Professor Lassen has deviated advisedly from Mr. Colebrooke, it is necessary to examine the passage more in detail. The following are his reasons for the version he has made:

"Hæc posterioris versus (*drishté* etc.) interpretatio, sicuti scholiastarum suffragiis probatur, a grammatica postulatur. Quod ideo moneo, ne leviter rationem, a Colebrookio, V. summo, in hoc versu enarrando initam deseruisse censear. Is enim: 'nor is the inquiry superfluous, because obvious means of alleviation exist: for absolute and final relief is not thereby accomplished.' Sed vereor, ne vir summus constructionem particulæ *chét* sententiam claudentis et a negatione exceptæ male intellexerit. De qua re dixi ad Hitop. procem. d. 28. Ex interpret. Colebrook. construendum esset: *drishté* sc. *sati* (i. e. *yadyapi drishtam vidya té*) *sá* (*jijnásá*) *apárthá na ékánt—abhávát*‡. Sed ut omittam, particulæ *chét* nullum omnino relinqui locum in sententia, *na* inopportuno versus loco collocatum esse, non potes quin concedas. Male omnino se habet tota sententia et claudicat. Equidem construo: *drishté sá* (*jijnásá*) *apárthá* (*bhavati*) *chét* (*tathápi*) *na* (*apárthá bhavati*) *ékánta—abhávát*‖. Prorsus similiter dicitur *nábhávát* infr. v. 8. Ablativum igitur *ekántyatyantoh*

---

* दुःखत्रयेणांतःकरणवर्त्तिना प्रतिकूलतया चेतनाशक्तेरभिसंबन्धोऽभिघातः। † असह्यसंबन्धः। ‡ दृष्टे सति (यद्यपि दृष्टं विद्यते) सा (जिज्ञासा) अपार्था न एका—भावात्। ‖ दृष्टे सा (जिज्ञासा) अपार्था (भवति) चेत् (तथाऽपि) न (अपार्था भवति) एकान्त—भावात्।

abhávát, non ad *drishté* refero cum Colebrookio, sed ad negationem, quæ cum supplementis suis apodosin constituit. Nam quæ post *chénna* sequuntur verba, ad apodosin pertinere semper observavi. Quam grammatica postulare videtur, patitur præterea loci tenor enarrationem, imo melior evadit sententia. Ad *drishté* enim relatis istis verbis, id tantum dicitur, rerum visibilium cognitione non attingi posse philosophiæ finem, liberationem absolutam et perpetuam a doloribus; mea posita enarratione non id tantum docetur, sed additur etiam hoc: finem istum posse attingi, licet alio cognitionis genere. Tres omnino positiones altero hemistichii versu continentur: philosophiæ (id enim valet *gignásá*, i. e. cognitionis desiderium) finem esse emancipationem a doloribus certam et omne tempus transgredientem; deinde ad eum non perveniri ea via quæ primum initur, quia obvia quasi sit, i. e. remediorum a sensibilibus rebus petitorum ope; denique ea remedia cognoscendi desiderium posse expleri. Sed aliter atque Colebrookius hasce sententias inter se conjungit noster, et per conditionem effert, quod ille per negationem enuntiat."

In this view of the meaning of the verse, there is a refinement that does not belong to it, and which is not Indian: arguments are often elliptically and obscurely stated in Sanscrit dialectics, but one position at a time is usually sufficient for even Brahmanical subtlety. The only position here advanced is, that the cure of worldly evil is not to be effected by such remedies as are of obvious and ordinary application, as they can only afford temporary relief. Death itself is no exemption from calamity, if it involves the obligation of being born again.

The version proposed by Professor Lassen rests upon his notion of the grammatical force of the expression *chénna* or *chét*, 'if,' *na*, 'not:' the former he would refer to the prior member of the sentence, the latter to the subsequent expressions. But this division of the compound is not that which is most usual in argumentative writings. The phrase is an elliptical negation of a preceding assertion, *chét* referring to what has been said, implying, 'if you assert or believe this;' and *na* meeting it with a *negatur*, 'it is not so:' then follows the reason or argument of the denial. Thus in the *Muktávalí:* 'But why should not Darkness be called a tenth *thing*, for it is apprehended by perception? If this be said, it is not so (*iti chén-na*); for it is the consequence of the non-existence of absolute light, and it would be illogical to enumerate it amongst things*.' So in the *Nyáya Sútra Vritti:* 'If by a disturbance in the assembly there be no subsequent speech, and through the want of a reply there be defeat; if this be urged, it is not so (*iti chén-na*), because there has been no opportunity for an answer †.' Again in the *Sánkhya Pravachana Bháshya.* Sútra:—'If it be said that Prakriti is the cause of bondage, it is not so, from its dependent state‡.' Comment:—'But bondage may be occasioned by Prakriti. If this be asserted, it is not so. Why? Because in the relation of bondage, Prakriti is dependent upon conjunction, as will be explained in the following precept ‖.' Also in the *Vedánta Sára Vivriti:* 'If in consequence of such texts of the Védas as "let sacrifice be performed as long as life endures" their performance is indispensable, and constant and occasional rites must be celebrated by those engaged in the attainment of true knowledge; and if, on the other hand, the attainment of true knowledge is distinct from the observance of ceremonies; then a double duty is incumbent on those wishing to eschew the world. If this be asserted, it is not so (*iti chén-na*), from the compatibility of severalty with union, as in the case of articles of khayar or other wood §:' that is, where there are several obligations, that which is most essential

---

* ननु दशमं द्रव्यं तमः कुतो नोक्तं तद्धि प्रत्यक्षेण गृह्यत इति चेन्न आवश्यकतेजोऽभावेनोपपत्तौ द्रव्यान्तरकल्पनाया अन्याय्यत्वात्। † सभाक्षोभादिना चेदननुभाषणमेव उत्तराप्रतिपत्त्या चेदप्रतिभेति चेन्न उत्तरावसराभावात्। ‡ प्रकृतिनिबन्धाच्चेन्न तस्या अपि पारतंत्र्यं। ‖ ननु प्रकृतिनिमित्ताद्बन्धो भवत्विति चेन्न यतस्तस्या अपि बन्धकत्वे संयोगपारतंत्र्यमुत्तरसूत्रे वक्ष्यमाणमस्ति। § ननु यज्ञादीनां यावज्जीवं वाक्येनावश्यकर्त्तव्यतया प्राप्तानां विविदिषार्थत्वे नित्यानित्यसंयोगः प्रसज्येत यदि च विविदिषार्थं यज्ञाद्यनुष्ठानमपरमिष्येत ततः संसारव्यावृत्सूनां द्विरनुष्ठानं स्यादितिचेन्न खादिरादिवत् संयोगपृथक्त्वोपपत्तेः।

may be selected from the rest. In the same work we have an analogous form used affirmatively; as, 'But how by the efficacy of knowledge, after the dissipation of ignorance, in regard to the object (of philosophy), can the true nature of the essentially happy (being) be attained? for as he is eternally existent, knowledge is not necessary to establish his existence. If this be asserted, it is true (*iti chét; satyam*). Brahme, one essentially with felicity, is admitted to be eternal, but in a state of ignorance he is not obtained; like a piece of gold which is forgotten (and sought for), whilst it is hanging round the neck*.' Here it would be impossible to refer *satyam* to the succeeding member of the sentence, as the apodosis being separated from it, not only by the sense, but by the particle *api*. Passages of this description might be indefinitely multiplied, but these are sufficient to shew that the construction in the sense adopted by Mr. Colebrooke is common and correct.

Accordingly his version is uniformly supported *scholiastarum suffragiis*. Thus in the *S. Bháshya*, as we have seen, the passage is explained, *drishťé sá apárthá chét évam manyasé na ékánta*, &c.; 'If by reason of there being obvious remedies, *you think* indeed the inquiry superfluous, no (it is not so), from their not being absolute and permanent.' So in the *S. Tatwa Kaumudí*, after stating the objection at length, the commentator adds, *nirákaroti, na iti;* '(the author) refutes it (by saying), no, not so:' *kutah*, 'why?' *ékántatyantatoh abhávát* †. The *S. Chandriká* is to the same effect, or still more explicit: 'There being obvious means, the inquiry is superfluous, the conclusion being otherwise attained: if (this be urged) such is the meaning (of the text), (the author) contradicts it; no, it is not so ‡. This commentator giving the very reading, *drishťé sati*, which Professor Lassen argues Mr. Colebrooke's version would errone-

---

* नन्वविद्यानिवृत्तेर्विद्यासाध्यत्वेन प्रयोजनत्वेऽपि कथं स्वरूपानन्दस्य तथात्वं तस्य नित्यप्राप्तत्वेन विद्यासाध्यत्वाभावादिति चेत् सत्यं नित्यं प्राप्तमप्यानन्दात्मब्रह्मस्वरूपमविद्यावस्थायां विस्मृतकण्ठगतचामीकरवदनवाप्तं भवति ।

† निराकरोति नेति । कुतः । एकान्त—अभावात् ।

‡ दृष्टे सति सा जिज्ञासा अपार्था अन्यथासिद्धास्तीति चेदित्यर्थः । निषेधयति नेति ।

ously require. The remaining scholiast, Ráma Krishna, adopts the comment of the *Chandriká* word for word, and consequently the commentators are unanimous in support of the translation of Mr. Colebrooke.

With respect to the passages referred to by Professor Lassen as establishing the connexion of the negative with the latter member of the sentence, instead of its being absolute, it will be seen at once that they are not at all analogous to the passage in our text. They are declaratory, not argumentative; and the terms following the negative particle are the parts or circumstances of the negative, not the reasons on which it is grounded. Thus in the *Hitopadesa:* 'What will not be, will not be; if it will be, it will not be otherwise *.' So in v. 8. of the *Káriká:* 'The non-apprehension of nature is from its subtlety, not from its nonentity †.' In neither of these is there any reference to a foregone position which must be admitted or denied, nor is the negative followed by the reasons for denial, as is the case in our text.

These considerations are more than sufficient to vindicate, what it was scarcely perhaps necessary to have asserted, Mr. Colebrooke's accuracy; and they are now also somewhat superfluous, as I have been given to understand that Professor Lassen acknowledges the correctness of his interpretation. The commentary of Gaurapáda distinctly shews that nothing more is intended by the text, than the unprofitableness of recourse to visible or worldly expedients for the relief or removal of worldly pain. In subjoining therefore the gloss of Váchespati Misra, with a translation, it is intended rather to illustrate the doctrines of the text, and the mode of their development by native scholiasts, than further to vindicate the correctness of the translation.

'‡But verily the object of the science may not need inquiry, 1. if there be no pain in the world; 2. if there be no desire to avoid it; 3. if there be no means of extirpating it. The impossibility of extirpating it is

---

* यदभावि न तद्भावि भाविचेन्नतदन्यथा । † सौक्ष्म्यात्तदनुपलब्धि नैतदभावात् । ‡ एवं हि न शास्त्रविषयो जिज्ञास्येत यदि दुःखं नाम जगति न स्यात् । सद्वा न जिहासितं । जिहासितं स्याद्वाशक्यं समुच्छेदं ।

twofold; either from the eternity of pain, or from ignorance of the means of alleviation: or, though it be possible to extirpate pain, yet that knowledge which philosophy treats of may not be the means of its removal; or again, there may be some other and more ready means. In the text, however, it is not said that pain does not exist, nor that there is no wish to avoid it. *From the embarrassment of the three kinds of pain.*—A triad of pain, three kinds: they are the *ádhyátmika*, 'natural;' *ádhibhautika*, 'extrinsic;' and *ádhidaivika*, 'superhuman.' The first is of two kinds, bodily and mental: bodily is caused by disorder of the humours, wind, bile, and phlegm; mental is occasioned by desire, wrath, covetousness, fear, envy, grief, and want of discrimination. These various kinds of pain are called inseparable, from their admitting of internal remedies. The pain that requires external remedies is also twofold, *ádhibautika* and *ádhidaivika*. The first has for its cause, man, beasts, deer, birds, reptiles, and inanimate things; the second arises from the evil influence of the planets, or possession by impure spirits (*Yakshas, Rákshasas, Vináyakas,* &c.). These kinds of pain, depending upon the vicissitudes arising from the quality of foulness, are to be experienced by every individual, and cannot be prevented. Through the obstruction occasioned by the three kinds of pain abiding in spirit, arises embarrassment, or

---

अशक्यसमुच्छेदता च द्वेधा । दुःखस्यनित्यत्वाद्वा तदुच्छेदोपायापरिज्ञानाद्वा । शक्यसमुच्छेदत्वेऽपि च शास्त्रविषयस्य ज्ञानस्यानुपायत्वाद्वा । सुकरोपायान्तरस्य सद्भावाद्वा । तत्र न तावद्दुःखं नास्ति नाप्यजिहासितमित्युक्तं । दुःखत्रयाभिघातादिति । दुःखानां त्रयं दुःखत्रयं । तत्खल्वाध्यात्मिकमाधिभौतिकमाधिदैविकं चेति । तत्राध्यात्मिकं द्विविधं शारीरं मानसं च । शारीरं वातपित्तश्लेष्मणां वैषम्यनिमित्तं । मानसं कामक्रोधलोभमोहभयेर्ष्याविषादविशेषदर्शननिबन्धनं । सर्वं चैतदन्तरोपायसाध्यत्वादाध्यात्मिकं दुःखं । बाह्योपायसाध्यं च दुःखं द्वेधा । आधिभौतिकमाधिदैविकं च । तत्राधिभौतिकं मानुषपशुमृगपक्षि सरीसृपस्थावरनिमित्तं । आधिदैविकं यक्षराक्षसविनायकग्रहाद्यावेशनिबन्धनं । तदेतत् प्रत्यात्मवेदनीयं दुःखं रजःपरिणामभेदो

confinement of the sentient faculty. The capability of knowing the impediment occasioned by such pain, is considered the cause of the desire to avoid it; for though pain may not be prevented, yet it is possible to overcome it, as will be subsequently explained. Pain then being generated, inquiry is to be made into the means of its removal. *Tad apaghátaké: tad* refers here to the three kinds of pain, *tad* having the relation dependent upon its being used as a subordinate (relative) term. *The means* (hetu) *of removing.*—These are to be derived from philosophy, not from any other source: this is the position (of the text). To this a doubt is objected; *As there are obvious means, the inquiry is superfluous; if so*—. The sense is this: Be it admitted that there are three kinds of pain; that the rational being wishes to escape from them; that escape is practicable; and that means attainable through philosophy are adequate to their extirpation; still any investigation by those who look into the subject is needless; for there do exist obvious (visible) means of extirpation, which are easily attainable, whilst the knowledge of philosophical principles is difficult of attainment, and to be acquired only by long study, and traditional tuition through many generations. Therefore,

---

न शक्यं प्रत्याख्यातुं । तदनेन दुःखत्रयेणान्तःकरणवर्त्तिना प्रतिकूलतया चेतनाशक्तेरभिसम्बन्धोऽभिघातः । एतावता प्रतिकूलवेदनीयत्वं जिहासाहेतुरुक्तः । यद्यपि न सन्निरुध्यते दुःखं तथापि तदभिभवः शक्यः कर्तुमित्युपरिष्टान्निवेदयिष्यते । तथा चोपपन्नं तदपघातके हेताविति । तस्य दुःखत्रयस्यापघातकस्तदपघातकः । उपसर्ज्जनस्यापि बुध्यानिःकृष्य तदापरमर्शः ॥ तदपघातकश्च हेतुः शास्त्रव्युत्पाद्यो नान्य इत्याशयः ॥ तत्र शंकते । दृष्टे सापार्था चेत् । अयमर्थः । अस्तु दुःखत्रयं जिहासतु तच्चेतनः भवतु च तच्छक्यहानं सहतां च शास्त्रगम्य उपायास्तदुच्छेत्तुं तथाप्यत्र जिज्ञासा प्रेक्षवतामयुक्ता । दृष्टस्यैवोपायस्य तदुच्छेदकस्य सुकरस्य विद्यमानत्वात् । तत्वज्ञानस्य त्वनेकजन्माभ्यासपरम्परायास साध्यतयाऽतिदुष्करत्वात् । तथा च लौकिकानामाभाणकः । अर्के चेन्मधु विन्देत किमर्थं पर्वतं व्रजेत् इष्टस्यार्थस्य

according to the popular saying, "Why should a man who may find honey in the *arkka* flower, go for it to the mountain?" so what wise man will give himself unnecessary trouble, when he has attained the object of his wishes. Hundreds of remedies for bodily affections are indicated by eminent physicians. The pleasures of sense, women, wine, luxuries, unguents, dress, ornaments, are the easy means of obviating mental distress. So in regard to extrinsic pain, easy means of obviating it exist in the skill acquired by acquaintance with moral and political science, and by residing in safe and healthy places, and the like; whilst the employment of gems and charms readily counteracts the evils induced by superhuman agency. This is the objection. (The author) refutes it; *it is not so.* Why? From these means *not being absolute or final. Ekánta* means the certainty of the cessation of pain; *atyanta*, the non-recurrence of pain that has ceased. (In obvious means of relief there is) the non-existence of both these properties; the affix *tasi*, which may be substituted for all inflexions, being here put for the sixth case dual;—as it is said; "From not observing the (invariable) cessation of pain of various kinds, in consequence of the employment of ceremonies, drugs, women, moral and political studies, charms, and the like, their want of certain operation (is predicated); so is their temporary influence, from

---

सम्प्राप्तौ को विद्वान् यत्नमाचरेदिति । सन्ति चोपायाः शतशः शारीरदुःखप्रतीकारायेषत्करा भिषजां वरैरुपदिष्टाः । मानसस्यापि तापस्य प्रतीकाराय मनोज्ञस्त्रीपानभोजनविलेपनवस्त्रालङ्कारादिविषयसम्प्राप्तिरुपाय ईषत्करः । एवमाधिभौतिकस्यापि दुःखस्य नीतिशास्त्राभ्यासकुशलतानिरत्ययस्थानाध्यासनादिः प्रतीकारहेतुरीषत्करः । तथाधिदैविकस्य दुःखस्य मणिमन्त्राद्युपयोगः सुकरः प्रतीकारोपाय इति । निराकरोति । नेति । कुतः । एकान्तात्यन्ततोऽभावात् । एकान्तो दुःखनिवृत्तेरवश्यं भावः । अत्यन्तो दुःखस्यनिवृत्तस्य पुनरनुत्पादः । तयोरेकान्तात्यन्तयोरभावात् । एकान्तात्यन्ततोऽभाव इति षष्ठी द्विवचनस्थाने सार्व्वविभक्तिकस्तसि । एतदुक्तं भवति । यथा विधिरसायनकामिनी नीतिशास्त्राभ्यासमन्त्राद्युपयोगेऽपि तस्य तस्या

observing the recurrence of pain that had been suppressed. Although available, therefore, the obvious means of putting a stop to pain are neither absolute nor final, and consequently this inquiry (into other means) is not superfluous." This is the purport (of the text).'

The *Sánkhya Chandriká* and *S. Kaumudí* are both to the same effect, and it is unnecessary to cite them. The original *Sútras* of Kapila, as collected in the *S. Pravachana*, and commented on by Vijgnyána Bhikshu, confirm the view taken by the scholiasts.

Sútra:—'The final cessation of the three kinds of pain is the final object of soul *.'

Comment:—'The final cessation of these three kinds of pain, the total cessation of universal pain, whether gross or subtle (present or to come), is the final, supreme object of soul †.'

Sútra:—'The accomplishment of that cessation is not from obvious means, from the evident recurrence (of pain) after suppression ‡.'

Comment:—'The accomplishment of the final cessation of pain is not (to be effected) by worldly means, as wealth, and the like. Whence is this? Because that pain of which the cessation is procured by wealth and the like is seen to occur again, when that wealth and the rest are exhausted ||.'

ध्यात्मिकादेर्दुःखस्य निवृत्तेरदर्शनादनैकान्तिकत्वं । निवृत्तस्यापि पुनरुत्पत्ति दर्शनादनात्यन्तिकत्वमिति । सुकरोऽप्यैकान्तिकात्यन्तिकदुःखनिवृत्तेर्न दृष्ट उपाय इति नापार्था जिज्ञासेति ॥

* अथ त्रिविधदुःखात्यन्तनिवृत्तिरत्यन्तपुरुषार्थः ।

† एषां त्रिविधदुःखानां यात्यन्तनिवृत्तिः स्थूलसूक्ष्मसाधारण्येन निःशेषतो निवृत्तिः सोऽत्यन्तः परमःपुरुषार्थः ।

‡ न दृष्टात्तत्सिद्धिर्निवृत्तेरनुवृत्तिदर्शनात् ।

|| लौकिकादुपायाद्धनादेरत्यन्तदुःखनिवृत्तिसिद्धिर्नास्ति । कुतः । धनादिना दुःखनिवृत्तेः पश्चाद्धनक्षये पुनरपि दुःखानुवृत्तिदर्शनात् ।

II.

THE revealed mode is like the temporal one, ineffectual, for it is impure; and it is defective in some respects, as well as excessive in others. A method different from both is preferable, consisting in a discriminative knowledge of perceptible principles, and of the imperceptible one, and of the thinking soul.

BHÁSHYA.

Although the inquiry is to be directed to other than to obvious remedies, yet it is not to be directed to such as are derivable from revelation, as means of removing the three kinds of pain. *Anusravati*, 'what man successively hears;' *ánusravika*, 'that which is thence produced, revealed mode;' that is, established by the Védas: as it is said; "We drank the juice of the acid asclepias; we became immortal; we attained effulgence; we know divine things. What harm can a foe inflict on us? How can decay affect an immortal?" (This text of the Véda refers to) a discussion amongst Indra and other gods, as to how they became immortal. In explanation it was said, "We were drinkers of *soma* juice, and thence became immortal," that is, gods: further, "We ascended to, or attained, effulgence, or heaven; we knew divine, celestial, things. Hence then, assuredly, what can an enemy do to us? What decay can affect an immortal?" *dhurtti* meaning 'decay' or 'injury:' 'What can it do to an immortal being?'

It is also said in the Védas, that final recompense is obtained by animal sacrifice: "He who offers the *aswamédha* conquers all worlds, overcomes death, and expiates all sin, even the murder of a Brahman." As, therefore, final and absolute consequence is prescribed in the Védas, inquiry (elsewhere) should be superfluous; but this is not the case. The text says, *the revealed mode is like the temporal one—drishíavat;* 'like, same as the temporal,' *drishténa tulya.* What is that revealed mode, and whence is it (ineffectual)? *It is impure, defective in some respects, and excessive in others.* It is impure from (enjoining) animal sacrifices; as, "according to the ritual of the *aswamédha*, six hundred horses, minus three, are offered at midday." For though that is virtue which is enjoined by the Védas and laws, yet, from its miscellaneous character, it may be affected by impurity. It is also said; "Many thousands of Indras and other gods have passed away in successive ages, overcome by time; for time is hard to overcome." Hence therefore, as even Indra and the gods perish, the revealed mode involves defective cessation of pain. Excess is also one of its properties, and pain is produced by observing the superior advantages of others. Here, therefore, by excess, *atiśaya*, is understood the unequal distribution of temporal rewards, as the consequence of sacrifice; the object of the ritual of the Védas being in fact in all cases temporal good. Therefore the revealed mode is like the temporal one. What then is the preferable mode? If this be asked, it is replied, *One different from both.* A mode different from both the temporal and revealed is preferable, being free from impurity, excess, or deficiency. How is this? It is explained (in the text: *It consists in a discriminative knowledge*, &c. Here, by *perceptible principles*, are intended *Mahat* and the rest, or Intellect, Egotism, the five subtile rudiments, the eleven organs (of perception and action), and the five gross elements. The *imperceptible one* is *Pradhána* (the chief or great one). *The thinking soul, Purusha* (the incorporeal). These twenty-five principles are intended by the (three) terms *vyakta*, *avyakta*, and *jna*. In discriminative knowledge of these consists the preferable mode; and he who knows them knows the twenty-five principles (he has perfect knowledge).

The difference between the perceptible, and imperceptible, and thinking principles, is next explained.

COMMENT.

Having taught that worldly means of overcoming worldly evil are ineffectual, it is next asserted that devotional remedies, such as the rites enjoined by the Védas, are equally unavailing; and knowledge of the three parts or divisions of existence material and spiritual, is the only mode by which exemption from the infirmities of corporeal being can be attained.

The Védas are inefficient, from their inhumanity in prescribing the shedding of blood: the rewards which they propose are also but temporary, as the gods themselves are finite beings, perishing in each periodical revolution. The immortality spoken of in the Védas is merely a long duration, or until a dissolution of the existent forms of things *. The Védas also cause, instead of curing, pain, as the blessings they promise to one man over another are sources of envy and misery to those who do not possess them. Such is the sense given by GAURAPÁDA to *atiśaya*, and the *S. Tatwa Kaumudí* understands it also to imply the unequal apportionment of rewards by the Védas themselves: 'The *jyotishtoma* and other rites secure simply heaven; the *vájapéya* and others confer the sovereignty of heaven: this is being possessed of the property of excess (inequality) †.'

In like manner, the original aphorism of KAPILA affirms of these two modes, the temporal and revealed, that there 'is no difference between them ‡,' and that 'escape from pain is not the consequence of the latter ||,' because 'recurrence is nevertheless the result of that immunity which is attainable by acts (of devotion) §,' as 'the consequences of acts are not eternal **.' Here however a dilemma occurs, for the Véda also says, 'There is no return (regeneration) of one who has attained the sphere of Brahma by acts (of devotion) ††.' This is explained away by a Sútra of Kapila, which declares that the Véda limits the non-regeneration of one who has

---

* अमृतत्वाभिधानं चिरस्थेमानमुपलक्षयति यदाह आभूतसम्प्लवं स्थानममृतत्वं भाष्यते ॥ विष्णु पुराणं ॥ † ज्योतिष्टोमादयः स्वर्गमात्रसाधनं वाजपेयादयः स्वराज्यस्येत्यतिशययुक्तत्वं । ‡ अविशेषश्चोभयोः । || नानुश्रविकादपि तत् सिद्धिः । § कर्म्मसाध्यत्वेन पुनरावृत्तिः । ** कर्म्मसाध्यस्य चानित्यत्वे । †† कर्म्मणा ब्रह्मलोकगतस्यानावृत्तिः ।

attained the region of Brahmá to him who, when there, acquires discriminative wisdom*.

This discriminative wisdom is the accurate discrimination of those principles into which all that exists is distributed by the *Sánkhya* philosophy. *Vyakta*, 'that which is perceived, sensible, discrete;' *Avyakta*, 'that which is unperceived, indiscrete;' and *Jna*, 'that which knows, or discriminates:' the first is matter in its perceptible modifications; the second is crude, unmodified matter; and the third is soul. The object of the *S. Káriká* is to define and explain these three things, the correct knowledge of which is of itself release from worldly bondage, and exemption from exposure to human ills, by the final separation of soul from body.

III.

Nature, the root (of all), is no production. Seven principles, the *Great* or intellectual one, &c., are productions and productive. Sixteen are productions (unproductive). Soul is neither a production nor productive.

BHÁSHYA.

Múla (the root) *prakriti* (nature) is *pradhána* (chief), from its being the root of the seven principles which are productions and productive; such nature is the root. *No production.*—It is not produced from another: on that account nature (*prakriti*) is no product of any other thing. *Seven principles.*—*Mahat* and the rest; from its being the great (*mahat*) element; this is Intellect (*Buddhi*). *Intellect and the rest.*—The seven principles are, 1. Intellect; 2. Egotism; 3—7. The five subtile rudiments. These seven are productions and productive: in this manner: Intellect is produced from the *chief* one (nature). That again produces Egotism, whence it is productive (*prakriti*). Egotism, as derived from Intellect, is a produc-

* तत्र प्राप्तविवेकस्यानावृत्तिश्श्रुतिः ।

tion; but as it gives origin to the five subtile rudiments, it is productive. The subtile rudiment of sound is derived from Egotism, and is therefore a production; but as causing the production of ether, it is productive. The subtile rudiment of touch, as generated from Egotism, is a production; as giving origin to air, it is productive. The subtile rudiment of smell is derived from Egotism, and is therefore a production; it gives origin to earth, and is therefore productive. The subtile rudiment of form is a production from Egotism; as generating light, it is productive. The subtile rudiment of flavour, as derived from Egotism, is a production; it is productive, as giving origin to water. In this manner the *Great* principle and the rest are productions and productive. *Sixteen are productions;* that is, the five organs of perception, the five organs of action, with mind, making the eleventh, and the five elements: these form a class of sixteen which are productions, the term *vikára* being the same as *vikriti.* Soul is neither a production nor productive. These (principles) being thus classed, it is next to be considered by what and how many kinds of proof, and by what proof severally applied, the demonstration of these three (classes of) principles, the perceptible, the imperceptible, and the thinking soul, can be effected. For in this world a probable thing is established by proof, in the same mode as (a quantity of) grain by a *prastha* (a certain measure), and the like, or sandal and other things by weight. On this account what proof is, is next to be defined.

COMMENT.

In this stanza the three principal categories of the Sánkhya system are briefly defined, chiefly with regard to their relative characters.

Existent things, according to one classification, are said to be fourfold: 1. *prakriti;* 2. *vikriti;* 3. *prakriti-vikriti;* and *anubhaya rúpa,* neither *prakriti* nor *vikriti.* *Prakriti,* according to its ordinary use, and its etymological sense, means that which is primary, that which precedes what is made; from *pra, præ,* and *kri,* 'to make.' This, however, is further distinguished in the text into the *múla prakriti;* the *prakriti* which is the root and substance of all things except soul, matter or nature; and secondary, special, or relative *prakriti,* or every production that in its turn becomes primary to some other derived from it. By *prakriti* may therefore be understood the matter of which every substance primarily or secondarily is composed, and from which it proceeds, the primary, or, as Mr. Colebrooke renders it, 'productive' principle of some secondary substance or production. This subsequent product is termed *vikriti*, from the same root, *kri*, 'to make,' with *vi*, implying 'variation,' prefixed. *Vikriti* does not mean a product, or thing brought primarily into existence, but merely a modification of a state of being, a new development or form of something previously extant. We might therefore consider it as best rendered by the term 'development,' but there is no objection to the equivalent in the text, or 'product.' In this way, then, the different substances of the universe are respectively nature, or matter, and form. Crude or radical matter is without form. Intellect is its first form, and Intellect is the matter of Egotism. Egotism is a form of Intellect, and the matter of which the senses and the rudimental elements are formed: the senses are forms of Egotism. The gross elements are forms of the rudimental elements. We are not to extend the materiality of the grosser elements to the forms of visible things, for visible things are compounds, not simple developments of a simple base. Soul comes under the fourth class; it is neither matter nor form, production nor productive. More particular definitions of each category subsequently occur.

IV.

Perception, inference, and right affirmation, are admitted to be threefold proof; for they (are by all acknowledged, and) comprise every mode of demonstration. It is from proof that belief of that which is to be proven results.

BHÁSHYA.

Perception;—as, the ear, the skin, the eye, the tongue, the nose, are the five organs of sense; and their five objects are respectively, sound, feel, form, flavour, and odour: the ear apprehends sound; the skin, feel; the eye, form; the tongue, taste; the nose, smell. This proof is called, (that which is) seen (or perception). That object which is not ascertainable either by its being present, or by inference, is to be apprehended from *right affirmation;* such as, INDRA, the king of the gods; the northern *Kurus;* the nymphs of heaven; and the like. That which is not ascertainable by perception or inference, is derived from apt (or sufficient) authority. It is also said; "They call scripture, right affirmation; right, as free from error. Let not one exempt from fault affirm a falsehood without adequate reason. He who in his appointed office is free from partiality or enmity, and is ever respected by persons of the same character, such a man is to be regarded as apt (fit or worthy)." In these three are comprised all kinds of proof. JAIMINI describes six sorts of proof. Which of those then are not proofs? They are, presumption (*arthápatti*), proportion (*sambhava*), privation (*abháva*), comprehension (*pratibhá*), oral communication (*aitihya*), and comparison (*upamána*). Thus: "Presumption" is twofold, 'seen' and 'heard.' 'Seen' is where in one case the existence of spirit is admitted, and it is presumed that it exists in another. 'Heard;' DEVADATTA does not eat by day, and yet grows fat: it is presumed then that he eats by night. "Proportion;" By the term one *prastha*, four *kuravas* are equally designated. "Privation" is fourfold; prior, mutual, constant, and total. 'Prior;' as, DEVADATTA in childhood, youth, &c. 'Mutual;' as, Water jar in cloth. 'Constant;' as, The horns of an ass; the son of a barren woman; the flowers of the sky. 'Total' privation, or destruction; as when cloth is burnt, or as from contemplating withered grain, want of rain is ascertained. In this manner privation is manifold. "Comprehension;" as, The part of the country that lies between the Vindhya mountains on the north and Sahya mountains on the south, extending to the sea, is pleasant. By this sentence it is intended to express that there are many agreeable circumstances comprehended in that country, the name of the site indicating its several products. "Oral communication;" as, When people report there is a fiend in the fig-tree. "Comparison;" The Gavaya is like a cow; a lake is like a sea. These are the six kinds of proof; but they are comprised in the three; for presumption is included in inference, and proportion, privation, comprehension, oral communication, and comparison, are comhended in right affirmation. Therefore from the expressions (in the text), *they comprise every mode of demonstration, and are admitted to be threefold proof*, it is said, that by these three kinds of proof, proof is established. *Belief of that which is to be proven results from proof*.—The things to be proven are, Nature, Intellect, Egotism, the five subtile rudiments, the eleven organs, the five gross elements, and Soul. These five and twenty principles are classed as the perceptible, the imperceptible, and the percipient; and some are verifiable by perception, some by inference, and some by authority; which is the threefold proof.

The definition of each kind (of proof) is next given.

COMMENT.

The work pauses in its enumeration of the physical and metaphysical principles of the system, to define its dialectical portion, or the proofs which may be urged in support of its principles.

The doctrine that there are but three kinds of proof, is said to be supported by a text of the Védas: 'Soul is either to be perceived, to be learned from authority, or to be inferred from reasoning *.' It is opposed to the tenets of the *Naiyáyikas* and *Mímánsakas*, the former of whom describe four kinds, and the latter six kinds of proof. The proofs of the logicians are, *pratyaksha* †, 'perception;' *anumána* ‡, 'inference;' *upamána* ‖, 'comparison;' and *śabda* §, 'verbal authority.' Of these, comparison and verbal authority are included by the *Sánkhyas* under right affirmation; the term *ápta* ** meaning 'fit, right,' and being applied either to the Védas ††, or to inspired teachers ‡‡, as subsequently explained. The *Mímánsakas* do recognise six kinds of proof; but GAURAPÁDA has either stated them incorrectly, or refers to a system different from that now found in the best authorities of this school. KUMÁRILA BHATTA alludes

---

* आत्मा वा द्रष्टव्यः श्रोतव्यो मन्तव्यः। † प्रत्यक्षं। ‡ अनुमानं।
‖ उपमानं। § शब्दः। ** आप्त। †† आगम। ‡‡ आचार्य्य।

to the sixfold proof of an older scholiast or *Vrittikára*, but those six proofs are, as Mr. Colebrooke states, perception, inference, comparison, presumption, authority, and privation; and the author of the *Sástra dípiká* excludes expressly *sambhava, pratibhá*, and *aitihya* from the character of proofs. With regard to the terms specified, it may be doubted if exact equivalents can be devised. *Arthápatti* is literally, 'attainment of meaning;' conjecture or presumption, 'inference;' from which it differs only in the absence of the predicate or sign from which the subject is inferred. The illustrations of the commentator do not very clearly explain the purport of the two kinds of this proof, 'seen' and 'heard.' In the *Sástra dípiká* the first is exemplified by the sentence, "Devadatta is alive, but not in his house; it is presumed therefore that he is abroad." 'Heard,' *sruta*, is referred to the Védas, and applies to the interpretation of precepts by the spirit as well as the letter, as in a direction to offer any particular article, it may be presumed, that should that not be procurable, something similar may be substituted. Váchespati also considers *arthápatti* to be comprised in inference, as well as *sambhava*, 'identity' or 'proportion.' Privation, he argues, is only a modification of perception; and *aitihya*, or 'report,' is no proof at all, the person with whom it originates being undetermined. *Pratibhá* he does not mention. The concluding expressions of Gaurapáda, *Pratijánvása sanjnánam*, are of questionable import, and there is possibly some error in the copy. The 'objects of proof,' *prameya*, are, according to the Sankhyá, all the principles of existence. *Siddhi*, 'accomplishment, determination,' in the last hemistich, is explained by *pratíti*, 'trust, belief.'

V.

Perception is ascertainment of particular objects. Inference, which is of three sorts, premises an argument, and (deduces) that which is argued by it. Right affirmation is true revelation.

BHÁSHYA.

Drishta 'seen,' or *pratyaksha,* 'perception,' is application or exertion of the senses in regard to their several objects, as of the ear, and the rest, to sound, &c. *Inference is of three kinds,* subsequent, antecedent, analogous. Inference antecedent is that which has been previously deduced; as, rain is inferred from the rising of a cloud, because formerly rain had been the consequence. Subsequent; as, having found a drop of water taken from the sea to be salt, the saltness of the rest also is inferred. Analogous; as, having observed their change of place, it is concluded that the moon and stars are locomotive, like CHAITRA: that is, having seen a person named CHAITRA transfer his position from one place to another, and thence known that he was locomotive, it is inferred that the moon and stars also have motion (because it is seen that they change their places). So observing one mango tree in blossom, it is inferred that other mango trees also are in flower. This is inference from analogy.

Again; *premises an argument, and* (*deduces*) *that which is argued by it. That* inference. Premises a prior argument; that is, the thing which has a predicate is inferred from the predicate, as, a mendicant (is known) by his staff; or it premises the subject of the argument, when the predicate is deduced from that of which it is predicated, as, having seen a mendicant, you say, this is his triple staff. *Right affirmation is true revelation.*—*Ápta* means *ácháryas,* 'holy teachers,' as Brahmá and the rest. *Sruti* means 'the Védas.' 'Teachers and Védas' is the import of the compound, and that which is declared by them is true revelation.

In this manner threefold proof has been described. It is next explained by what sort of proof ascertainment is to be effected, and of what objects.

COMMENT.

The three kinds of proof, perception, inference, and right affirmation, are here more particularly explained.

The first is defined, 'what severally relates to, or is engaged in, an object of sense*. *Adhyavasáya* is explained by VÁCHESPATI, 'Knowledge, which is the exercise of the intellectual faculty†.' NÁRÁYANA explains it, 'That by which certainty is obtained‡.' The organs do not of themselves apprehend objects, but are merely the instruments by which they are approximated to the intellect: 'neither does intellect apprehend them (rationally), being, as derived from (*prakriti*) matter, incapable of sense; but the unconscious impressions or modifications of intellect, derived through the senses, are communicated to soul, which, reflecting them whilst they are present in the intellect, appears by that reflection actually affected by wisdom, pleasure, and the like §.'

The explanation given by GAURAPÁDA of the three kinds of inference is not exactly conformable to the definitions of the logicians, although the same technical terms are employed. Thus in the *Nyáya Sútra Vritti*, in the comment on the *Sútra* of Gautama ¶, we have the following: 'Threefold inference. Prior, that is, cause; characterized by, or having, that (cause); as inference of rain from the gathering of clouds. Posterior, effect; characterized by it, as inference of rain from the swelling of a river. Analogous (or generic); characterized as distinct from both effect and cause, as the inference of any thing being a substance from its being earthy **.' Here then we have inference *a priori*, or of effect from cause;

---

* प्रतिविषयाध्यवसायः—विषयं प्रति वर्त्तते । † अध्यवसायो बुद्धिव्यापारो ज्ञानं । ‡ अध्यवसीयते निश्चीयतेऽनेन । § बुद्धितत्वं हि प्राकृतत्वादचेतनमिति तदीयोऽध्यवसायोऽप्यचेतनो घटादि वत् । एवं बुद्धितत्वस्य सुखादयोऽपि परिणामभेदा अचेतनाः । पुरुषस्तु सुखाद्यननुषङ्गी चेतनः । सोऽयं बुद्धितत्ववर्त्तिनाज्ञानसुखादिना तत्प्रतिविम्बित छायापत्त्याज्ञानसुखादिमानिव भवतीति । ¶ त्रिविधमनुमानं पूर्ववच्छेषवत् सामान्यतोदृष्टं च । ** त्रिविधमिति पूर्वं कारणं तद्वत् तल्लिंगकं यथा मेघोन्नतिविशेषेण वृष्ट्यनुमानं । शेषः कार्य्यं तल्लिंगकं शेषवत् यथा नदीवृद्ध्या वृष्ट्यनुमानं । सामान्यतो दृष्टं कार्य्यकारणभिन्नलिंगकं यथा पृथिवीत्वेन द्रव्यत्वानुमानं ।

inference *a posteriori*, or of cause from effect; and inference from analogy, or community of sensible properties; for *samányato drishtam* is 'that which is recognised from generic properties, its own specific properties being unnoticed *.' The *S. Chandriká* gives a similar, or logical, explanation of the three kinds of inference.

The definition of inference in general is the subject of the first member of the second hemistich. The expressions *linga* † and *lingí* ‡ are analogous to 'predicate and subject,' or the mark, sign, or accident by which any thing is characterized, and the thing having such characteristic mark and sign. Thus *linga* is explained by logicians by the term *vyápya* ||, and *lingí* by *vyápaka* §; as in the proposition, There is fire, because there is smoke, the latter is the *linga, vyápya,* 'major or predicate;' and fire the *lingí* or *vyápaka,* the 'minor or subject,' or thing of which the presence is denoted by its characteristic. Inference, then, is a conclusion derived from previous determination of predicate and subject; or it is knowledge of the points of an argument depending on the relation between subject and predicate; that is, 'Unless it were previously known that smoke indicated fire, the presence of the latter could not be inferred from the appearance of the former ¶.' This is what the logicians term *paramersha,* 'observation or experience.' *Ápta* **, according to GAURAPÁDA, means *ácharya;* and *ápta srutí* †† implies 'holy teachers and holy writ.' NÁRÁYANA expounds it in a similar manner ‡‡, and adds, that *ápta* means *Íswara,* or 'god,' according to the theistical *Sánkhya* ||||. VÁCHESPATI explains the terms similarly, though more obscurely. *Ápta* is equivalent with him to *prápta,* 'obtained,' and *yukta,* 'proper, right;' and *ápta sruti* is 'both that which is right and traditional, holy knowledge §§;' for *sruti* is defined to be 'knowledge of the pur-

---

* अदृष्टस्वलक्षणस्य सामान्यदर्शनमनुमानमित्यर्थः । † लिंगं ‡ लिंगिन् । || व्याप्यं । § व्यापकं । ¶ तद्व्याप्यव्यापकपक्षधर्म्मता ज्ञानपूर्व्वकमनुमानमित्यनुमानसामान्यं लक्षितं । ** आप्त । †† आप्तश्रुती । ‡‡ वाक्यार्थगोचरयथार्थज्ञानवानाप्तः । |||| सेश्वरमते ईश्वर एव आप्तः । §§ आप्तश्चासौ श्रुति श्चेत्याप्तश्रुतिः ।

port of texts derived from holy writ; which knowledge is of itself proof, as obtained from the Védas, which are not of human origin, and fit to exempt from all fear of error *.' The first term, *vákya,* is explained to signify, 'the Véda is the teacher of religion †;' and the expression *vákyártha* is equivalent to *dherma,* 'religion or virtue.' 'Religion is heard by it; as, "Let one desirous of heaven perform the *jyotishtoma* sacrifice:" such is a text (of scripture) ‡.' The texts of the Védas and of other inspired works are authority, as having been handed down through successive births by the same teachers as Jaigíshavya says, 'By me living repeatedly in ten different great creations ‖.' So 'the Véda was remembered by Kapila from a former state of being §.' The *Mímánsakas* distinguish between *ápta vákya* and *véda vákya:* the former is human, the latter inspired, authority.

VI.

Sensible objects become known by perception; but it is by inference (or reasoning) that acquaintance with things transcending the senses is obtained: and a truth which is neither to be directly perceived, nor to be inferred from reasoning, is deduced from revelation.

BHÁSHYA.

By inference from analogy; of things beyond the senses—the ascertainment of existing things which transcend the senses. Nature and soul are

---

* श्रुतिवाक्यजनितं वाक्यार्थज्ञानं तच्च स्वतः प्रमाणमपौरुषेयवेदजनितत्वेन सकलदोषशंकाविनिमुक्तेर्युक्तं। † धर्म्मबोधकः श्रुतिः। ‡ श्रूयते धर्म्मोऽनेन यथा ज्योतिष्टोमेन स्वर्गकामो यजेतेति वाक्यं। ‖ दशमहासर्गेषु विपरिवर्त्तमानेन मया। § आदिविदुषश्चकपिलस्य कल्पादौ कल्पान्तराधीतश्रुतिस्मरणसम्भवः।

not objects of sense, and are to be known only by reasoning from analogy. For as the predicates *Mahat* and the rest have the three qualities, so must that of which they are effects, the chief one (nature), have the three qualities; and as that which is irrational appears as if it was rational, it must have a guide and superintendent, which is soul. That which is perceptible is known by perception; but that which is imperceptible, and which is not to be inferred from analogy, must be learnt from revelation, as, INDRA, the king of the gods; the northern *Kurus;* the nymphs of heaven: these depend upon sacred authority. Here some one objects, Nature or soul is not apprehended, and what is not apprehended in this world does not exist; therefore these two are not, any more than a second head, or a third arm. In reply it is stated, that there are eight causes which prevent the apprehension of existing things.

COMMENT.

In this verse, according to the translation followed, the application of the three different kinds of proof to three different objects is described: according to a different version, only one class of objects is referred to, those which transcend the senses, and of which a knowledge is attainable only by inference from analogy, or by revelation.

The *S. Tatwa Kaumudí* concurs with the *S. Bháshya* in understanding the terms of the text, *sámányato drishtát**, to refer to *anumánát*†, intending 'inference from analogy‡.' A similar explanation occurs in the *S. Pravachana Bháshya:* 'Thence, from reasoning by analogy, the determination of both, of nature and soul, is effected‖.' It appears therefore that in this place the text does not refer either to perception or to inference in general, as evidence of perceptible things, but solely to inference

---

* सामान्यतो दृष्टात् । † अनुमानात् । ‡ तु शब्दः प्रत्यक्ष पूर्व्ववद्भ्यां विशिनष्टि । सामान्यतो दृष्टादनुमानादध्यवसायादतीन्द्रियाणां ।

‖ सामान्यतो दृष्टादुभयसिद्धिः—तत्र सामान्यतो दृष्टादनुमानात् । अथ प्रकृतिपुरुषयोः सिद्धिरित्यर्थः ।

from analogy, as proof of imperceptible objects. For inference *a priori* or *a posteriori* regards things not necessarily beyond the cognizance of the senses, like nature and soul, but those only which are not at the moment perceptible, as fire from smoke, rain from floods or clouds, and the like. It might be preferable, therefore, to render the verse somewhat differently from the text, or, 'It is by reasoning from analogy that belief in things beyond the senses is attained; and imperceptible things, not thereby determined, are to be known only from revelation.' The version of Mr. Colebrooke, in which he is followed by Professor Lassen ("Æqualitatis intellectus est per perceptionem: rerum quæ supra sensus sunt per demonstrationem vel hac non evictum, quod præter sensus est, probatur revelatione"), rests apparently upon the authority of the *S. Chandriká* and *S. Kaumudí*. '*Sámányatas* has the affix *tasi* in the sense of the sixth (possessive) case. The ascertainment of all objects appreciable by the senses, whether actually perceived or not, is by perception: therefore knowledge of earth and the other elements is by sense; but knowledge of things beyond the senses, as nature and the rest, is from inference *.'

When inference from analogy fails, then, according to all the authorities, the remaining proof, or revelation, must be had recourse to, agreeably to the Sútras; 'Oral proof is fit instruction,' and 'fit instruction is communication of the proofs by which the nature of both *prakriti* and *purusha* may be discriminated †.'

VII.

From various causes things may be imperceptible (or unperceived); excessive distance, (extreme) nearness, defect of the organs, inatten-

---

* सामान्यत इति षष्ठ्यन्तात्तसि तथा चेन्द्रिययोग्यस्य सर्वस्यापेक्षित स्यानपेक्षितस्य च दृष्टात् प्रत्यक्षादेव सिद्धिस्तेन पृथिव्यादीनां प्रत्यक्षादेव सिद्धिरिति भावोऽतीन्द्रियाणां प्रकृत्यादीनां सिद्धिरनुमानात् । † आप्तोपदेशः शब्दः—उभयसिद्धिः प्रमाणात्तदुपदेशः ।

tion, minuteness, interposition of objects, predominance of other matters, and intermixture with the like.

BHÁSHYA.

Non-perception of things here existing may proceed from, their *remoteness*, as of Vishnumitra, Maitra, and Chaitra, dwelling in different countries; or their *propinquity*, as the eye does not see the collyrium applied to the eyelids; from *defect of the organs*, as sound and form are undiscernible by the deaf and the blind; from *inattention*, as a person whose thoughts are distracted does not apprehend what is said to him, however intelligibly; from *minuteness*, as the small particles of frost, vapour, and smoke in the atmosphere are not perceived; from *interposition*, as a thing hidden by a wall; from *predominance of others*, as the planets, asterisms, and stars are invisible when their rays are overpowered by those of the sun; from *intermixture with the like*, as a bean in a heap of beans, a lotus amongst lotuses, a myrobalan amongst myrobalans, a pigeon in a flock of pigeons, cannot be perceived, being confounded in the midst of similar objects. In this way non-perception of actually existing things is eightfold.

Be it granted, that whatever is to be ascertained (by any means) is; by what cause is apprehension of nature and soul prevented, and how is it to be effected?

COMMENT.

Reasons are here assigned why things may not be perceived, although they actually exist.

The terms of the text, as illustrated by the comment, are easily understood: the particle *cha*, in connexion with the last, is considered to imply the existence of other impediments besides those enumerated, such as non-production, as of curds from milk *. But these circumstances, for

---

* चकारोऽनुक्तसमुच्चयार्थः तेनानुद्भवोऽपि संगृहीत यथा क्षीराद्यवस्थायां दध्यनुद्भवान्न दृश्यते ।

the most part, account for the non-perception of perceptible things, and it is still to be considered why nature and soul, which are not amongst things ordinarily perceptible, are not perceived *.

VIII.

It is owing to the subtilty (of nature), not to the non-existence of this original principle, that it is not apprehended by the senses, but inferred from its effects. Intellect and the rest of the derivative principles are effects; (whence it is concluded as their cause) in some respects analogous, but in others dissimilar.

BHÁSHYA.

From subtilty the non-perception of that nature. Nature is not apprehended (by the senses) on account of its subtilty, like the particles of smoke, vapour, and frost, which are in the atmosphere, although not perceived there. How then is it to be apprehended? *Its perception is from its effects.* Having observed the effects, the cause is inferred. Nature is the cause, of which such is the effect. Intellect, egotism, the five subtile rudiments, the eleven organs, the five gross elements, are its effects. That effect may be *dissimilar* from nature: 'nature,' *prakriti;* 'the chief one,' *pradhána;* dissimilar from it: or it may be *analogous*, of similar character; as in the world a son may be like or unlike his father. From what cause this similarity or dissimilarity proceeds, we shall hereafter explain.

Here a doubt arises, from the conflicting opinions of teachers, whether intellect and other effects be or be not already in nature. According to the Sánkhya doctrine, the effects are in nature; according to the

---

* नन्वतिदूरत्वादिषु मध्ये प्रकृत्याद्युपलम्भे किं प्रतिबन्धकं।

Bauddhas and others, they are not; for that which is, cannot cease to be; and that which is not, can by no means be: this is a contradiction. Therefore, it is said—

COMMENT.

Nature is said to be imperceptible, from its subtilty: it must be therefore inferred from its effects.

The effects are the products of nature, or intellect, egotism, and the rest; some of which are of a similar, and some of a dissimilar character, as subsequently explained.

Effect, according to the Sánkhya system, necessarily implies cause, as it could not exist without it*: but on this topic there are different opinions, thus particularized by VÁCHESPATI: '1. Some say, that that which is may proceed from that which is not. 2. Some say, that effect is not a separately existent thing, but the revolution of an existent thing. 3. Some say, that that which is not may proceed from that which is. 4. The ancients assert, that that which is comes from that which is (or *ens* from *ens*). By the three first propositions the existence of nature would not be proved; for,

'1. The materiality of the cause of the world, of which the qualities goodness, foulness, and darkness are the natural properties, comprises sound and other changes of its natural condition, and is diversified by pleasure, pain, and insensibility; but if that which is, is born from that which is not, how can that insubstantial cause which is not, comprehend pleasure, pain, form, sound, and the like? for there cannot be identity of nature between what is and what is not.

'2. If sound, and other diversified existences, were but revolutions of one existent thing, yet that which is could not proceed from such a source, for the property of manifold existence cannot belong to that which is not twofold: the notion of that which is not manifold through its comprising manifold existence is an obvious error.

---

* कार्य्यात्कारणमात्रं गम्यते ।

'3. The notion of the Kanabhakshas, Akshacharanas, and others, that that which is not may proceed from that which is, excludes the comprehension of effect in cause, as that which is and that which is not cannot have community: consequently the existence of nature is not proved; and in order to establish its existence, the existence of effect in it must first be determined *.'

Of the doctrines here alluded to, the first is said to be that of some of the Buddhists, who deny the existence of *prakriti*, or any universal cause, or of any thing which they cannot verify by perception. The second is that of the Védántis, who maintain that all that exists is but the *vivarttas*, literally the 'revolutions'—the emanations from, or manifestations of, one only universal spirit. It might be said that the Sánkhya seems to teach a similar doctrine, in as far as it refers all that exists, exclusive of spirit, to one common source, and makes all else identical with *prakriti*. It differs however in this, that it regards the substances evolved from the radical *prakriti* as substantial existences, as effects or products of a cause which exists no longer except in its effects. The Védántis, on the other hand, maintain that it is cause which is eternal, and that effects are

---

* केचिदाहुरसतः सज्जायत इति । एकस्य सतो विवर्त्तः कार्य्यजातं न वस्त्वित्यपरे । अन्ये तु सतोऽसज्जायत इति । सतः सज्जायत इति वृद्धाः । तत्र पूर्व्वस्मिन् कल्पत्रये प्रधानं न सिध्यति सुखदुःखमोहभेदवत् स्वरूपपरिणामशब्दाद्यात्मकं हि जगत् कारणस्य प्रधानत्वं सत्वरजस्तमः स्वभावत्वं । यदि पुनरसतः सज्जायेत असन्निरूपाख्यं कारणं कथं सुखादिरूपशब्दाद्यात्मकं स्यात् सदसतोस्तादात्म्यानुपपत्तेः ॥ अथैकस्य सतो विवर्त्तः शब्दादिप्रपंचस्तथापिसतः सज्जायत इति न स्यात् नास्याद्वयस्य प्रपंचात्मकं । अपित्वप्रपंचस्य प्रपंचात्मकतया प्रतीतिर्भ्रम एव ॥ येषामपि कणभक्षाक्षचरणादीनां सत एव कारणादसतो जन्म तेषामपि सदसतोरेकत्वानुपपत्तेर्न कार्य्यात्मकं कारणमिति न प्रधानसिद्धिः ॥ अतः प्रधानसिद्ध्यर्थं प्रथमं तावत् सत्कार्य्यं प्रतिजानीते ॥

only its present operations. The popular form of Védántism asserts, indeed, that nothing exists but cause, and that its effects, or all that appears to exist, are unrealities, illusions, the phantoms of a dream: but the commentator on the *Sánkhya Pravachana* declares, that the doctrine of *máyá*, or 'illusion,' is modern, and is contrary to the Védas, and that those who advocate it are nothing but disguised Bauddhas: 'The cause of the bondage of soul asserted by those concealed Bauddhas, the modern advocates of *máyá*, is here refuted *.' In the third case we have the authors specified as *Kanabhakshas*, 'Feeders upon little,' or upon atoms, perhaps; and *Akshacharanas*, 'Followers of controversy;' contemptuous terms for the *Vaiśéshikas*, who maintain the origin of all things from primæval atoms, or monads; and who may therefore be said to deduce what is not—the insubstantial forms of things—from actual corpuscular substance.

The fourth or ancient doctrine, that that which is comes from that which is, *ens* from *ens*, *τὸ ὂν* from *τὸ ὄν*, is the converse of the celebrated dogma of antiquity, *ex nihilo, nihil fit;* and although in this place it is especially restricted to the relation of certain effects to a certain cause, yet it comes to the same thing as regards the world in general, the things of which cannot be derived from no primary existent thing; agreeably to the Sútra of KAPILA; 'The production of a thing cannot be from nothing †;' *Οὐδὲν γίνεται ἐκ τοῦ μὴ ὄντος*: not only according to Democritus and Epicurus, but according to all the ancient philosophers, who, Aristotle states, agreed universally in the physical doctrine, that it was impossible for any thing to be produced from nothing: *Τούτων δὲ τὸ μὲν ἐκ μὴ ὄντων γίνεσθαι ἀδύνατον· περὶ γὰρ ταύτης ὁμογνωμόνουσι τῆς δόξης ἅπαντες οἱ περὶ φύσεως.* Phys. I. 4.

---

* नवीनामपि प्रच्छन्नबौद्धानां मायावादिनां बन्धहेतुत्वं निराकृतं ।

† नावस्तुनो वस्तुसिद्धिः ।

IX.

Effect subsists (antecedently to the operation of cause); for what exists not, can by no operation of cause be brought into existence. Materials, too, are selected which are fit for the purpose: every thing is not by every means possible: what is capable, does that to which it is competent; and like is produced from like.

BHÁSHYA.

From there being no instrumental cause of *what exists not*—non-existent, what is not—there is no making what is not: therefore effect is. In this world there is no making of what is not; as, the production of oil from sand: therefore the instrumental cause produces what is, from its having been formerly implanted. Hence perceptible principles, which are effects, exist in nature.

Further, *from selection of materials.*—*Upádána* is '(material) cause,' from the selection of it: thus, in life, a man who desires a thing, selects that by which it may be produced; as he who wishes for curds, takes milk, not water (for their material cause). Thence effect is.

Again, *every thing is not by every means possible.* The universal possibility of every thing is not; as of gold in silver, &c. or in grass, dust, or sand. Therefore, from the non-universality of every thing in every thing, effect is.

Again, *what is capable does that to which it is competent;* as, a potter is the capable agent; the implements, the lump of clay, the wheel, rag, rope, water, &c. (are capable), by which he makes the jar, which is capable of being so made from earth. Thence effect is.

Lastly, *like is produced from like.* Such as is the character of cause, in which effect exists, such also is the character of effect; as, barley is produced from barley, rice from rice. If effect was not (did not pre-exist), then rice might grow from pease; but it does not, and therefore effect is.

By these five arguments, then, it is proved that intellect and the other characteristics do (pre)exist in nature; and therefore production is of that which is, and not of that which is not.

COMMENT.

Arguments are here adduced to shew that the effects or products of nature are comprised in, and coexistent with, their cause or source; consequently they are proofs of the existence of that primary cause or source.

It is laid down as a general principle, that cause and effect are in all cases coexistent, or that effect exists anteriorly to its manifestation; *sat-káryyam** in the text meaning 'existent effect prior to the exercise of (efficient) cause †;' or, as the phrase also of the text *asadakaranát* ‡ is explained, 'If effect prior to the exercise of (efficient) cause does not exist, its existence cannot by any means be effected ‖.' The expression *sat-káryyam*, therefore, is to be understood throughout as meaning 'existent effect,' not the effect of that which exists: and the object of the stanza is to establish the existence of cause from its effects, and not of effects from the existence of cause, as Professor Lassen has explained it: "Quænam sint rationes docetur quibus evincatur mentem ceteraque principia effecta esse a τῷ ὄντι." Mons. Pauthier (*Traduction de la Sánkhya Káriká*, 105) is more correct in his view of the general purport of the verse; "Ce qui n'existe pas ne peut arriver à l'état d'effet;" but he has mistaken the particulars—the *reasons* why that which is not can never be, for the *means* which would be fruitlessly exercised for its production: it is not that such existence cannot be effected "par la co-opération d'aucune cause matérielle," &c., but *because* an effect requires an adequate material cause, and the like.

* सत्कार्य्यं। † सत्कार्य्यं प्राक् कारणव्यापारादितिशेषः। ‡ असदकरणात्। ‖ असच्चेत् कारणव्यापारात् पूर्व्वं कार्य्यं नास्य सत्त्वं केनापि कर्त्तुं शक्यं।

Not only has the meaning of this verse been misapprehended by its translators, but the doctrine which it conveys seems to have been somewhat misconceived by high authority. M. Cousin, referring to this passage, observes, "L'argumentation de Kapila est, dans l'histoire de philosophie, l'antécédent de celle d'Ænésidème et Hume. Selon Kapila il n'y a pas de notion propre de cause, et ce que nous appelons une cause n'est qu'une cause apparente relativement à l'effet qui la suit, mais c'est aussi un effet relativement à la cause qui la précède, laquelle est encore un effet par la même raison, et toujours de même, de manière que tout est un enchainement necessaire d'effets sans cause véritable et indépendente." M. Cousin then supports his view of the doctrine by selecting some of the arguments contained in the text; as, "That which does not exist cannot be made to exist;" and, "Cause and effect are of the same nature:" and he adds, as a third, that "il ne faut pas s'occuper des causes, mais des effets, car l'existence de l'effet mesure l'énergie de la cause; donc l'effet équivaut la cause." In this instance, however, he is scarcely justified by his authority, whose object is not to dispense with the consideration of cause altogether, but to prove its existence from that of its effects. Kapila, therefore, is far from asserting that "il n'y a pas de cause," although he may so far agree with the philosophers referred to, in recognising no difference between *material cause* and *material effects:* for it must be remembered, that it is of material effects, of substances, that he is speaking. His doctrine is, in fact, that on which Brown enlarges in his lectures on power, cause, and effect—that "the forms of a body are the body itself; and that all the substances which exist in the universe are every thing which truly exists in the universe, to which nothing can be added which is not itself a new substance: that there can be nothing in the events of nature, therefore, but the antecedents and consequents which are present in them; and that these accordingly, or nothing, are the very causes and effects which we are desirous of investigating." Lect. on the Philosophy of the Human Mind, p. 175. KAPILA, however, has not asserted a series of antecedents and consequents without beginning; and whatever we may conceive of his *múla-prakriti*, his original and unoriginated substance whence all substances proceed, it is a fixed point from which he starts, and the existence of which he deduces from its effects: the mutual and correlative existence of which, with their cause, he endeavours to establish by arguments, which, as regarding a curious and not uninteresting part of the Sánkhya philosophy, it may be allowable to recapitulate a little more in detail.

1. *Asadakaranát;* 'Because efficient or instrumental cause cannot make or produce that which is not.' Professor Lassen renders this, 'E nulla nonentis efficacitate, nonens nil efficit. *Asat* in this passage, however, is the object, not the agent; and *karana* is employed technically to denote the efficient or operative cause, the energy of which would be exerted in vain, unless applied to materials that existed: that which does not exist cannot be brought into existence by any agent. It would be useless to grind the sesamum for oil, unless the oil existed in it: the same force applied to sand or sugar-cane would not express oil. The appearance or manifestation of the oil is a proof that it was contained in the sesamum, and consequently is a proof of the existence of the source whence it is derived. This dogma, in its most comprehensive application, is of course the same with that of the Greeks, that nothing can come from nothing, and makes the creation of the universe dependent upon preexisting materials. Here, however, the application is limited and specific, and as Sir Graves Haughton, in his vindication of Mr. Colebrooke's exposition of the Védanta philosophy, has justly observed, it means no more than that things proceed from their respective sources, and from those sources alone; or that certain sequents follow certain antecedents, and indicate consequently their existence.

2. *Upádána grahanát;* 'From taking an adequate material cause: a fit material cause must be selected for any given effect or product.' There is no difference of opinion as to the purport of *upádána;* 'Such as the substance evolved, such is that from which it is evolved;' or as illustrated by Gaurapáda, 'He who wishes to make curds will employ milk, not water:' but this being the case, the effects which we behold, or infer, must proceed from something similar to themselves, and consequently prove the existence of that substance. 'The relation between cause and effect is the generation of effect; but there can be no relation

(between cause and) a non-existent effect, and therefore effect is*," and consequently so is cause.

3. 'From the unfitness of all causes for every effect;' *sarva sambhavábhávát*. There must be an identity of character between the sequent and its antecedent, and the existence of one indicates that of the other: a jar is made with clay, cloth with yarn; the latter material could not be used to fabricate a water-pot, nor clay to weave a garment. If this was not the case, all things would be equally fit for all purposes,

. . . ex omnibus rebus
Omne genus nasci possit.

It is not, however, here intended to assert, that "idonea causa non est ulla quam *sad, τὸ ὄν*," but that the effect must have a determinate existence in that cause, and can be the only effect which it can produce; as in the commentary on this expression in the *S. Pravachana Bháshya*: 'If effect prior to production do not exist in cause, there would be no reason why cause should not produce one non-existent effect, and not another †.'

4. *Saktasya sakyákaranát;* 'From the execution of that which the agent is able to do.' Active or efficient causes can do only that to which they are competent: the potter and his implements fabricate a water-jar, not a piece of cloth; they are not competent to the latter, they are capable of the former. If effect did not pre-exist, if it were not inseparable from cause, power, or the exertions of an agent, and the employment of means, might derive from any antecedent one consequence as well as another.

5. *Káranabhávat;* 'From the nature of cause;' that is, from its being of the same nature or character with effect, and consequently producing its like; or, according to VÁCHESPATI, 'from the identity of cause with effect ‡:' 'Cloth is not different from the threads of which it is woven,

* कार्य्येण संबद्धं कारणं कार्य्यस्य जनकं संबन्धश्च कार्य्यस्यासतो न सम्भवति तस्मात्सदिति। † उत्पत्तेः प्राक् कारणे कार्य्यासत्तायां हि न कोऽपि विशेषोऽस्ति येन कंचिदसन्तं जनयेन्नेतरमिति। ‡ कार्य्यस्य कारणात्मत्वात्।

for it is made up of them *.' Here, then, we have precisely the discovery of modern philosophy, "that the form of a body is only another name for the relative position of the parts that constitute it; and that the forms of a body are nothing but the body itself:" (Brown's Lectures:) a discovery which, simple as it may appear to be, dissipated but recently the illusion of 'substantial forms,' which had prevailed for ages in Europe. It seems, however, to have been familiar to Hindu speculation from the remotest periods, as the commentator on the *S. Pravachana*, and the author of the *S. Chandriká*, cite the Védas in its confirmation: 'Before production there is no difference between cause and effect †.' There is good reason, however, to think that the conclusion drawn from the doctrine by the Védas was very different from that of the Sánkhyas, being the basis of Pantheism, and implying that before creation the great First Cause comprehended both cause and effect: the texts illustrating the dogma being such as, 'The existent τὸ ὄν verily was unevolved‡—This, the Existent, was, oh pupil, before all things ‖—The Unborn was verily before all §.' The Sánkhyas, like some of the old Grecian philosophers, choose to understand by *tad*, *idam*, τὸ ὄν, τὸ ἕν, 'the comprehensive, eternal, material cause.'

From the arguments thus adduced, then, it is concluded that effect is, *sat káryam* ¶; that is, that it exists in, and is the same with, cause; or, as GAURAPÁDA has it, *mahat* and the other characteristics of *pradhána* are in *pradhána*. *Sat káryam* is therefore neither 'ponendum est existens (*sad*) emphatice ita dictum τὸ ὄντως ὄν, per se ens,' nor 'effectus existentis, ab existente effectum, effectum a τῷ ὄντι:' the question is, whether effect exists or not before production; and not whether it is produced 'a τῷ ὄντι an a τῷ μὴ ὄντι.' It is the production, or appearance, OF that which is or is not; not the production of any thing BY that which is or is not; agreeably to the Sútra of KAPILA: 'There is no production of that which

---

* न पटस्तन्तुभ्यो भिद्यते तद्धर्म्मत्वात् । † उत्पत्तेः प्रागपि कार्य्यस्य कारणाभेदः श्रूयते । ‡ तद् होवमव्याकृतमासीत् । ‖ सदेव सौम्येदमग्रासीत् । § अजमेवेदमग्रास । ¶ सत् कार्य्यं ।

is not, as of a man's horn*—The production of that which is not is impossible, as would be that of a human horn†.' Agreeably to the same doctrine also is the reply made in the Sútras to the objection, that if effect exists already, existence is superfluously given to it; 'It is absurd to produce what is already extant‡.' The answer is, 'It is not so; for the actual occurrence or non-occurrence of production depends upon manifestation‖:' that is, the present existence of an effect is not the production of any thing new, but the actual manifestation of a change of form of that which previously existed: something like the notions which Aristotle ascribes to ancient philosophers, that all things were together, and that their generation was merely a change of condition: Ἦν ὁμοῦ τὰ πάντα καὶ τὸ γίνεσθαι τοιόνδε καθέστηκεν ἀλλοιοῦσθαι: and it is curious enough to find the doctrine illustrated almost in the words of Hobbes: "Faciendum est quod faciunt statuarii, qui materiam exculpentes, supervacaneam *imaginem non faciunt* sed inveniunt;" or as Vijnyána Bhikshu has it, 'The active exertion of the sculptor produces merely the manifestation of the image which was in the stone§.'

Although however, as identical with cause, and regarded as proofs of its existence; effects or products, in their separated or manifested condition regarded as forms only, possess properties different from those of their source or cause: these differences are detailed in the next stanza.

X.

A discrete principle is causable, it is inconstant, unpervading, mutable, multitudinous, supporting, mergent, conjunct, governed. The undiscrete one is the reverse.

---

* नासदुत्पादो नरशृंगवत् । † नरशृङ्गतुल्यस्यासत उत्पादो न सम्भवति । ‡ नभावि भावयोगश्चेत् । ‖ नाभिव्यक्तिनिवन्धनौ व्यवहाराव्यवहारौ । § शिलामध्यस्थप्रतिमाया लैङ्गिकव्यापारेणाभिव्यक्तिमात्रं ।

BHÁSHYA.

Discrete; intellect and the other effects. *Causable;* that of which there is cause; the term *hetu* meaning 'cause,' as synonymous with *upádána, kárana,* and *nimitta.* Nature is the cause of a discrete principle; therefore discrete principles, as far as the gross elements inclusive, have cause: thus, the principle intellect has cause by nature; egotism by intellect; the five rudiments and eleven organs by egotism; ether by the rudiment of sound; air by that of touch; light by that of form; water by that of taste; and earth by that of smell. In this way, to the gross elements inclusive, a discrete principle has cause. Again, *it is inconstant,* because it is produced from another; as a water-jar, which is produced from a lump of clay, is not constant. Again, *it is unpervading,* not going every where: a discrete principle is not like nature and soul, omnipresent. Again, *it is mutable;* it is subject to the changes which the world undergoes: combined with the thirteen instruments, and incorporated in the subtile frame, it undergoes worldly vicissitudes, and hence is mutable. *It is multitudinous;* it is intellect, egotism, the five rudiments, and eleven organs; and the five gross elements are *supported* by the five rudiments. *It is mergent;* subject to resolution; for at the period of (general) dissolution, the five gross elements merge into the five rudiments; they, with the eleven organs, into egotism; egotism into intellect; and intellect merges into nature. *Conjunct;* conjoined, made up of parts, as sound, touch, taste, form, and smell. *Governed;* not self-dependent; for intellect is dependent on nature, egotism on intellect, the rudiments and organs on egotism, and the gross elements on the rudiments. In this way the governed or subject discrete principle is explained: we now explain the undiscrete.

The undiscrete one is the reverse. An undiscrete principle is the contrary in respect to the properties attributed to the discrete: that, is causable; but there is nothing prior to nature, whence follows its non-production, and therefore it is without cause. A discrete principle is inconstant; an undiscrete is eternal, as it is not produced. The primary elements are not produced from any where; that is, nature. A discrete principle is unpervading; nature is pervading, going every where. A discrete principle is mutable; nature immutable, from the same omnipresence. Discrete principles are multitudinous; nature is single, from its causality: "Nature is the one cause of the three worlds;" thence nature is single. Discrete principles are dependent; the undiscrete one is independent, from its not being an effect: there is nothing beyond nature of which it can be the effect. A discrete principle is mergent; the undiscrete immergent (indissoluble), being eternal: intellect and the rest, at the period of general dissolution, merge respectively into one another; not so nature; and that therefore is immergent (indissoluble). A discrete principle is conjunct (or compound, made up of parts); nature is uncompounded, for sound, touch, flavour, form, and odour, are not in (crude) nature. Discrete principles are governed; the undiscrete is independent, it presides over itself. These are the properties in which discrete and undiscrete principles are dissimilar: those in which they are similar are next described.

COMMENT.

It was stated in the eighth stanza, that intellect and the other effects of nature were in some respects similar, and in others dissimilar, to their cause: the properties in which the dissimilarity consists are here enumerated.

The generic term used for the effects or products of primæval nature (*vyakta**) means, in its etymological and commonly received senses, that which is evident or manifest, or that which is individual or specific; from *vi*, distributive particle, and *anja*, 'to make clear or distinct.' The purport is therefore sufficiently well expressed by the equivalent Mr. Colebrooke has selected, 'discrete,' detached from its cause, and having a separate and distinct existence. Nature (or primary matter) is the reverse of this, or *avyakta* †, 'undiscrete, unseparated, indistinct.' If *natura* were substituted for *tellus*, these lines of Lucretius would illustrate the application of the terms in question:

---

* व्यक्त । † अव्यक्त ।

Multa modis multis multarum semina rerum
Quod permixta gerit tellus *discretaque* tradit.

Discrete or separated effect or principle (meaning by principle a *tatwa*, or category, according to the Sánkhya classification of the elements of existent things) is described by its properties, and they are the same which are specified in the original Sútra. 1. *Hétumat* *, 'having cause, or origin;' *hetu* implying 'material, efficient, and occasional cause;' 2. *Anitya* †, 'temporary;' for whatever has cause has beginning, and whatever has a beginning must have an end. At the same time this is to be understood of them in their actual or present form or condition: 'Of their own nature (or as one with their cause) they are eternal, but they are perishable by their separate conditions ‡.' So in the Sútras 'destruction' is explained 'resolution into cause ‖.' 3. 'Unpervading §:' 'Every one of the effects of nature is not observable in every thing, they are dispersed as different modifications ¶.' *Vyápti* is the essential and inherent presence of one thing in another, as of heat in fire, oil in sesamum, &c. 4. *Sakriya* **, 'mutable,' or 'having action:' perhaps 'movable' or 'migratory' would perfectly express the sense; for the phrase is explained to signify that the effects of nature migrate from one substance to another: 'Intellect and the rest leave one body in which they were combined, and enter into the composition of another: this is their transition: the transition of the gross elements earth and the rest, composing body, is well known ††.' 5. 'Multitudinous:' many, *anéka* ‡‡ being repeated in various objects and persons, as 'the faculties in different individuals, and the elements in different forms ‖‖.' 6. Supported

---

* हेतुमत् । † अनित्य । ‡ सर्व्वकार्य्याणां स्वभावतो नित्यत्वम वस्थाभिर्विनाशित्वं च । ‖ नाशः कारणलयः । § अव्यापि । ¶ सर्व्वपरिणामि न व्याप्नोति । ** सक्रियं । †† बुद्ध्यादय उपात्तं देहं त्यजन्ति देहान्तरंश्चोपाददत इति तेषां परिस्पन्दः शरीरपृथिव्यादीनां च परिस्पन्दः प्रसिद्धः । ‡‡ अनेक । ‖‖ प्रतिपुरुषं बुद्ध्यादीनां भेदात् पृथिव्याद्यपि शरीरघटादिभेदेन ।

by, referable to, *ásrita**; as an effect may be considered to be upheld by its cause, or an individual referable to a species; as trees form a wood. 7. 'Mergent,' *linga* †; that which merges into, or is lost or resolved into, its primary elements, as subsequently explained. Intellect and the rest are the *lingas*, signs, marks, or characteristic circumstances of nature: and when they lose their individuality, or discrete existence, they may be said to have been absorbed by, or to have fused or merged into, their original source. Although, therefore, the application of *linga* as an attributive in this sense is technical, the import is not so widely different from that of the substantive as might at first be imagined. VÁCHESPATI, explaining the term, has, '*Linga*, the characteristic of *pradhána*, for these principles, *buddhi* and the rest, are its characteristics, as will be hereafter explained ‡:' and the author of the *S. Chandriká* has, '*Linga* is that which characterizes, or causes to be known ||;' it is the *anumápaka* §, 'the basis of the inference:' 'For this effect (of nature) is the parent of the inference that an undiscrete cause exists ¶.' (See also Com. on v. 5. p. 24.) According to these interpretations, 'predicative' or 'characteristic' would perhaps be a preferable equivalent; but 'mergent' or 'dissoluble**' is conformable to the *S. Bháshya*. The commentator on the *S. Pravachana* explains it by both terms 'inferential' or 'resolvable:' 'Effect is termed *linga*, either from its being the ground of inference of cause, or from its progress to resolution ††.' 8. 'Combined, conjunct,' *sávayava* ‡‡; explained by VÁCHESPATI, 'mixing,' *misrana* ||||, or 'junction,' *samyoga* §§, as the elements combine with one another. It might be said, then, that nature is a compound, as its products combine with it; but this is not so, for their union with nature is not mere 'mixture or conjunction,

---

* आश्रित। † लिंग। ‡ लिंगं प्रधानस्य यथा चैते बुद्ध्यादयः प्रधानस्य लिंगमुपरिष्टाद्वक्ष्यति। || लिंगं लिंगयति ज्ञापयति। § अनुमापकं। ¶ भवति हि कार्य्यमिदं कारणस्याव्यक्तस्यानुमिति जनकं। ** लययुक्तं। †† कारणानुमापकत्वाल्लयगमनाद्वाच लिंगं कार्य्यं जातं। ‡‡ सावयव। |||| मिश्रण। §§ संयोगः।

but identification from the sameness of the cause and effect*:' a notion which distinguishes the *pradhána* of the Sánkhyas from the first principles of those Grecian philosophers, who, if their doctrines have been rightly represented, taught that substances existed either as distinct particles of an aggregate, or component parts of a mixture, in their original form. In the Sánkhya they separate or reunite as one and the same. 10. 'Governed†:' the effects of nature depend upon its existence, and each in its turn produces its peculiar effect or product, in furtherance of the influence of nature, or in consequence of its existence, without which they would cease to be, and their effects would be null; as, 'In the effect of egotism, which intellect has to produce, the fulfilment of nature is regarded; otherwise intellect, being ineffective, would not be able to produce egotism‡.'

The properties of nature, or the undiscrete principle, are the reverse of these; it has no cause; it has no end; it is omnipresent; it is immutable; it is single; it is self-sustained; it is the subject, not the predicate; it is entire, or one whole; it is supreme.

Although the especial object of the text here is the dissimilarity between the effects of nature and their material cause, yet the term *avyakta* applies equally to *purusha*, or 'soul,' also an invisible or undiscrete principle; and accordingly soul differs from discrete principles in the same circumstances as nature. In the properties, therefore, of non-causability, constancy, omnipresence, immutability, singleness, self-support, substantiveness, entireness, and supremacy, soul and nature correspond. They differ, however, in other respects, and particularly in those in which nature and its effects assimilate, as enumerated in the succeeding stanza.

---

* न तु प्रधानस्य बुद्ध्यादिभिः संयोगस्तादात्म्यात्। † परतन्त्र।

‡ बुद्ध्या हि स्वकार्य्येऽहंकारे जनयितव्ये प्रकृत्यापूरोऽपेक्ष्यत अन्यथा क्षीणा सती नालमहंकारं जनयितुमिति।

XI.

A DISCRETE principle, as well as the chief (or undiscrete) one, has the three qualities: it is indiscriminative, objective, common, irrational, prolific. Soul is in these respects, as in those, the reverse.

BHÁSHYA.

Has the three qualities: it is that of which goodness, foulness, and darkness are the three properties. A discrete principle is *indiscriminative;* discrimination does not belong to it: that is, it cannot distinguish which is a discrete principle and which are properties, or that this is an ox, that is a horse: such as the properties are, such is the principle; such as is the principle such are the properties; and the like. *Objective;* a discrete principle is to be enjoyed (made use of), from its being an object to all men. *Common;* from being the common possession of all, like a harlot. *Irrational;* it does not comprehend pain, pleasure, or dulness. *Prolific;* thus, egotism is the progeny of intellect; the five rudiments and eleven organs of egotism; and the five gross elements of the five rudiments. These properties, to *prolific* inclusive, are specified as those of a discrete principle; and it is in them that the *chief (or undiscrete) one* is similar: "Such as is a discrete principle, such is the chief (or undiscrete) one." Therefore as a discrete principle has three qualities, so has the undiscrete, or that of which intellect and the rest, having the three qualities, are the effects: so in this world effect is of the like quality with cause, as black cloth is fabricated with black threads. A discrete principle is indiscriminative; so is the chief one, it cannot discern that qualities are distinct from nature, that qualities are one thing, and that nature is another; therefore the chief one is indiscriminative. A discrete principle is objective; so is the chief one, from its being the object of all men. A discrete principle is common; so is the chief one, being common to all things. A discrete principle is irrational; so is the chief one, as it is not conscious of pain, or pleasure, or dulness. Whence is this inferred? From the irrationality of its effects; from an irrational lump of clay proceeds an irrational water-pot. Thus has (nature) the chief one been explained. ***Soul is in these respects, as in those, the reverse:*** this is now explained.

Reverse of both the discrete and undiscrete principles. Soul is the reverse of both, thus: Discrete and undiscrete have (the three) qualities; soul is devoid of qualities: they are indiscriminative; soul has discrimination: they are objects (of sense or fruition); soul is not an object (of sense or fruition): they are common; soul is specific: they are irrational; soul is rational; for inasmuch as it comprehends, or perfectly knows, pleasure, pain, and dulness, it is rational: they are prolific; soul is unprolific; nothing is produced from soul. On these grounds soul is said to be the reverse of both the discrete and undiscrete principles.

It is also said, ***as in those***, referring to the preceding verse; for as the chief (or undiscrete) principle is there said to be without cause, &c. such is the soul. It is there stated that a discrete principle is causable, inconstant, and the like; and that the undiscrete one is the reverse; that is, it has no cause, &c.; so soul is without cause, being no production. A discrete principle is inconstant; the discrete one is constant; so is soul; and it is immutable also, from its omnipresence. A discrete principle is multitudinous; the undiscrete is single; so is soul. A discrete principle is supported; the undiscrete is unsupported; so is soul. A discrete principle is mergent; the undiscrete immergent (indissoluble); so is soul; it is not in any way decomposed. A discrete principle is conjunct; the undiscrete one uncombined; so is soul; for there are no (component) parts, such as sound, &c., in soul. Finally, discrete principles are governed; the undiscrete one is independent; so is soul, governing (or presiding over) itself. In this way the common properties of soul and nature were described in the preceding stanza; whilst those in which they differ, as possession of the three qualities, and the like, are specified in this verse. Next follows more particular mention of these three qualities, with which both discrete principles and the undiscrete one are endowed.

COMMENT.

In this verse the properties common to crude nature and to its products are specified, continuing the reference to the eighth verse, in which it was asserted, that in some respects the effects of nature and nature itself were analogous. This being effected, the text proceeds to state that soul has not the properties which are common to nature and its products, but possesses those which are peculiar to the former; agreeing therefore in some respects with crude nature, but dissimilar in every respect to its effects or products.

The three qualities *, or *satwa* †, 'goodness,' *rajas* ‡, 'foulness,' and *tamas* ‖, 'darkness,' which are familiar to all the systems of Hindu speculation, are more particularly described in the next verse; soul has them not. *Pradhána*, 'the chief one,' crude nature, and its products, have not discrimination, *viveka* §, the faculty of discerning the real and essential differences of things, of 'distinguishing between matter and spirit, of knowing self; the exercise of which is the source of final liberation (from existence) ¶.' By the term 'objective**' is intended that which may be used or enjoyed, such as the faculties of the mind, and the organs of sense; or such as may be perceived by observation, *vijnána* ††: such nature, or *pradhána*, may also be considered as the origin of all things inferable by reason. Soul, on the contrary, is the observer or enjoyer, as afterwards explained. *Achétana* ‡‡, 'irrational;' that which does not think or feel, unconscious, non-sentient; as in the *Meghadúta*; 'Those afflicted by desire seek relief both from rational and irrational objects ‖‖;' explained either 'living and lifeless §§,' or 'knowing and ignorant ¶¶;' *chétaná**** being defined 'knowledge of right and wrong,' or 'of what ought, and what ought not, to be done †††.'

The general position, that the properties of soul are the reverse of

---

* गुणाः । † सत्व । ‡ रजस् । ‖ तमस् । § विवेक । ¶ यद्यप्यन्योन्यभेदज्ञानं विवेकज्ञानं तथाप्यात्मविशेष्यकमेव तन्मोक्षकारणं भवति । ** विषय । †† विज्ञान । ‡‡ अचेतन । ‖‖ कामार्त्ताहि प्रकृतिकृपणाश्चेतनाचेतनेषु । §§ प्राण्यप्राणिषु । ¶¶ विवेचकाविवेचकेषु । *** चेतना । ††† कार्य्याकार्य्यविवेचना ।

those of the products of nature, requires, however, some modification in one instance. A discrete principle is said to be multitudinous, many, *aneka* *; consequently soul should be single, *eka* †; and it is so, according to the *S. Bháshya* ‡. On the other hand, the *S. Tatwa Kaumudí* makes soul agree with discrete principles, in being multitudinous: 'The properties of non-causability, constancy, and the rest, are common to soul and nature; multitudinousness is a property common to (soul and) an undiscrete principle ‖.' The *S. Chandriká* confirms the interpretation, 'The phrase *tathá cha* implies that (soul) is analogous to the undiscrete principle in non-causality and the rest, and analogous to discrete principles in manifold enumeration §.' This is, in fact, the Sánkhya doctrine, as subsequently laid down by the text, ver. 18, and is conformable to the Sútra of KAPILA; 'Multitude of souls is proved by variety of condition ¶:' that is, 'the virtuous are born again in heaven, the wicked are regenerated in hell; the fool wanders in error, the wise man is set free **.' Either, therefore, GAURAPÁDA has made a mistake, or by his *éka* is to be understood, not that soul in general is one only, but that it is single, or several, in its different migrations; or, as Mr. Colebrooke renders it (R. A. S. Trans. vol. I. p. 31), 'individual.' So in the Sútras it is said, 'that there may be various unions of one soul, according to difference of receptacle, as the etherial element may be confined in a variety of vessels ††.' This singleness of soul applies therefore to that particular soul which is subjected to its own varied course of birth, death, bondage, and liberation; for, as the commentator observes, 'one soul is born, not

---

* अनेक। † एक। ‡ अनेकं व्यक्तमेकमव्यक्तं तथा पुमानप्येकः। ‖ अहेतुमत्त्वनित्यत्वादि प्रधानसाधर्म्यमस्ति पुरुषस्य एवमनेकत्वं व्यक्तसाधर्म्यं। § तथा चाव्यक्तसरूपोऽप्यहेतुमत्त्वादिना एवं व्यक्तसरूपोऽप्यनेकसंख्ययेति। ¶ जन्मादि व्यवस्थातः पुरुषबहुत्वं। ** पुण्यवान् स्वर्गे जायते पापी नरके अज्ञो भ्रम्यते ज्ञानी मुच्यते। †† उपाधिभेदेऽप्येकस्य नानायोग आकाशस्य घटादिभिः।

another (in a regenerated body) *.' The singleness of soul therefore, as asserted by GAURAPÁDA, is no doubt to be understood in this sense.

XII.

THE qualities respectively consist in pleasure, pain, and dulness; are adapted to manifestation, activity, and restraint; mutually domineer; rest on each other; produce each other; consort together; and are reciprocally present.

BHÁSHYA.

The qualities goodness, foulness, and darkness, are severally the same as what is agreeable, what is disagreeable, and what is indifferent: thus goodness is all that is pleasure, *príti* meaning 'pleasure;' being one with (or consisting of) that (pleasure): foulness is one with, or consists of, disagreeableness (*apríti*): darkness consists of, or is the same with, dulness; *vishâda* meaning *móha*, 'dulness, stupidity.' Next, *are adapted to manifestation*, &c.; *artha* signifying 'competency' or 'fitness.' Goodness, then, is for the sake of manifestation; it is fit for, or adapted to it: foulness is for activity; darkness for restraint: that is, the qualities are connected with, or possessed of, manifestation, action, and *inertia*. *They mutually domineer:* they are mutually paramount, sustaining, productive, cooperative, and coexistent. Thus, they are said to domineer mutually; that is, they severally prevail or predominate over each other, or they are displayed by the properties of pleasure, pain, or dulness. When goodness is dominant, it overpowers foulness and darkness by its own properties, and is exhibited or identified with light and joy. When foulness predominates, it overpowers goodness and darkness, and exists in pain and action. When darkness triumphs, it suppresses goodness and foul-

---

* एकः पुरुषो जायते नापरः ।

ness, and is supreme as one with insensibility and inaction. So *they rest on each other:* the qualities combine with one another, like binary atoms. *They produce each other*, as the lump of clay generates the earthen jar. *They consort together*, as males and females cohabit: as it is said, "Goodness is the consort of foulness, foulness of goodness; darkness is called the consort of both:" that is, they are respectively associates. *They are reciprocally present:* they abide or exist reciprocally, according to the text, "qualities abide in qualities" (that is, the same qualities may be regarded as different, according to their different effects): thus, a beautiful and amiable woman, who is a source of delight to every one else, is the cause of misery to the other wives of her husband, and of bewilderment (insensibility) to the dissolute: and in this manner she is the cause of the influence of all three qualities. Thus also, a king, assiduous in protecting his people, and curbing the profligate, is the cause of happiness to the good, of misery and mortification to the bad: here foulness (activity) produces the effects of goodness and darkness. So darkness, by its investing nature, produces the effects of goodness and foulness, as clouds, overshadowing the heavens, cause delight upon earth, animate by their rain the active labours of the husbandman, and overwhelm absent lovers with despair. In this manner the three qualities are reciprocally present (or perform the functions of one another).

COMMENT.

The three qualities are here described, by their effects and relations; by the production of pleasure, pain, and indifference; and by the manner in which they are detached or combined in their operations and influence.

The terms *príti* and *apríti* are here used as synonymes of *sukha*, 'pleasure,' and *dukha*, 'pain;' *vish//áda* as a synonyme of *moha*, 'bewilderment, stupefaction, dullness, or insensibility.' The composition of *átma* with these terms, *prítyátmaka*, implies 'essential or inseparable presence,' like that of life or soul in the living body. An exact equivalent for such a compound can scarcely perhaps be supplied, but the sense may be conveyed by such expressions as 'consists of, comprehends, is one or identical with,' and the like. *Átma* is here used also to shew that the properties have positive existence; that is, pleasure is not the mere absence of pain; pain is not the mere absence of pleasure; as, 'Negatives could not be essential ingredients in any thing: pleasure, pain, and insensibility are therefore entities; the word *átma* implying being, existence, existent nature, or property *.'

The absolute and relative influence of the several qualities is sufficiently illustrated by GAURAPÁDA; but VÁCHESPATI understands the text as in some respects differently constructed. Instead of considering the last term, *vrittaya* †, as a distinct condition, *anyonyavrittaya* ‡, expounded in the *S. Bháshya, parasparam varttanté* ||, they are reciprocally present,' he interprets *vritti* by *kriyá*, 'act, operation, function,' and compounds it with each of the foregoing terms §. In all other respects his explanation of the terms coincides with that of the elder commentator. The passage quoted by GAURAPÁDA is cited by VÁCHESPATI, with some difference, from the Védas: 'As it is said in the *ágama*, all universally present are the associates of each other: goodness is the partner of foulness, foulness of goodness; both are the companions of darkness, and darkness is said to be the associate of both. Their original connexion, or disjunction, is never observed ¶.' The *Chandriká* concurs with the *S. Tatwa Kaumudí* in the explanation of *vritti* **. This commentary likewise offers some additional interpretation of the terms *príti*, &c. Thus *príti* is said to

---

* नेतरेतराभावाः सुखादयोऽपि तु भावाः । आत्मशब्दस्य भाववचनात् । † मिथुनवृत्तयश्च । ‡ अन्योन्यवृत्तयः । || परस्परं वर्त्तन्ते । § सा च (वृत्तिः) प्रत्येकमभिसम्बध्यते यथान्योन्याभिभववृत्तयोऽन्योन्याश्रयवृत्तयोऽन्योन्यजननवृत्तयोऽन्योन्यमिथुनवृत्तयः । ¶ भवति चात्रागमे । अन्योन्यमिथुनाः सर्व्वे सर्व्वत्रगामिनश्चवै रजसो मिथुनं सत्वं सत्वस्य मिथुनं रजः तमसश्चापि मिथुने ते सत्वरजसी उभे उभयोः सत्वरजसोर्म्मिथुनं तम उच्यते नैषामादिः संप्रयोगो विप्रयोगो वोपलभ्यते । ** अन्योन्यपदं वृत्तिपदं च चतुर्ष्वन्वेति ।

comprise 'rectitude, gentleness, modesty, faith, patience, clemency, wisdom:' *apríti*, besides 'misery,' implies 'hatred, violence, envy, abuse, wickedness:' and *vishāda* is not only 'insensibility,' but 'tardiness, fear, infidelity, dishonesty, avarice, and ignorance. Whenever either of these is observed, it is referable to the corresponding quality *.'

In speaking of qualities, however, the term *guna* is not to be regarded as an insubstantial or accidental attribute, but as a substance discernible by soul through the medium of the faculties. It is, in fact, nature, or *prakriti*, in one of its three constituent parts or conditions, unduly prominent; nature entire, or unmodified, being nothing more than the three qualities in equipoise, according to the Sútra, '*Prakriti* is the equal state of goodness, foulness, and darkness †:' on which the commentator remarks, '*Satwa* and the rest are "things," not specific properties, from their being subject to combination or disjunction, and from their having the properties of lightness, heaviness, and strength ‡:' and again, 'From the construction of intellect and the rest endowed with the three properties, like cords wherewith to bind the victim the soul ‖.' So in the *S. Sára*, 'Goodness and the rest are not the faculties of that (*prakriti*), being of the same nature §'—'Such expressions as "qualities of nature" are to be understood (in the same sense) as (the term) "the trees of a forest" ¶:' that is, the forest is nothing different from the trees of which it is the aggregate, although particular trees or clumps may sometimes be indivi-

---

* अत्र प्रीतिः सुखमुपलक्षणमार्जवमार्द्दवह्रीश्रद्धा क्षमानुकम्पाज्ञानादीनां । अप्रीतिर्दुःखमुपलक्षणं प्रद्वेषद्रोहमत्सरनिन्दानिकृतीनां । विषादो मोह उपलक्षणं विप्रलम्भभयनास्तिक्य कौटिल्यकार्प्पण्याज्ञानादीनां यत्रै तदुपलभ्यते तत्र तादृग्गुणः प्रत्येतव्य इति भावः ।

† सत्वरजस्तमसां साम्यावस्था प्रकृतिः ।

‡ सत्वादीनि द्रव्याणि न वैशेषिका गुणाः संयोगवियोगवत्वात् लघुत्वचलत्वगुरुत्वादिधर्म्मत्वाच्च ।

‖ पुरुषपशुबन्धकत्रिगुणात्मकमहदादि रज्जुनिर्म्मातृत्वाच्च ।

§ सत्वादीनामतद्धर्म्मत्वं तद्रूपत्वात् ।

¶ प्रकृतेर्गुणा इत्यादि वाक्यं तु वनस्य वृक्षा इति बोध्यं ।

dualized. In like manner nature is not different from the qualities, but is the aggregate of them. 'Ingredients or constituents of nature,' therefore, would be a preferable term perhaps to 'quality;' but 'quality' is the more ordinary acceptation of the word *guna,* and it may therefore be used, remembering only the distinction made by the Sánkhyas of its materiality, as a constituent part of nature itself; the qualities being, in fact, only the conditions of things, and therefore not separable from the things themselves. It may be thought possible that there is some connection between the *gunas* which are the constituents of *prakriti*, and the qualities, passions, or affections of primary matter of the older philosophers, alluded to by Aristotle; from the changes produced by which on one unaltered substance all things originated: Τῆς μὲν οὐσίας ὑπομενούσης, τοῖς δὲ πάθεσι μεταβαλλούσης, τοῦτο στοιχεῖον καὶ ταύτην τῶν ὄντων τὴν ἀρχὴν φασιν εἶναι. Metaph. I. 3. Another analogy may be conjectured in the identification of the two *gunas*, *satwa* and *rajas*, with *príti*, 'affection,' and *apríti*, 'aversion,' as they thus correspond with the φιλία and νεῖκος, the 'love' and 'strife' of Empedocles, as the principles of creation; respectively the source of what is good or evil.

The sense in which the several terms for the three *gunas* is employed is sufficiently clear from the explanation given of them in the text; and the meaning of the equivalents which Mr. Colebrooke has assigned them must be understood according to the same interpretation. Prof. Lassen renders them *essentia, impetus,* and *caligo;* which, similarly understood, are equally unobjectionable: but as the name of a 'quality,' *satwa,* is not perhaps well rendered by 'essence,' or even by 'existence,' which is its literal purport, 'goodness,' denoting exemption from all imperfection, seems to be preferable. *Impetus* is rather the effect of *rajas,* than the quality; and the term 'foulness,' derived from its etymology from *ranj,* 'to colour or stain,' will better comprehend its characteristic results. The quality bears a striking analogy to the *perturbatio* of the Stoics, and might be rendered by that word, or by 'passion,' in its generic acceptation. 'Darkness,' or *caligo,* expresses both the literal and technical signification of *tamas.*

XIII.

GOODNESS is considered to be alleviating and enlightening: foulness, urgent and versatile: darkness, heavy and enveloping. Like a lamp, they cooperate for a purpose (by union of contraries).

BHÁSHYA.

Goodness is alleviating, &c.—When goodness predominates, the frame is light, the intellect is luminous, and the senses are acute. *Foulness is urgent and versatile.*—What urges, urgent, exciting: as a bull, upon seeing another bull, exhibits vehement excitement; that is the effect of foulness. Foulness is also seen to be versatile; that is, a person under its influence is capricious. *Darkness is heavy and enveloping.*—Where darkness prevails, the members of the body are heavy, the senses obtuse, or inadequate to the performance of their functions. But here it may be said, If these qualities are contraries to one another, what effect can they produce by their several purposes, and how therefore can it be said, *they cooperate, like a lamp, for a* (*common purpose*). Like a lamp, their operation is for a (common) purpose: as a lamp, which is composed of the opposites, a wick, oil, and flame, illuminates objects, so the qualities of goodness, foulness, and darkness, although contrary to one another, effect a (common) purpose.

This question involves another. It was said (in ver. 11) that a discrete principle, as well as the chief one, has the three qualities, and is indiscriminative, objective, and the like. Admitting this to be true of the chief one (or nature), how is it ascertained that intellect and the rest have also the three qualities, and are indiscriminative, and the like? This is next explained.

COMMENT.

The description of the three qualities is continued in this verse.

Goodness is alleviating; laghu, 'light;' it is matter, elastic and elevating, generating upward and lateral motion, as in the ascent of flame, and the currents of the air. It is the cause of active and perfect functionality also in the instruments of vitality*; *enlightening*, *prakásakam*, 'making manifest,' the objects of the senses. The term *ishṫam*, meaning ordinarily 'wished, desired,' imports in the text merely *drishṫam*, 'seen, regarded, considered'—'by the Sánkhya teachers †.' *Foulness is urgent and versatile.*—The qualities of goodness and darkness are both inert and inoperative, even with regard to their own peculiar consequences; and it is only by the restless activity and stimulating agency of the quality of foulness that they are roused to action; *upashṫambhakam* ‡ being here explained to signify 'stimulating, impelling,' *udyotakam*, *prĕŕakam* ||, contrary to its usual sense of 'opposing, hindering.' It might be supposed to imply some relation to the primitive *shṫabhi* §, 'stop, hinder, oppose, be stupid;' inasmuch as the idea appears to be that of action consequent upon obstruction, or *inertia*, 'reaction.' Thus, as illustrated in the *S. Bháshya*, a bull displays excitement on beholding, or being opposed by, another. The *S. Tatwa Kaumudí* has, 'The qualities goodness and darkness, on account of their own *inertia*, are inoperative, in regard to the exercise of their own effects, until excited by foulness. Having been roused from inactivity, they are made to put forth vigour and energy; and therefore foulness is said to be urgent ¶.' The *Chandriká* is to the same effect:- 'The meaning is this: From the production of combination and activity by foulness, the definition of that quality is excitement and versatility **.' It is not necessary, however, to take into consideration the sense of the primitive *shṫabhi*, for *upashṫambhaka* is not derived from that root, but from *stambhu* ††, a *Sautra* root; which therefore, although the meanings of

---

* करणानां वृत्तिपटुत्वहेतुर्लाघवं। † सांख्याचार्य्यैः। ‡ उपष्टम्भकं। || उद्योतकं प्रेडकं। § ष्टभि। ¶ सत्वतमसी स्वयमक्रियतया स्वकार्य्यप्रवृत्तिं प्रत्यवसीदतो रजसोपष्टभेते। अवसादात् प्रच्याव्य उत्साहं प्रयत्नं कार्य्येते। तदिदमुक्तमुपष्टम्भकं रज इति। ** रजसैव संश्लेष क्रिययोरुपलम्भात् प्रेडकत्वं सक्रियत्वं च रजसो लक्षणमितिभावः। †† स्तम्भु।

shtabhi are usually also assigned to it, may take the import required by the text, of 'urging' or 'exciting.'

The quality of darkness is 'heavy,' *guru*, causing sluggishness of body and dulness of mind. It is also *varanaka*, 'surrounding, enveloping,' so as to obstruct light, retard motion, &c.

But these qualities, although contraries, cooperate for a common purpose; as the cotton, the oil, and the flame, although mutually destructive, combine in a lamp to give light. The common object of the qualities is the fulfilment of the purpose of soul, as is subsequently explained.

XIV.

INDISCRIMINATIVENESS and the rest (of the properties of a discrete principle) are proved by the influence of the three qualities, and the absence thereof in the reverse. The undiscrete principle, moreover, (as well as the influence of the three qualities,) is demonstrated by effect possessing the properties of its cause (and by the absence of contrariety).

BHÁSHYA.

That which is the property of indiscriminativeness and the rest is proved from the influence of the three qualities in *mahat* and the other discrete principles: but this is not proved in the undiscrete; therefore it is said, *by the absence the reverse of it:* the reverse of it; the absence; the non-existence of the reverse of that: thence the undiscrete principle is established; as, where there are threads, there is cloth; the threads are not one thing, and the cloth another. Why so? From the absence of the reverse (they are not contraries to each other). In this manner the discrete and undiscrete principles are established. The latter is remote, the former is near: but he who perceives discrete principles, perceives the undiscrete one also, as there is no contrariety between them. Hence also the undiscrete one is proved *by effect possessing the properties of cause* in this world: such as is the nature of the cause, such is that of the effect;

thus, from black threads black cloth is made. In the same manner, as the characteristics of intellect and the rest are their being indiscriminative, objective, common, irrational, prolific, such as they are, such the undiscrete is proved essentially to be. From the influence of the three qualities, indiscriminativeness and the rest are proved to be in discrete principles; and from there being no difference between them (and the undiscrete), and from essential identity of the properties of cause and effect, the undiscrete principle also is demonstrated.

But it is replied, this cannot be true; for in this world that which is not apprehended is not; but the undiscrete one is, although not applicable.

COMMENT.

It was stated in ver. 8, that *mahat* and the other effects of *prakriti* were in some respects like, and in others unlike, to their original. The circumstances in which they were dissimilar were specified in ver. 10, and those in which they agreed in ver. 11. In the latter stanza, the first of the concurrent properties that was named was that of their possessing the three qualities; and in verses 12 and 13 it was explained what was meant by the three qualities. In the present stanza it is asserted, that as the effects of *prakriti* have the three qualities, they must have, as a necessary consequence, the other properties, want of discrimination and the rest, enumerated in ver. 11; and that as they have them, their origin, or *prakriti*, must have them also, as there is no essential difference between the properties of cause and effect.

The influence of goodness, foulness, and darkness, or the varied affections and conditions of all substances, is the obvious cause of perplexity, or want of discrimination, &c.; being, in fact, the same state or condition. *Traigunya* is the influence or any consequence of the three *gunas*. The next expression is variously interpreted.

Mr. Colebrooke renders *tad viparyaya abhávát**, 'and from the absence thereof in the reverse;' that is, the absence of want of discrimination, &c.

---

* तद्विपर्य्ययाभावात् ।

in that subject which is the reverse of the material products of nature, as, for instance, soul, is a negative proof of their existence in the former. The properties of contraries are contrary. Soul and matter are contraries, and consequently their properties are mutually the reverse of each other: but one property of soul is freedom from the three qualities, whilst that of matter, or any material product of *prakriti*, is their possession; consequently the former must be capable, and the latter incapable, of discrimination. The same may be said of the other properties of *mahat* and the rest. Thus VÁCHESPATI observes: 'It (the assertion) is first plainly or affirmatively expressed in the natural order: it is then put negatively, or in the inverted order; *from the absence thereof in the reverse;* from the absence of the three qualities in soul, as the reverse of the products of *prakriti*, in regard to want of discrimination and the like *.' The *S. Chandriká* has a similar explanation: 'The reverse of that want of discrimination; where that is that is the reverse (of *mahat*, &c.), or soul: for in soul there are not the three qualities; or, where there is not want of discrimination there are not the three qualities, as in soul †:' intimating, therefore, that *tad*, 'thereof,' may refer either to the three qualities *traigunya*, or to want of discrimination, &c.

There is, however, another sense attached to the expression; and *the reverse* is understood not to signify soul, or any thing contrary to *mahat* and the rest, but to imply contrariety or incompatibility in the properties of their origin, or *prakriti:* that is, indiscriminativeness and the rest are the properties of *mahat*, &c. not only from their possessing the three qualities, but because there is nothing contrary to indiscriminativeness, &c. in *prakriti*. This proposition is indicated by VÁCHESPATI, who, after explaining the passage as above, adds, 'Or it may be understood as

---

* स्फुटत्वादन्वयेनोक्तं । व्यतिरेकेणाह । तद्विपर्य्ययाभावादविवेक्यादिविपर्य्यये पुरुषे त्रैगुण्याभावात् ।

† तस्याविवेकित्वस्य विपर्य्ययो यत्र सस्तद्विपर्य्यय आत्मा तत्र त्रैगुण्याभावात्तथा च यत्राविवेकित्वाभावस्तत्र त्रैगुण्याभाव आत्मवदिति ।

taking for its two subjects *vyakta* and *avyakta* (discrete and undiscrete matter), and by the inverted proposition (or negatively) asserting that there is no reason (to the contrary) arising from one being exempt from the three qualities *.' The same is more explicitly stated by GAURAPÁDA. The absence of indiscriminativeness, he observes, as deduced from the influence of the three qualities, relates in the first instance to *vyakta*, 'discrete matter,' not to *avyakta*, or 'indiscrete:' but the same must apply to the latter also, because there is no property belonging to it which is incompatible with, or the reverse of, the properties of the *vyakta*, or 'discrete matter,' *mahat*, &c.; as in the case of the cloth and the threads of which it is woven, there is no incompatibility between them.

The first portion of the stanza having shewn, then, either simply that discrete matter is possessed of indiscriminativeness, &c. or that both it and indiscrete matter are equally devoid of discrimination, proceeds to draw the conclusion that such an indiscrete cause must exist, endowed with properties similar to those of its indiscrete effects, because there is no difference of property between cause and effect; agreeably to the Sútra, 'The three qualities, insensibility and the rest, belong to both (*prakriti* and its products) †:' and VÁCHESPATI observes, 'Effect is seen to be the same in its properties with cause. As the properties of the threads, &c. are identical with those of cloth and the like, so the attributes of pleasure, pain, and insensibility, evidenced in the effects, which are distinguished as *mahat* and the rest, are proofs that similar conditions must belong to their cause: the existence of *pradhána* or *avyakta*, as a cause, of which pleasure, pain, and insensibility are the conditions, is consequently established ‡.'

---

* अथ वा व्यक्ताव्यक्ते पक्षीकृत्य अन्वयाभावेन त्रैगुण्यावीत एव हेतुर्वक्तव्यः । † त्रिगुणाचेतनत्वादिद्वयोः । ‡ कार्य्यं हि कारणगुणात्मकं दृष्टं । यथा तन्त्वादिगुणात्मकं पटादि तथा महदादिलक्षणेनापि कार्य्येण सुखदुःखमोहरूपेण स्वकारणगतसुखदुःखमोहात्मना भवितव्यं तथा च तत्कारणं सुखदुःखमोहात्मकं प्रधानमव्यक्तं सिद्धं भवति ।

XV.

Since specific objects are finite; since there is homogeneousness; since effects exist through energy; since there is a parting (or issue) of effects from cause, and a reunion of the universe,—

BHÁSHYA.

The undiscrete principle is cause: this is the completion of the construction of the sentence. *Since specific objects are finite:* as in the world, wherever the agent is, his limits are observed: thus, a potter makes certain jars with certain portions of clay; so with intellect: intellect and the other characteristics (of nature) are finite, as specific effects of it. Intellect is one, egotism is one, the subtile rudiments are five, the organs eleven, the gross elements five: from the limitation of these species nature is their cause, which produces finite discrete principles. If nature were not the cause, then discrete principles would have no limit: from the measure (or limit) of specific objects, therefore, nature exists, whence discrete principles are produced. *Since there is homogeneousness:* as in the world, that which is notorious is observed; for having seen a religious student engaged in sacred study, it follows that his parents were assuredly of the Brahmanical tribe: so having observed that *mahat* and the other characteristics have the three qualities, we conclude what their cause must be; and in this way from homogeneousness the chief one exists. *Since effects exist through energy:* in life, that which is effective in any thing is active in the same: a potter is able to make a jar, therefore he makes a jar, not a piece of cloth. *Since there is a parting of effect from cause:* the chief one is cause; that which makes is cause, that which is made is effect: the separation of cause and effect: thus; a jar is competent to hold curds, honey, water, milk; not so is its cause, or the lump of clay; but the lump of clay produces the jar, the jar does not produce the lump of clay. So having observed intellect and the other effects, it is inferred that cause must have been separated, of which these discrete principles are detached portions. Again, *since there is a reunion of the universe* (*vaiswarúpa*). *Viswa* here means 'the world;' *rúpa*, 'individualization' (or specific form): the abstract condition of the form of the world is the universe: *from its reunion*, nature exists (as cause); whence there is no mutual separation of the five gross elements, earth &c., composing the three worlds; or, the three worlds are comprised in the gross elements. The five gross elements are earth, water, fire, air, ether; which at the season of general dissolution return in the order of creation to a state of non-separation, or into the modified five subtile rudiments: they and the eleven organs reunite in egotism; egotism resolves into intellect; and intellect into nature. Thus the three worlds, at the period of general dissolution, reunite in nature; and from such reunion of the discrete and undiscrete principles, like that of curds and milk, it follows that the undiscrete principle is cause.

COMMENT.

The sentence is incomplete, the government being in the first member of the following verse; *káranam asti-avyaktam*, 'There is (a general) cause (which is undiscrete).' Hitherto the subjects discussed have been the existence of effects, and their correspondence or disagreement with their cause. It is now shewn that cause exists imperceptible, or undiscrete.

From specific effects being finite: from the certain or definite measure of the varieties of discrete principles, as one intellect, one egotism, five rudiments, and the like. If there were no certain and defined cause, the effects would be indefinite and unlimited: the water-jar, however, must be limited by the earth of which it consists, and which, as a distinct body, is no longer extant. 'Homogeneousness,' *samanwaya*, is defined 'the common nature of different things*,' as the property of generating pain, pleasure, and dulness, which is possessed by intellect and the rest. *Effects exist through energy:* 'through the energy, ability, or power of cause they

---

* भिन्नानां समान रूपता ।

become active*:' A parting, or issue, of effect from cause, and final reunion of the separated effect. *Vaiswarúpa* is merely a synonyme of *kárya*, 'effect;' that which is of various, or every, sort of form, or nature. The evolution of effect from unseparated cause is illustrated by comparing nature to a tortoise, the limbs of which are at one time protruded, and at another retracted within the shell: 'As when the limbs which are in the body of the tortoise protrude, then they are distinguished, or (it is said) this is the body, those are the limbs: so when they are withdrawn into it they are undistinguished (from the body)†.' *S. Tatwa Kaumudí.* In like manner the water-jar or the diadem exist in the lump of clay or of gold, but are distinguished from it only when individually manifested; they become mere clay or gold again on losing their detached condition: thus earth and the rest exist in the subtile rudiments; those and the organs of sense and action in egotism; egotism in intellect; and intellect in nature: when manifested or put forth they are separated or distinguished from their several sources, but at the period of universal dissolution lose their distinct form, and become progressively one with their common original: the existence of which therefore, as their undiscrete cause, is proved both by their appearance or separation, and disappearance or reunion.

XVI.

There is a general cause, which is undiscrete. It operates by means of the three qualities, and by mixture, by modification, as water; for different objects are diversified by influence of the several qualities respectively.

---

* कारणशक्तितः कार्य्यं प्रवर्त्तते । † यथा कूर्म्मशरीरे सन्त्येवाङ्गानि निःसरन्ति विभज्यन्त इदं कूर्म्मशरीरमेतान्यस्याङ्गानीति । एवं निविशमानानि तस्मिन्नऽव्यक्तीभवन्ति ।

BHÁSHYA.

That which is known as the undiscrete principle is the cause; whence intellect and the other effects proceed. *It operates by means of the three qualities.*—That in which are the three qualities, goodness, foulness, and darkness, is the (aggregate of the) three qualities. What then is that? The equipoised condition of goodness, foulness, and darkness, is the chief one (nature). Also, *from mixture.*—In like manner as the Ganges unites into one river the three streams that descend upon the head of Rúdra, so the (aggregate of the) three qualities, the undiscrete, produces a single discrete principle; or, as many threads combined form one piece of cloth, so the undiscrete generates intellect and the rest from the interweaving of the three qualities: and thus from the influence of the three qualities and their aggregation the discrete world proceeds. But if discrete principles proceed from one undiscrete, then one form should be common to all. This objection is invalid; for it is *by modification, like water, from a variety in the receptacles of the several qualities*, that the three worlds, derived from one undiscrete principle, assume different conditions of being. The gods are united with pleasure, mankind with pain, animals with dulness; so that a discrete principle, emanating from one nature, becomes modified, like water, according to the diversified receptacles of the qualities. *Prati prati* implies 'several order:' *guná sraya*, 'a receptacle of the qualities,' by the difference of that receptacle (according to that several receptacle) in which it is lodged. Discrete principles are varied from modification; as the simple element water, when fallen from the atmosphere, is diversely modified as various fluids, according to its various combinations, so from one *pradhána* proceed the three worlds, which are no longer of one (uniform) character. In the divinities the quality of goodness predominates, foulness and darkness are inert; therefore they are supremely happy. In men the quality of foulness abounds, and goodness and darkness are inert; therefore they are supremely miserable. In animals goodness and foulness are inactive, and darkness prevails; and therefore they are supremely insensible.

In these two stanzas the existence of nature (*pradhána*) has been determined: in the next place, that of soul is to be established.

COMMENT.

In this verse, besides the conclusion drawn from the arguments in the preceding stanza, it is here explained how nature, which is one, produces diversified effects. This is said to be through the influence of the three qualities, the combination or several predominance of which in various objects is attended with a modification and diversity of that which is essentially one and the same.

'Modified condition,' according to VÁCHESPATI, 'is the character of the three qualities, which are never for a moment stationary*,' except when creation is not: and from this constant vicissitude ensues combination in different proportions, or the predominance of one or other in different objects; for they are always combined, or mixed, in different proportions. This is the mixture, the blending, or contention of the qualities which the text intends. Hence proceeds the modification of the original matter; as rain water, falling upon different trees, is modified as the juice of their different fruits. 'As simple water shed by the clouds, coming into contact with various situations, is modified as sweet, sour, bitter, pungent, or astringent, in the character of the juice of the cocoa-nut, palm, bèl karanja, and wood-apple †.' *S. Tatwa Kaumudí*. So, according to Cudworth, the Italic philosophers maintained that the forms and qualities of bodies were only different modifications of primary matter. "The same numerical matter," he observes, "differently modified, causing different phantasms in us, which are therefore vulgarly supposed to be forms and qualities in the things, as *when the same water is successively changed and transformed* into vapour, snow, hail, and ice." Intellect. System, III. 426.

It may be doubted if the latter portion of the verse should not be

---

* परिणामस्वभावा त्रिगुणा नापरिणम्य क्षणमवतिष्ठन्ते । † यथा वारिदमुक्तमुदकमेकरसमपि तत्तद्भूमिविकारानासाद्य नारिकेलतालीविल्व चिरविल्वामलक कपित्थफलरसतया परिणतमपि मधुराम्लतिक्तकटुकषाय तया विकल्पते ।

preferably rendered, 'By modification, like water, according to the receptacle, or subject, of the qualities *.' Such is evidently the sense in which the *S. Bháshya* understands it, and such appears to be that of the above illustration; the simple water being modified, as sweet, sour, &c., according to the tree by which it is absorbed, and the fruit of which it constitutes the juice. So certain objects are fitted for certain qualities; as the gods for goodness, men for foulness, animals for darkness; and nature is modified in them accordingly; that quality predominating which is conformable to the receptacle: the question here being, not the origin of things, but of their different properties. Váchespati, however, seems to make the diversity of objects depend upon the qualities, not the difference of qualities upon the subject; explaining the phrase *prati gunásraya vishéshát*, 'The difference which is produced by the recipience of each several quality; thence, &c.†' The *Chandriká* has the same explanation, adding, 'Diversity is from diversity (different ratio) of qualities ‡.' There is no incompatibility, indeed, in the two views of the meaning of the text, as the variety of things depends upon the difference or disproportion of the three primary qualities, whether those qualities modify, or be modified by, the subject to which they belong: in either case the variety is not a different thing, it is only a modification of the same thing, *pradhána*.

XVII.

Since the assemblage of sensible objects is for another's use; since the converse of that which has the three qualities, with other properties (before mentioned), must exist; since there must be superintendence; since there must be one to enjoy; since there is a tendency to abstraction; therefore, soul is.

---

* प्रतिप्रतिगुणाश्रयविशेषात् । † एकैकगुणाश्रयेण यो विशेषस्तस्मात् । ‡ गुणवैषम्याद्वैषम्यं ।

BHÁSHYA.

As it is said, "Liberation is obtained by discriminative knowledge of discrete and undiscrete principles;" and whereas the undiscrete has been shewn to be distinct from the discrete by five arguments (ver. 9), so soul being, like the undiscrete principle, subtile (not cognizable by the senses), its existence is now established by inference. *Soul is.*—Why? *Because the assemblage of objects is for another's use.*—The assemblage of intellect and the rest is for the use of soul: this is inferred from the irrationality (of nature and its effects), like a bed. In like manner as a bed, which is an assemblage of bedding, props, cords, cotton, coverlid, and pillows, is for another's use, not for its own; and its several component parts render no mutual service; thence it is concluded that there is a man who sleeps upon the bed, and for whose use it was made: so this body, which is an assemblage of the five elements, is for another's use; or, there is soul, for whose enjoyment this enjoyable body, consisting of an aggregate of intellect and the rest, has been produced.

Again, soul is, *because the reverse of that which has the three qualities has been declared:* as it was stated in a former verse (11), 'A discrete principle has the three qualities, is indiscriminative, objective, &c.;" and it is added, "Soul is in these respects the reverse."

Again, soul is, *because there must be superintendence.*—As a charioteer guides a chariot drawn by horses able to curvet, to prance, to gallop, so the soul guides the body: as it is said in the *Shashṫhi Tantra,* "Nature, directed by soul, proceeds."

Soul is, *because there must be an enjoyer.*—In like manner as there must be some one to partake of food flavoured with sweet, sour, salt, pungent, bitter, and astringent flavours, so, as there is no capability of fruition in intellect and the other products of nature, there must be soul, by which this body is to be enjoyed.

Again, soul is, *because there is a tendency to abstraction.*—*Kaivalya* is the abstract noun, derived from *kevala*, 'sole, only'—for, on account of, that (abstraction); the practice of it: from the exercise of (or tendency to) abstraction (for the sake of its own separation or detachment) it is inferred that soul is. That is, Every one, whether wise or unwise, equally desires imperishable release from succession of worldly existence.

It is next to be determined whether this soul be but one superintendent over all bodies, like the string that supports all the gems of a necklace; or whether there be many souls presiding severally over individual bodies.

COMMENT.

Arguments for the existence of soul as a distinct principle are here adduced.

The existence of soul is established by inference: a bed implies a sleeper; nature, made up of its effects, is for the production of pain, pleasure, and insensibility, of which soul alone is conscious *. But admitting that the assemblage is for the benefit of another, why should that other be soul? because soul is not a similar aggregate; it is not made up of qualities and the like, but is the reverse of nature in these respects, as was explained in verse 11: or, as the commentator on the Sútra, *Sanhata parárthatwát* †, observes, because the property of pain or pleasure, which is identical with body, must be different from that which enjoys the one, or suffers the other. *Because there must be an enjoyer.*—The existence of an enjoyer implies the existence of both pleasure and pain; election between which cannot be made by intellect and the rest, which are inseparable from them, and it must be the act of something else, which is soul. 'Intellect and the rest are the things to be used (*bhogya*) or perceived (*driśya*), and consequently imply one who perceives ‡.' *S. Tatwa Kaumudi.*

The term *kaivalya*, rendered 'abstraction,' signifies 'detachment from the world;' or, as it is explained, 'absolute suppression of the three kinds of pain, as a property of sacred writ, holy sages, and inspired teachers or prophets. It must therefore be something different from intellect and the

---

* सुखदुःखमोहात्मकतया व्यक्तादयः सर्वे संघाताः। † संहतपरार्थत्वात्। ‡ भोग्या दृश्या बुद्ध्यादयो न च द्रष्टारमन्तरेण दृश्यता युक्ता तेषां तस्माददस्ति द्रष्टा दृश्यबुद्ध्याद्यतिरिक्तः स चात्मेति।

rest, which are the same thing as pain, and cannot effect a separation from their own essence *.' *S. Tatwa Kaumudí*. So VIJNÁNA BHIKSHU explains *kaivalya*, 'absolute extirpation of pain †.'

The arguments in the text for the existence of soul are so many original aphorisms of KAPILA; as, 1. 'Soul is distinct from body, &c.‡:' 2. 'From an aggregate being for another's use ‖:' 3. 'From (the properties of) soul being the converse of the three qualities, &c.§:' 4. 'From superintendence ¶:' 5. 'From the tendency to abstraction **.' The commentator notices a different reading of the last Sútra 'From nature not being competent to abstraction:' but this he considers erroneous ††. The fifth book of the *S. Pravachana* contains other Sútras affirmative of the separate existence of soul.

XVIII.

SINCE birth, death, and the instruments of life are allotted severally; since occupations are not at once universal; and since qualities affect variously; multitude of souls is demonstrated.

BHÁSHYA.

Life and death, and the instruments (*of life*).—From the several allotment of these: this is the meaning of the text. Thus, if there was but one soul,

---

* शास्त्राणां महर्षीणां दिव्यलोचनानां च। कैवल्यं चात्यन्तिकदुःखत्रयप्रशमलक्षणं न बुद्ध्यादीनां सम्भवति ते हि दुःखात्मकाः कथं स्वभावाद्विमोचयितुं शक्यन्ते।

† दुःखात्यन्तोच्छेदः।

‡ शरीरादिव्यतिरिक्तः पुमान्।

‖ संहतपरार्थत्वात्।

§ त्रिगुणादिविपर्य्ययात्।

¶ अधिष्ठानाच्चेति।

** कैवल्यार्थं प्रवृत्तेश्च।

†† अकैवल्यार्थं प्रकृतेः। इति सूत्रपाठः प्रामादिकत्वादुपेक्षणीयः।

then when one was born, all would be born; when one died, all would die; if there was any defect in the vital instruments of one, such as deafness, blindness, dumbness, mutilation, or lameness, then all would be blind, deaf, dumb, maimed, and halt: but this is not the case; and therefore, from the several apportionment of death, birth, and instruments of life, multiplicity of soul is demonstrated. *Since occupations are not at once universal.*—*Yugapat* means, 'at one time.' *Not at once;* or, at one time. *Occupation:* as engaging in acts of virtue and the like are not observed to occur at one moment; but some are busy with virtuous, others with vicious, actions; some cultivate indifference to the world, and some acquire true wisdom: therefore, from the non-contemporaneousness of occupation, multitude of souls is concluded. Also, *since qualities affect variously.*—From the contrary nature of the qualities multitude of souls is proved; as, in birth in general, one endowed with the quality of goodness is happy; another with that of foulness is wretched; and a third having that of darkness is apathetic: hence, therefore, multitude of souls is proved.

Soul is not agent: this is next declared.

COMMENT.

The multitudinous existence of soul, or the individual incorporation of soul in different bodies, is here maintained.

Birth is defined to be the association of soul with body; death, its detachment: soul being always existent, and not in itself subject to birth or death; as in the *S. Pravachana Bháshya**: also the *S. Tatwa Kaumudí;* 'Life is the combination of soul with the pains incident to body, &c.; not any modification of soul. Death is the abandonment of those bodies, &c.; not the destruction of soul †.' The instruments of life are

* जन्ममरणे चात्र नोत्पत्तिविनाशौ पुरुषनिष्ठत्वाभावात्

† देहेन्द्रियादिवेदनाभिः पुरुषस्यसम्बन्धो जन्म न तु पुरुषस्यपरिणामः । तेषामेव देहादीनां परित्यागो मरणं न त्वात्मनो विनाशः ।

the organs of perception and action, with egotism and intellect. 'Allotment,' *niyama*, properly 'rule, regulation,' is explained by *vyavasthá*, which may import 'distribution;' as, 'The distribution is in regard to different souls in several bodies *:' so also the Sútra of KAPILA; 'From the distribution of life, &c. follows the multitudinousness of soul †.' The term is especially understood, however, of the distribution which is laid down by religious and legal authorities, 'a prescribed distribution or allotment,' as the commentator on the Sútra observes, after stating, 'The virtuous man is happy in heaven,' &c. (see p. 48), 'Souls are many, as otherwise there would not be the occurrence of such division, or appointment of conditions, as is laid down in the Véda and the law ‡.' If soul were one, all the accidents, vicissitudes, and interests of existence would simultaneously affect all individuals.

But though manifold, as individualized, this individual soul is one and unchanged, through all its migrations into various forms, until its final liberation. It is the disguise which is changed, not that which wears it, as has been before explained (p. 48).

The multiplied existence of soul is in especial contradiction to the doctrine of the Védántis, of the universality of one supreme soul of the world, from which all human souls are derived, as in such texts as this; 'One only existent soul is distributed in all beings; it is beheld collectively or dispersedly, like the reflection of the moon in still or troubled water. Soul, eternal, omnipresent, undisturbed, pure, one, is multiplied by the power of delusion, not of its own nature ‖.' This is undoubtedly the doctrine of the Védas, and the Sánkhya teachers, who profess to receive those works as authority, are obliged to interpret the texts

---

* प्रतिक्षेत्रं पुरुषभेदे भवति व्यवस्था । † जन्मादिव्यवस्थातः पुरुषबहुत्वं । ‡ इत्यादेः श्रुतिस्मृतिव्यवस्थाया विभागस्यान्यथानुपपत्त्या पुरुषा बहवः । ‖ एक एव हि भूतात्मा भूते भूते व्यवस्थितः । एकधा बहुधा चैव दृश्यते जलचन्द्रवत् । नित्यः सर्व्वगतोह्यात्मा कूटस्थो दोषवर्ज्जितः । एकः स भिद्यते शक्त्या मायया न स्वभावात् ।

unfavourable to their dogmas in a peculiar manner. Thus the Sútra of KAPILA asserts, 'There is no contradiction (to the doctrine of many souls) in the unity of the Védas, from its reference to the comprehensiveness of genus *:' that is, Soul, considered as genus, is but one; its nature and properties are common to all souls, individualized and manifold in connection with individual aggregates of the products of nature. 'Genus here means community, unity of nature; such is the purport of the unity of the Védas; not indivisibility, from the absence of any motive (for its continuing undivided). This is the meaning of the Sútra †.' The subject is discussed at considerable length by VIJNÁNA BHIKSHU; but, notwithstanding his arguments, it is clear that the Sánkhya doctrine is contradictory to that of the Védas.

The doctrines of those Grecian philosophers, who maintained the immateriality and eternity of soul, conformed to that of the Védas. As far as we are able to learn of the doctrines of Pythagoras, he taught that human souls were portions of one supreme soul. Plato held the souls of men to be emanations from God, through the soul of the world. Souls and bodies were both portions of the τὸ ἓν, the 'one existent,' of the Stoics; and even Aristotle appears to have conceived the human soul to be an intellectual energy, derived from an eternal intelligence. Cudworth asserts that none of the ancient philosophers maintained the Sánkhya notion of the eternity of individual souls. "It doth not follow," he remarks, "because they held souls to be ingenerable, that therefore they supposed souls to have existed from all eternity of themselves unmade. This was never asserted by theist or atheist. The philosophic theists, who maintained *æternitatem animorum*, did, notwithstanding, assert their essential dependence upon the Deity, like that of the lights upon the sun, as if they were a kind of eternal effulgency, emanation, or eradiation, from an eternal Sun." Intell. Syst. III. 429.

---

* नाद्वैतश्रुतिविरोधो जातिपरत्वात् । जातिः सामान्यमेकरूपत्वं तत्रैवाद्वैतश्रुतीनां तात्पर्य्यान्नत्वखण्डत्वं प्रयोजनाभावादित्यर्थः ।

XIX.

And from that contrast (before set forth) it follows, that soul is witness, solitary, bystander, spectator, and passive.

BHÁSHYA.

And from that contrast: the contrast of the possession of the three qualities. *Contrast:* reverse. Soul is void of qualities, is discriminative, enjoyer, &c. The contrast is that presented by these attributes of soul; and thence, the qualities of goodness, foulness, and darkness being agents (active), *it follows that soul is (passive) witness.* This sentence is syntactically connected with the preceding, regarding the multitudinousness of soul. The qualities, as agents, act; a witness neither acts nor desists from action. Again, *abstraction* (detachment) is an attribute (of soul); the property of being sole is detachment or abstraction, difference or distinctness (from all others); that is, it is distinct, or separate, from the three qualities. Next, *being a bystander* (is an attribute of soul): the condition of a middle man (or looker-on, or neutral). Soul is a bystander, like a wandering mendicant: as a vagrant ascetic is lonely and unconcerned, whilst the villagers are busily engaged in agriculture, so soul does not act where the qualities are present. Hence also proceed the properties of being a *spectator* and *passive.* From being a bystander, soul is a spectator, and is not a performer of those acts (which it contemplates). The three qualities, goodness, foulness, and darkness, engage in acts in the relation of agent and act; not soul: and in this manner the existence of soul is demonstrated.

But if soul is a non-agent, how does it exercise volition? as, I will practise virtue, I will not commit crime: here soul must be the agent; for if soul is not the agent (then these purposes cannot be entertained). This is a dilemma: to explain which it is said—

COMMENT.

In the preceding verse it was stated that soul was many; in this, its other attributes are enumerated.

The conjunction *cha*, in the term *tasmát-cha*, connects the sentence with the preceding, or with *bahutwam*, 'multitudinousness.' The contrast alluded to is that intimated in ver. 14, and is this: Soul has not the three qualities, it is discriminative, it is perceptive, it is specific, it is rational, it is unprolific; being the reverse, in these respects, of nature and its effects. Not being an object of sense, but percipient of such objects, it observes and testifies to the existence of nature and its products, like an evidence in a lawsuit being plaintiff and defendant. 'That which is irrational cannot observe, and that to which an object is apparent is a witness *.' Solitariness is 'exemption from the three kinds of pain †;' or, in fact, total abstraction from the world: this is the necessary consequence of being devoid of the three qualities, which are essentially the same with pleasure, pain, and dulness; and from them, therefore, soul is equally free. From the same cause, absence of qualities and insusceptibility of agreeable or disagreeable emotions, proceeds the next property of soul, that of being a bystander; *madhyastha*, 'neutral, indifferent, unconcerned;' *udásína*, 'neither rejoicing in pleasure, nor sorrowing in pain.' Qualities, and particularly foulness, are indispensable to activity; and being without them, soul is consequently inert: the same is considered to be also the necessary result of its being 'discriminative and unprolific, or unproductive ‡.' VIJNÁNA BHIKSHU restricts the term *sákshí*, 'witness,' to the sense of 'beholder,' distinguishing it from the other term, to which such a translation is more applicable, *drashtri*, as importing one who has the object near to, or before, his eyes; the latter implies seeing in general: hence he says, 'Soul witnesses or contemplates *buddhi* (intellect), and sees the other principles ‖.'

---

* चेतनोहि द्रष्टा भवति नाचेतनः साक्षी च दर्शितविषयो भवति ।

† आत्यन्तिकदुःखत्रयाभावः कैवल्यं ।

‡ विवेकित्वादप्रसवधर्म्मित्वाच्चाकर्त्तेति सिद्धं ।

‖ बुद्धेरेव साक्षी पुरुषोऽन्येषां तु द्रष्टृमात्रमिति ।

XX.

Therefore, by reason of union with it, insensible body seems sensible; and though the qualities be active, the stranger (soul) appears as the agent.

BHÁSHYA.

Here soul is said to be possessed of sensation; and in connection with it, intellect and the other predicates of nature assuming the appearance of sense seem sentient: as in life, a jar with cold water appears to be cold, with warm water seems to be warm; so intellect and the rest, from *union with it*, with soul, *seem sensible*. But the qualities perform the active application (of sense), not the soul: for although in common it is said, soul is the doer, the goer, yet soul is not the agent. How so? *Though the qualities be active,* (soul) *the stranger appears as the agent*. There being activity of the qualities, soul, which is indifferent, or inactive, appears as if it was the agent; which it is not. Here is an illustration: as a man who is not a thief, being taken up along with thieves, is suspected to be a thief also; so soul, being connected with the three active qualities, is supposed, though inert, to be active also.

In this manner the distinction of the perceptible, imperceptible, and thinking principles (ver. 2. p. 13) has been explained; from the discrimination of which liberation is obtained. It is next expounded why the union of the two (chief) principles, nature and soul, takes place.

COMMENT.

It is here taught that the sentient faculty resides in soul, and not, as it appears to do, in the products of nature; and that activity resides in the qualities, not, as it appears to do, in soul.

The term *chétaná*, from *chit*, 'to reflect,' means in general 'reason, intelligence;' but it is here applied to the possession or exercise of every faculty proper to a sentient and thinking being. It is the attribute of soul only, as will be more distinctly made clear when the functions of the senses, of consciousness, and intellect are explained, and they are shewn to be merely the vehicles or instruments through which ideas and notions are conveyed. They seem, however, to act independently, but this is merely from their *union* with, or, more correctly, proximity to, soul; *samyoga* being explained by the commentators to mean here merely *sannidhána*, 'approximation.' In like manner, soul, which is contemplative, not active, mover, though itself unmoved, appears to be active through a similar contiguity. 'I am sentient; wishing to do, I do: here a common origin or subject of action and reflection is apprehended*.' *S. Tatwa Kaumudí*. But this is an error, as the site or subject of action and reflection is distinct †. The term *linga* in the first line is explained to denote *mahat* and the subtile products of *pradhána*. *Udásína*, 'indifferent,' is said also to mean 'inert ‡.'

But it appears that there are passages in the Védas and in the law-books which attribute agency to soul, and knowledge to *buddhi* ‖: and to meet this is supposed to be the purpose of the aphorism, 'Agency from affection, intelligence from propinquity §;' that is, 'The apparent agency of soul is from the affection (or operation) of *buddhi;* the apparent intelligence of *buddhi* (understanding) is from the proximity of soul; neither is actual. Their mutual transfer of properties is like that of fire and iron in a heated bar, or of the sun and water, in the reflected rays of the former from the latter ¶.' *S. Prav. S.* In like manner the *S. Chandriká* exemplifies the doctrine by reference to *buddhi*, the organ of the understanding; and furnishes also an example of the sense in which *chétaná*,

---

* चेतनोऽहं चिकीर्षन् करोमीति कृतिचैतन्ययोः सामान्याधिकरण्यमनुभवसिद्धं । † यतश्चैतन्यकर्त्तृत्वे भिन्नाधिकरणे युक्तितः सिद्धे तस्माद्भ्रान्तिरिति । ‡ औदासीन्यमकर्त्तृत्वं । ‖ पुरुषस्य कर्त्तृत्वं बुद्धेरपि चैतन्यं च श्रुतिस्मृत्योरुच्यमानं । § उपरागात् कर्त्तृत्वं चित्सान्निध्यात् । ¶ पुरुषस्य यत् कर्त्तृत्वं तद्बुद्ध्युपरागात् बुद्धेश्चया चित्ता सा पुरुषसान्निध्याद् एतदुभयं न वास्तवमित्यर्थः । यथाग्न्ययसोर्यथा वा जलसूर्य्ययोः परस्परं संयोगविशेषात् परस्परैकधर्म्मव्यवहारः ।

'intelligence,' is to be understood: 'Thence the effect (of *pradhána*), the category *buddhi*, which is unintelligent, is as it were intelligent, (seems to be that which says) I know, becomes as it were endowed with knowledge *:' that is, it is not the understanding, but soul, that knows. This, however, applies equally to all the other products of nature, as far as to the subtile rudiments, whether individually considered, or as composing subtile body †. They are all non-sentient, or irrational and inert. Their activity depends on combination with the qualities; their sentient power on proximity to soul: and the conjoint presence of these two properties leads to the erroneous belief that soul is agent, as well as sentient.

XXI.

For the soul's contemplation of nature, and for its abstraction, the union of both takes place, as of the halt and blind. By that union a creation is framed.

BHÁSHYA.

The union of soul with nature is for its contemplation (of nature); that is, soul contemplates nature (in the state of) intellect and the other effects to the gross elements inclusive. For that object is the union of nature with soul; and the same union, which is also for the abstraction (of the latter), is *like the association of the halt and blind*. As, a lame man and a blind man, deserted by their fellow-travellers, who in making their way with difficulty through a forest had been dispersed by robbers, happening to encounter each other, and entering into conversation so as to inspire mutual confidence, agreed to divide between them the duties of walking and of seeing; accordingly the lame man was mounted on the

---

* तस्मादचेतनमपि लिङ्गं बुद्धितत्वं चेतनावदिव जानामीति ज्ञानवद्भवति । † लिङ्गं महदादि सूक्ष्मपर्य्यन्तं ।

blind man's shoulders, and was thus carried on his journey, whilst the blind man was enabled to pursue his route by the directions of his companion. In the same manner the faculty of seeing is in soul, not that of moving; it is like the lame man: the faculty of moving, but not of seeing, is in nature; which resembles, therefore, the blind man. Further, as a separation takes place between the lame man and the blind man, when their mutual object is accomplished, and they have reached their journey's end, so nature, having effected the liberation of soul, ceases to act; and soul, having contemplated nature, obtains abstractedness; and consequently, their respective purposes being effected, the connexion between them is dissolved.

Again, *By that*, by that union, *a creation is framed.*—As the birth of a child proceeds from the union of male and female, so the production of creation results from the connection of nature and soul.

The text next describes the particulars of all the products of nature.

COMMENT.

The object of the union of soul and nature, or the final liberation of the former by its knowledge of the latter, is here explained.

'Contemplation,' *darśana*, is considered to comprise 'fruition,' *bhoga*. As nature is devoid of sensibility and reflection, it can neither enjoy nor observe; and its existence would be therefore without an object, unless there were some other one capable both of observation and fruition *. This other one is soul. But, again, as pain is inseparable from nature, so enjoyed soul desires, after a season, to be loosed from the combination; and this detachment, or the liberation of purified soul, necessarily requires some one from which to be liberated: that some one is nature: consequently, for the fulfilment of their respective ends—the fruition of nature, and liberation of soul—their mutual cooperation and combination are essential. 'Abstraction,' *kaivalya*, is explained by VÁCHESPATI, 'The cause of the attribution of separation to purified soul, which cannot be

---

* भोग्यं प्रधानं भोक्तारमन्तरेण न सम्भवति ।

without previous union with nature *.' But these results cannot be attained without the evolution of the products of nature, and consequently they assume their several developments, or, in other words, *a creation is framed;* as it is only in the state of discrete principles that nature is to be contemplated by soul, and it is only by the exact appreciation of the same, and of their source, that soul can detach itself from nature. For both purposes, therefore, the world must exist, as developed from its material cause.

There are passages in the Védas, however, attributing creation to soul; as, 'That was from it—From this soul was ether produced †.' To this it is replied, that all that is herein intended is the attribution of the act of the inferior, or nature, to the superior, soul: 'As in the world it is said that a king triumphs or is defeated, when it is not he, but his army, that suffers a defeat or achieves a victory ‡.' *S. Prav. Sára.*

XXII.

FROM nature issues the great one; thence egotism; and from this the sixteenfold set: from five among the sixteen proceed five elements.

BHÁSHYA.

Nature (*prakriti*) is also termed 'the chief one' (*pradhána*), 'the supreme' (*brahme*), 'the undistinguished' (*avyaktam*), 'the multi-comprehending' (*bahudhánáka*) and *máyá*. Such are its synonymes. From that which is devoid of characteristic attributes, or from (crude) nature, the great one (*mahat*) is produced: this is also termed 'intellect' (*buddhi*); it is also called *ásuri*, or 'demoniac;' *mati*, or 'understanding;' 'notoriety'

---

* सत्वपुरुषान्यताख्यातिनिवन्धनं न च सत्वपुरुषान्यताख्यातिः प्रधानमन्तरेणे ति । † तत् तस्माद्वा एतस्मादात्मन आकाशः सम्भूतः । ‡ यथा लोके स्वशक्तिषु योधेषु वर्त्तमानौ जयपराजयौ राज्ञि उपचर्य्येते ।

(*khyáti*), 'knowledge' (*jnána*), 'wisdom' (*prajná*). From thence proceeds egotism, also called 'the origin of the elements,' &c. (*bhútádi*), 'the luminous' (*taijasa*), 'the modified' (*vaikrita*), 'conscience' (*abhimána*). *From this the sixteenfold set.*—*From this*, from egotism, the class of sixteen is derived. This consists of the five subtile elements, or the archetypes of sound, touch, form, flavour, and odour: the synonymes of *tan-mátra* are all words denoting 'subtile' (*sukshma*): also the eleven organs, the ear, the skin, the eye, the tongue, the nose, which are the five organs of perception; the voice, the hand, the foot, and the organs of excretion and generation, which are the five organs of action; and, besides these, mind, making the eleventh, and being an organ of both action and sensation. These constitute the class of sixteen produced from egotism. *From five among the sixteen.*—From the five subtile elements proceed the five gross elements: as it is said, "From the archetype sound, ether is produced; from touch, air; from form, light (or fire); from flavour, water; from odour, earth: and thus from these five rudiments the five gross elements proceed." As also it is said, "From discriminative knowledge of perceptible and imperceptible principles and the thinking soul (see ver. 2) liberation is obtained." Now, therefore, intellect and the rest, to the gross elements inclusive, forming twenty-three categories, have been specified (in the text); the undiscrete principle has been described (see ver. 15, 16); and soul has been explained (ver. 18, 19); and these constitute the *twenty-five tatwas* (physical and metaphysical categories of the Sánkhya system of philosophy). He who knows the universe to be composed of these principles—called *tatwas*, from the abstract of *tad*, 'that,' implying the abstract existence of those principles—as it is said, "He who knows the twenty-five principles, whatever order of life he may have entered, and whether he wear braided hair, a top-knot only, or be shaven, he is liberated: of this there is no doubt." (See p. 1.) The twenty-five categories are, nature, soul, intellect, egotism, the five subtile (or rudimental) elements, the eleven organs of sensation and of action, and the five gross elements.

It is stated in this stanza, *from nature issues the great one.* What is meant by that *great one* is next defined.

COMMENT.

The categories of the Sánkhya system have been before alluded to (ver. 3. p. 16), in explanation of their mutual relations, and of the properties which they have in common, or by which they are discriminated from one another; but we have them here enumerated in the order of their production, as prefatory to a detailed description of them and of their functions contained in the following stanzas.

The generic term for the twenty-five principles, *tattwa*, or as usually and with equal correctness written *tatwa*, is explained by GAURAPÁDA to mean 'the abstract existence,' *astitwa**, *οὐσία*, *essentia*, of *tat*†, THAT; that thing, which is the object of philosophical investigation, or which has a real existence, and must be known. The more common etymology, *tat*, 'that,' and *twam*, 'thou,' belongs to the Védánta system; as in the *Mahávákya*, *tat-twam asi*, 'that (supreme soul) thou art,' implies the identity of universal and individualized spirit.

We have in the scholia of GAURAPÁDA on this stanza some synonymes of nature and the two first principles, the analysis of which elucidates the ideas entertained of them by the Sánkhyas. The succeeding stanzas will afford an opportunity of adverting to the terms used for intellect and egotism, and we may here confine the inquiry to the synonymes of nature, or matter.

Prakriti, as has been previously mentioned (p. 17), intimates, that which precedes, or is prior to, making; that which is not made from any thing else. It is also used relatively, to signify that which is the source from which a product is derived; so that *mahat* is the *prakriti* of *ahankára*, &c. (see p. 18). Here, however, our business is with the primary source of all material products, and the term indicates merely that which preceded (*pra*) production (*kriti*); what that may have been is left wholly undefined or unimplied by the particular term. The same may be said of it agreeably to another etymology given in the *Sánkhya Sára*, where

---

* अस्तित्वं । † तत् ।

pra is interpreted by *prakrishta*, 'principal, chief, best,' analogously to its other denomination, *pradhána*, 'the chief.' *Pradhána* is derived from *pra*, 'principal,' and *dhá*, 'to hold:' 'that in which all generated effect is comprehended*.' The next synonyme, *avyakta*, 'the unseparated, the undistinguished, the unperceived,' has been also previously noticed (p. 41) as derived from *anja*, 'to make clear,' with *vi*, separative preposition, and the negative *a* prefixed: the term is of as frequent occurrence as either of the preceding, and is constantly used as a synonyme of *prakriti* in the Puranas and in Manu. *Brahme*, which is to be carefully distinguished from *Brahmá*, the personified creative power, is ordinarily applied either to the Védas or supreme spirit, and is an uncommon synonyme of *prakriti;* but as derived from *vriha*, 'to increase,' it implies the first principle of which the expansion becomes all perceptible objects. *Bahudhánaka* is derived, like *pradhána*, from *dhá*, 'to hold;' *dhánaka*, 'the holder' or 'comprehender' of *bahu*, 'much', of all things. *Máyá*, in its ordinary sense of 'illusion,' is applied to *prakriti*, not by the Sánkhyas, for they maintain the reality of existing things, but by the Védántis and Pauranikas, who regard creation as a delusion or as a sport of the Creator: it is derived from the root *má*, 'to measure,' and may here perhaps imply either 'comprehension,' like *pradhána*, or 'extension.' There is no explanation of the term by any of the Scholiasts. VIJNÁNA BHIKSHU quotes the Védas to shew that it is synonymous with *prakriti* †. In the *Sánkhya Sára* we have other synonymes, as, *sakti*, 'power,' δύναμις; *ajá*, 'the unborn, the unproduced;' *tamas*, 'darkness;' and *avidyá*, 'ignorance ||.'

Now what is to be considered as the sense of these words? By what equivalent is *prakriti* to be best rendered? Professor Lassen translates it *procreatrix*, but this seems to convey too much the idea of personality, and therefore, although very well agreeing with the original term as used by the Pauraniks, where *prakriti* is commonly personified, yet it can

---

* प्रधीयतेऽस्मिन् कार्य्यजातमिति प्रधानमुच्यते । † मायां तु प्रकृतिं विद्यादिति श्रुतौ । ‡ प्रकृतिः शक्तिरजा प्रधानमव्यक्तं तमो मायाऽविद्येत्यादयः प्रकृतेः पर्य्यायाः ।

scarcely be considered as indicative of that which not only produces, but is the thing produced, being at once the origin and substance of all things. Mr. Colebrooke has rendered the term sometimes by 'nature,' and sometimes by 'matter:' the former expresses both the parent and the progeny, and agrees in being also the constant subject of *prosopopeia*. It is therefore preferable to perhaps any synonyme that the English language can offer. At the same time the correct equivalent is 'matter,' *materia, quasi mater*, 'the substance and source of material things;' not, however, crude, visible, or divisible matter, but that first principle of the Pythagoreans and Platonists, and of Aristotle, which having neither parts, nor form, nor sense, nor quantity, nor any of the properties of body, was yet the one universal, incorporeal, invisible substance from which all bodies were derived. *Διὸ δὴ τὴν τοῦ γεγονότος ὁρατοῦ καὶ πάντως αἰσθητοῦ μητέρα καὶ ὑποδοχὴν μήτε γῆν μήτε ἀέρα μήτε πῦρ μήτε ὕδωρ λέγωμεν, μήτε ὅσα ἐκ τούτων μήτε ἐξ ὧν ταῦτα γέγονεν. ἀλλ' ἀνόρατον εἶδός τι καὶ ἄμορφον πανδεχές.* Timæus. See also the Physics, b. III. c. 6. That we are to understand this of the *prakriti* of the Sánkhyas is evident from the meaning of its several appellations. It is also said by VIJNÁNA BHIKSHU, that 'the world is merely modification of form, of which *prakriti* is the materiality *.' 'It is not individual or formal, but universal material †.' *S. Pr. Bháshya*. Its invisibility is, as we have seen (ver. 8. p. 29), attributed, not to its non-existence, but to its subtilty (*saukshmya*). *Prakriti* is also defined 'the equilibrium of the three qualities ‡;' and here it differs from the subject matter of Aristotle in having qualities. These qualities, however, whilst *prakriti* is yet unevolved, neutralize each other, and are scarcely qualities as regards primary nature, because their loss of equilibrium, or their activity, is concurrent with the discontinuance of *prakriti* as separate from its products. So far, however, *prakriti* may be considered as different from the brute matter of the ancient physiologists, that it produces

---

* परिणामरूपं जगदुपादानकत्वं तु प्रकृतिः । † पारछिन्नं न सर्व्वोपादानं—सर्व्वोपादानं प्रधानं न परिछिन्नं व्यापकमित्यर्थः । ‡ त्रिगुणसाम्यं ।

products of its own energy or power for a special cause, and is therefore more akin to the "plastic nature that acts, ἕνεκα τοῦ, for the sake of something." In the Sánkhya system, however, such nature is not distinct from matter itself, whilst it appears to be a different principle in the writings of the Greek philosophers, although not always very intelligibly described; for, as Cudworth observes of Aristotle, "he nowhere declares of this nature of his, whether it be corporeal or incorporeal, substantial or accidental." To conclude, we are to understand of the *prakriti* of the Sánkhyas, primary, subtile, universal substance, undergoing modification through its own energy, and for a special motive, by which it is manifest as individual and formal substance, varied according to the predominance of qualities, which are equipoised and inert in the parent, and unequal and active in the progeny.

XXIII.

Ascertainment is intellect. Virtue, knowledge, dispassion, and power are its faculties, partaking of goodness. Those partaking of darkness are the reverse.

BHÁSHYA.

The definition of intellect is *ascertainment*. Ascertaining (discerning, determining) is ascertainment: as in the seed the future germinating shoot is contained, so is determination (in intellect). This is a jar, this is cloth: that intellect which will so determine is so defined. This intellect has eight members, according to the twofold affection of goodness and darkness. The first kind, or intellect, *partaking of goodness*, is of four kinds, *virtue, knowledge, dispassion, power*. *Virtue* comprises humanity, benevolence, and acts of restraint (*yama*) and of obligation (*niyama*). The former are said in the *Pátanjala* to be, restraint of cruelty, of falsehood, of dishonesty, of incontinence, and of avarice: the latter are the obligations of purification, contentment, religious austerity, sacred study, and worship of God. *Knowledge* has for its synonymes, manifestation, certainty, light. It is of two kinds, external and internal. The former is (knowledge of) the Védas and their six subordinate branches, recitation, ritual, grammar, glossary, prosody, and astronomy; also (of) the *purānas*, and of logic, theology, and law. Internal knowledge is that of nature and soul, or (the discrimination that) this is nature, the equipoised condition of goodness, foulness, and darkness: this is soul, perfect, devoid of qualities, pervading, and sentient. By external knowledge worldly distinction or admiration is acquired; by internal knowledge, liberation. *Dispassion* is also of two kinds, external and internal. The former is the indifference of one who contemns sensible objects from observing their defects, or the trouble of acquiring and preserving them; the inconvenience of attachment to them; their liability to decay; and the injustice they cause. The latter is the indifference of one who is desirous of liberation, and looks upon nature as if it was a piece of witchcraft or a dream. *Power* is the abstract property of a superior (or divine) being: it is eightfold, (the capacity of) minuteness, magnitude, heaviness, lightness, reach, gratification of will, dominion, subjugation, and irresistible purpose. Atomic existence is meant by 'minuteness;' so that a person becoming atomically subtile or minute may traverse the world: 'magnitude' is said of one who may make himself a giant: 'lightness' is having limbs like the fibres of the lotus stalk, or like cotton, so as to be able to stand upon the tops of the filaments of a flower: 'reach' is attainment of a desired object by going to the place where it is situated, wherever that may be: 'gratification of will' is obtaining or effecting whatever is desired: 'dominion' is governing the three worlds, as a king: 'subjugation' is having all things subject: 'irresistible purpose' is compelling the site, rest, and motion of all things, from Brahmá to a block, agreeably to the will of the person endowed with this faculty. These are the four properties of intellect which soul obtains when the qualities of foulness and darkness are overcome by that of goodness.

But *those partaking of darkness are the reverse.*—When intellect is influenced by the quality of darkness, then its four properties are the reverse of the above; they are, vice, ignorance, passion, and weakness. In this manner intellect having eight members, as it is affected by goodness or foulness, is produced from the undiscrete principle having the three qualities.

Intellect has thus been explained. Egotism is next described.

COMMENT.

The first product of nature, or intellect, is here described by its properties.

Intellect (*buddhi*) is *adhyavasáya**. It is not easy to offer a satisfactory equivalent for this word, nor to understand precisely what is meant by it. In the *Amera Kosha* it occurs as a synonyme of *utsáha*†, 'effort, strenuous and continued effort, perseverance;' according to Rámásrama, 'possessing great power‡.' He derives it from *sho antakarmmani*‖, 'finishing, making end of,' with *adhi*§, 'over,' and *ava*¶, 'off;' that is, entirely or absolutely ending or effecting; as in the *Hitopadésa:* 'The precepts of knowledge confer not the least benefit on one who is afraid of exertion: of what use is a lamp to a blind man, though it be within his reach**.' In the *Mitákshara, utsáha* is explained, 'Effort (or perseverance) in the performance of acts accomplishing the objects of man ††.' In the *Bhatti Kávya* we have the word used in the sense of 'wish, purpose, determination:' 'The bird said to the monkeys, You have not studied the law, if at such a season you wish (or resolve) to die ‡‡.'

In a preceding passage (ver. 5) the phrase *prati vishaya adhyavasáya* ‖‖, 'ascertainment of several objects,' was given as the definition of *drishta*,

---

* अध्यवसायः। † उत्साहः। ‡ अतिशक्तिभाक्। ‖ षो अन्तकर्म्मणि। § अधि। ¶ अव। ** न स्वल्पमप्यध्यवसायभीरोः करोति विज्ञानविधिर्गुणं हि। अन्धस्य किं हस्ततलस्थितोऽपि प्रकाशयत्यर्थमिह प्रदीपः। †† पुरुषार्थसाधनकर्म्मारम्भोऽध्यवसायः। ‡‡ जगाद वानरान् पक्षी नाध्यगीध्वं स्मृतीः। यूयं संकुटितुं यस्मात् कालेऽस्मिनध्यवस्यथ। ‖‖ प्रतिविषयाध्यवसायः।

'perception;' and the explanation of the Scholiast, *buddhivyápára jnánam**, 'knowledge, which is the exercise of the intellectual faculty,' was cited (p. 23). The same commentator, VÁCHESPATI, here defines it, 'the specific function of intellect, not differing from intellect itself;' or, to quote the passage at length, 'Ascertainment is intellect, from the identity of the act and the agent, as will be explained. Every one who engages in any matter first observes, or considers; he next reflects, it is I who am concerned in this; and then *determines*, this is to be done by me; thence he proceeds to act: this is familiar to every one. Thence this ascertainment that such act is to be done is the determination of intellect, which is as it were endowed with reason, from the proximity of the sentient principle. This is the specific function of intellect, not differing from intellect itself; and the definition of intellect is ascertainment, as that comprehends both its generic and specific distinctions †.'

The explanation of the *S. Chandriká* is to the same effect: '*Adhyavasáya* is a sort of modified condition of intellect, as flame is of a lamp; it is certainty in this form, such an act is to be done by me ‡.'

These explanations, however, would rather seem to intimate intention, or volition, or, at least, the determination to act after reflection; but the determination or conclusion that such an act should be done, does not necessarily signify that it shall be done: it is only the conclusion or ascertainment of its fitness. This function of the intellect, also, is not indispensably connected with the notion of will; as in the example given

---

* बुद्धिव्यापारज्ञानं । † अध्यवसायो बुद्धिः । क्रिया क्रियावतोरभेदविवक्षया । सर्व्वो व्यवहर्त्ता आलोच्य मत्वाहमधिकृत इत्यभिमत्य कर्त्तव्यमेतन्मयेत्यध्यवस्यति ततश्च प्रवर्त्तत इति लोकसिद्धं । तत्र योऽयं कर्त्तव्यमिति विनिश्चयश्चितिसन्निधानादापन्नचैतन्याया बुद्धेः योऽध्यवसायो बुद्धेरसाधारणव्यापारस्तदभेदा बुद्धिः स च बुद्धेर्लक्षणं समानासमानजातीयव्यवच्छेदकत्वात् । ‡ अध्यवसायो मयेदं कर्त्तव्यमित्याकारनिश्चयो दीपशिखेव बुद्धिपरिणामावस्थाविशेषः ।

by GAURAPÁDA; where, in the simple conclusion after consideration, "this object is a jar; that, is a piece of cloth," no wish, or will, is indicated; no act follows. It is clear also that he considers *adhyavasáya* merely as the functions of intellect in exercise: they are in intellect, and part of it, as the germ is in the seed, until brought into activity. Intellect is only an instrument; that which, having received the ideas or images conveyed through the organs of sense, and the mind, constructs them into a conclusive idea, which it presents to soul. Its function in exercise, therefore, is ascertainment or certainty, as described in the *S. Pravachana Bháshya*, which explains *adhyavasáya*, 'the synonyme, as well as *buddhi*, of the great principle (*mahat*), and its specific function denominated ascertainment *.'

The other synonymes of this principle are, *buddhi*, derived from *budh*, 'to know,' 'knowing, intellect.' *Mahat*, 'great, the great principle;' 'The first and most important of the products of nature, and presiding over and pervading the whole †.' *Ásurí* ‡: this is a very unusual and questionable denomination. It occurs only in the *S. Bháshya*, and may be an error, perhaps for *śemushi*, one of the synonymes of *buddhi* in the *Amera kosha*. It cannot be connected with *asura*, 'a demon,' as if the faculty were incompetent to convey divine knowledge; for one of its properties, in connexion with the quality of goodness, is *jnyána*, 'true knowledge.' There is no good reason why it should be derived from ASURI, the pupil of KAPILA, unless allusion is made to some personification of intellect, as the bride of the sage. No explanation of the word is given in the *Bháshya*, and I must confess my inability to suggest one entitled to any confidence. *Mati* means 'understanding:' *manyaté anayá*, that by which any thing is understood. *Khyáti* properly signifies 'fame,' but here means 'notoriety, notion, familiar knowledge;' as in the *Smriti*,

---

* महत्तत्वस्य पर्य्यायो बुद्धिरित्यध्यवसायश्च निश्चयाख्यस्तस्यासाधारणी वृत्तिरित्यर्थः ।

† महत्त्वं स्वेतरसकलकार्य्य व्यापकत्वान्महैश्वर्य्याच्च मन्तव्यं ।

‡ आसुरी ।

'The great one it is, whence the familiar notions of the universe are always produced *.' *Jnyána* is usually the term for 'true or divine knowledge;' knowledge of matter and spirit leading to liberation; but it is here employed in its generic purport, 'that by which things are known.' The same may be said of *prajná*, which is also commonly used in the sense of 'true wisdom,' but here implies merely, 'that by which knowledge is obtained,' *prajnáyaté anayá*, as RÁMÁSRAMA expounds it. Several of these terms, in their technical, as well as literal application, bear an analogy to the νοῦς of Aristotle, and the φρόνησις of Plato. M. Cousin considers the category to be 'une sorte d'ame du monde.' It is, however, the instrument most proximate to soul, by which the latter perceives, wills, and acts.

Intellect is of two kinds, or has two sets of properties, as it is influenced or affected by the opposite qualities, goodness and darkness. The former are, 'virtue,' *dherma;* 'knowledge,' *jnyána;* 'dispassion,' *vairágya;* and 'power,' *aiswaryya.* The latter are their negatives, 'vice,' *adherma;* 'ignorance,' *ajnyána;* 'passion,' *avairágya;* and 'weakness,' *anaiswaryya.* These again comprehend specific varieties.

Dherma, 'virtue,' according to the *S. Bháshya*, comprehends morality and religion. The *S. Tatwa Kaumudí* explains it, 'The cause of happiness and liberation †.' As the source of prosperity and happiness in life, it is the discharge of religious and moral obligations‡; as the means of liberation, it is the observance of the eightfold *yoga*, or eight modes of contemplative devotion ‖. *Jnyána*, or 'knowledge,' is defined by the same Scholiast to be, 'distinct notion of the difference between the three qualities and soul §.' 'Dispassion,' *vairágya*, is the extinction of *rága*, 'colour,' or passion, which like dyes of various hues tinctures the soul ¶.'

---

* महानिति यतः ख्यातिर्लोकानां जायते सदा । † धर्म्मोभ्युदयनिःश्रेयसहेतुः । ‡ यागदानादिः । ‖ अष्टाङ्गयोगानुष्ठानं । § गुणपुरुषान्यताख्यातिर्ज्ञानं । ¶ रागादयः कषायाश्चित्तवर्त्तिनस्तेषामभावो वैराग्यं ।

'Power,' *aiswaryya*, is the possession of superhuman faculties. It is always termed eightfold, even in the *S. Bháshya*, although nine varieties are there named: one of them, however, 'heaviness,' *gariman*, finds no place among the definitions given there, any more than in other authorities. It may be supposed to be included under the faculty of magnitude.

The four first faculties, 'minuteness,' *animá;* 'lightness,' *laghimá;* 'reach,' *prápti;* and 'magnitude,' *mahimá;* are explained and illustrated every where much in the same way. According to Váchespati, the person endowed with the first can make his way into a solid rock: with the second, he may ascend to the solar sphere upon a sunbeam; or, as Moore has it, "may dance on a beam of the sun:" with the third, he can touch the moon with the tip of his finger: and with the fourth, he may expand himself so as to occupy all space. The latter four faculties are less distinctly defined, and are sometimes confounded: the shades of difference are indeed so slight, that they may all be resolved into one, 'absolute power over matter.' 'Gratification of will,' *prákámya*, is generally defined by *ichchhánabhigháta* *, 'unobstruction of wish;' or, as explained by Hémachandra, in his commentary on his own Lexicon, 'The wishes of a person possessing this faculty are unimpeded by the properties of material nature, such as form and the like; so that he can swim, dive, or float in earth as readily as in water †.' This is sometimes adduced in illustration of the meaning of the next faculty, but less accurately. That, is termed *vasitá*, which Váchespati defines, 'absolute subjugation of the elements and elementary beings ‡.' The *Chandriká* makes it 'independance on matter ||,' which is much the same as *prákámya;* and a similar confusion occurs in Rámásrama's commentary on Amera, for he illustrates it by 'swimming or diving on dry land §.' 'Subjugation of nature' is the usually accepted import; as Hémachandra, 'Thus as (with this faculty)

---

* इच्छानभिघातः ।

† नास्य भूतस्वरूपैर्मूर्त्त्यादिभिरिच्छाऽभिहन्यते भूमावुन्मज्जति निमज्जति यथोदके ।

‡ भूतभौतिकं वशी भवत्यवश्यं ।

|| गुणभूताद्यनधीनता ।

§ भूमावप्युन्मज्जनिमज्जने ।

any one determines the elements shall be, so they remain *.' The next faculty is 'dominion,' *ísitá*. According to VÁCHESPATI, it is 'disposition at will of the production, arrangement, and expenditure of the elements and elementary beings †.' NÁRÁYANA explains it, 'directing or impelling them at will ‡.' RÁMÁSRAMA interprets it *prabhutwa*, 'dominion, sovereignty; under which inanimate things obey command ‖.' The last faculty is termed *yatrakámávaśáyitá*. In RÁMÁSRAMA's commentary he reads the word *kámávaśáyitá* §; and the only variety he notices is that of the sibilant, which is sometimes, he observes, the dental, instead of the palatal letter ¶. According to the latter reading it is derived from *śí* **, 'to sleep;' to the former, from *shó* ††, 'to destroy:' in either, with *ava* prefixed, meaning, as RÁMÁSRAMA explains it, 'he who tranquillizes or destroys (that is, accomplishes) his desires ‡‡.' The reading of GAURAPÁDA is, however, *yatrakamávasáyitá*, as one compound; and the common definition of the term is 'true (infallible) purpose ‖‖,' wherever exercised: 'Whatever the person having this faculty intends or proposes must be complied with by that which is the subject of his purpose; the elements themselves must conform to his designs §§.' The *Chandriká* has, 'Whatever the will proposes, that it obtains ¶¶.' HÉMACHANDRA, in his text, gives the word as in the *Bháshya*, *yatrakámávasáyitwam*; and explains it, 'he who accomplishes his desires, to whatever they may be directed ***:' and he illustrates it by saying that 'an *arhat*, or Bauddha saint, can, by

* तेन यथा तानि (पृथिव्यादीनि) यथावस्थापयति तथावतिष्ठन्ते । † भूतभौतिकानां प्रसवव्यूहव्ययानामीष्टे । ‡ भूतभौतिकानां संकल्पमात्रेण प्रेरणं । ‖ प्रभुत्वं येनस्थावराण्याज्ञाकारिणः । § ईशिता वशिता चैव तथा कामावशायिता । ¶ कामावसायिता । ** शी । †† षो । ‡‡ कामानवशेते—अवस्यतिवा । ‖‖ सत्यसंकल्पता । §§ यथास्य संकल्पोभवति भूतेषु तथैव भूतानि भवन्ति । ¶¶ यत्कामस्तदवस्यति तत्प्राप्नोति । *** यत्रकामस्तत्रावश्यतीति ।

virtue of this faculty, convert poison into ambrosia, and administer it as means of vitality *.'

XXIV.

Consciousness is egotism. Thence proceeds a twofold creation. The elevenfold set is one: the five elemental rudiments are the other.

BHÁSHYA.

The elevenfold set: the eleven organs. *The five elemental rudiments:* elementary matter of five kinds, or the rudiments, sound, touch, form, flavour, and odour. What sort of creation proceeds from that which is thus defined is next explained.

COMMENT.

The third category is here specified, and described as the source of the senses and their respective objects.

The term here given as the synonyme and definition of 'egotism,' *ahankára* †, is *abhimána* ‡, translated 'consciousness.' The ordinary sense of both words is *pride,* and the technical import is 'the pride or conceit of individuality;' 'self-sufficiency;' the notion that 'I do, I feel, I think, I am,' as explained by Váchespati: 'I alone preside and have power over all that is perceived and known, and all these objects of sense are for my use. There is no other supreme except I; I am. This pride, from its exclusive (selfish) application, is egotism ‖.' The principle, therefore, is something more in Hindu metaphysics than mere consciousness,

---

* विषमप्यमृतकार्य्यं संकल्पतो भोजयं जीवयतीति । † अहंकारः । ‡ अभिमानः । ‖ यत् खल्वालोचितं मतं च तत्राहमधिकृतः शक्तः खल्वहमत्र मदर्था एवामी विषयाः मत्तो नान्योत्राधिकृतः कश्चिदस्त्यहमस्मि योऽभिमानः सोऽसाधारणव्यवहारत्वादहंकारः ।

or *conscience*. It might be better expressed, perhaps, by 'le moi,' as it adds to the simple conception of individuality the notion of self-property, the concentration of all objects and interests and feelings in the individual.

The other synonymes of this category express rather modifications of it, as the next stanza intimates. *Taijasa*, 'the active' or 'the ardent,' from *téjas* *, 'light, splendour, ardour,' refers to its animating or exciting influence on human actions, in connection with the quality of foulness. *Bhútádi* †, 'primitive element,' and *vaikrita* ‡, 'the modified,' as explained in the *Bháshya*, on the next verse, regard its being, in connection with darkness and goodness, the principle from which the organs and objects of sense proceed: for it must not be forgotten, that this category of egotism or consciousness has a physical, not a metaphysical character, according to the Sánkhya philosophy, being the organ or instrument by which the impression of individuality is conveyed to soul. It is in this capacity that it may be considered the primary element, the parent of the rudiments of the elements, or the objects of sense, and of the organs by which they are perceived. It is, in fact, the same with both these, as it is only by the application of our own senses to the objects of sense that we can become conscious of individual existence.

XXV.

FROM consciousness, affected by goodness, proceeds the good elevenfold set: from it, as a dark origin of being, come elementary particles: both issue from that principle affected by foulness.

BHÁSHYA.

When goodness predominates in egotism over darkness and foulness, that egotism is of the pure kind; the name of which, according to ancient

---

* तेजस् । † भूतादिः । ‡ वैकृतः ।

teachers, was *vaikrita*, 'the modified.' From this modified egotism the class of eleven organs is produced. *The good set:* perfect organs; adequate to their functions: the set is thence called *good.* Again; *from it, as a dark origin of beings, &c.*—When darkness predominates in egotism over goodness and foulness, that egotism is called *dark*, or, as it was named by the old masters, 'primitive element,' *bhútádi. From it come elementary particles;* the fivefold set. The first element of the elements is darkness; therefore it is usually called *the dark:* from that primitive element the fivefold rudimental set proceed. *Both issue from that principle affected by foulness:* that is, the egotism in which foulness predominates over goodness and darkness takes the denomination *taijasa*, 'the active;' and from that both proceed; both the eleven organs and five rudiments. For the pure egotism, which is *vaikrita*, 'the modified,' becoming so modified, produces the eleven organs: but to do this it takes active egotism for its assistant; for pure (*sátwika*) egotism is inert, and is only able to produce the organs when combined with the active. In like manner the dark egotism, or that which is called 'primitive element,' is inert, and becomes active only in union with the active, when it produces the five rudiments. Therefore it is said, both the organs of sense and their objects issue from the modification of egotism affected by foulness. The good elevenfold set proceeds from modified egotism, or that which is affected by the quality of goodness. They are next particularized.

COMMENT.

The products of egotism are here described as proceeding from three modifications of that principle, varied by the influence of the three qualities.

The terms used to designate the 'pure,' or *sátwika* principle; the 'dark,' or *támasa;* and the 'foul,' or *rájasa;* 'variety of egotism,' or *vaikrita, bhútádi,* and *taijasa;* have been explained. According to our text, as understood by the Scholiasts, the eleven organs of sense issue from pure or modified egotism, and the five rudiments from elemental egotism; both being influenced by ardent or active egotism.' The commentator on the *S. Pravachana* has a rather different explanation, interpreting *ékádaśaka*, 'eleventh,' not 'elevenfold:' according to him, this eleventh, which is mind, proceeds from the first kind of egotism; the other ten from the second kind; and the elements from the third. "*Sutra:* The pure eleventh (organ) proceeds from modified egotism. *Comment:* Eleventh, is mind, which in the class of sixteen organs and rudiments is of the quality of goodness; therefore it is born from egotism, affected by goodness, called *vaikrita*. This is the sense. Hence it follows, that from egotism, affected by foulness, proceed the other ten organs of sense; and from egotism, affected by darkness, proceed the rudiments *." This interpretation he defends by the authority of the law-books and Puranas; and he gives a similar turn, although rather indistinctly expressed, to the text of the *Káriká*. In the stanzas subsequent to this, to ver. 37, the organs of sense are fully described, and in ver. 38. the text returns to the elements. It is not necessary, therefore, to enter upon any explanation of them in this place. There is a remarkable expression in the *Bháshya*, which presents a notion familiar to all ancient cosmogonies. Gaurapáda says, 'the first of the elements was darkness †.' It is the first of the 'elements,' not the first of 'things;' for it was preceded by unevolved nature, and intellect, and it is itself a modified form of individuality. It therefore harmonizes perfectly well with the prevailing ideas in the ancient world, of the state of things anterior to elementary or visible creation, when "chaos was, and night," and when

> Nullus adhuc mundo præbebat lumina Titan,
> Nec nova crescendo reparabat cornua Phœbe.

In the influence of the quality of foulness, or passion, for the word *rajas* has both senses, may be suspected an affinity to the doctrine of an active principle, the moving mind, the *eros*, that set inert matter into motion, and produced created things.

---

* सात्विकमेकादशकं प्रवर्त्तते वैकृतादहंकारात् ॥ एकादशानांपूरणमेकादशकं मनः षोडशात्मगणमध्ये सात्विकमतस्तद्वैकृतात् सात्विकाहंकाराज्जायत इत्यर्थः। अतश्चराजसाहंकाराद्दशेन्द्रियाणि तामसाहंकाराच्च तन्मात्राणीत्यपि गन्तव्यं।

† भूतानामादिभूतस्तमः।

XXVI.

INTELLECTUAL organs are, the eyes, the ears, the nose, the tongue, and the skin: those of action are, the voice, hands, feet, the excretory organ, and that of generation.

BHÁSHYA.

Reckoning from the eye to the organ of touch, the organs are called 'intellectual.' Touched by it, the organ of touch, which is the skin: thence the term for the skin which is used (in the text), 'that which touches,' *sparśanaka.* Intellectual organs are five, as they ascertain or know (severally) five objects, or sound, touch, form, flavour, and smell. *Those of action, &c.*—They perform acts, whence they are called 'organs of action:' thus, the voice articulates; the hands variously manipulate; the feet effect motion; the excretory organ, excretion; and the sexual organ, generation. Thus are enumerated ten organs, five of intellect and five of action. The character and nature of the eleventh, or mind, is next described.

COMMENT.

The five instruments or means of perception and five of action, products of egotism, are enumerated in this stanza.

The term 'organs' is correctly applicable to the material instruments by which perception is exercised; but it is not to be understood of the gross corporeal bodies, the visible eye, ear, hand, &c., which are parts of gross body. The word 'senses' would therefore be a less equivocal term, only that it does not so distinctly convey the idea of an instrument which, though subtile, is substantial. The original word, *indriya,* is defined to mean whatever relates or belongs to *indra,* said to be a synonyme of soul, the senses being indicative, being marks or signs, of the presence of soul*:

---

* इन्द्रस्यात्मनश्चिह्नादिन्द्रियमुच्यते ।

accordingly each is denominated a *linga* (see p. 24), 'a characteristic feature or indication *.'

XXVII.

(In this set is) mind, which is both (an organ of sensation and of action). It ponders, and it is an organ as being cognate with the rest. They are numerous by specific modification of qualities, and so are external diversities.

BHÁSHYA.

Here, as one of the class of organs, *mind* is said to be *both*. Among the organs of sensation it is one of sensation, and among those of action it is an organ of action also. As it performs the function of the organs of sensation and of those of action it belongs to both. *It ponders* (or purposes); whence the term *sankalpaka*. *It is also an organ as being cognate with the rest;* for such is the meaning of the word *sádhermya*. The organs of sensation and action being (cognate or) produced, along with mind, from egotism affected by goodness, have this (property, of origin) in common with mind; and from this common property mind is an organ likewise.

Thus eleven organs are produced from egotism affected by goodness. What, then, is the function (*vritti*) of mind? Reflection (*sankalpa*) is its function. Sound and the rest are the functions of the organs of sensation. Speech and the rest are the functions of the organs of action. Now are these various organs, apprehending various objects, so created by *Íswara?* or are they self-generated? since nature, intellect, and egotism, are devoid of sense; and soul is devoid of action. Thence, according to the Sánkhya doctrine, a certain spontaneity is the cause (of the variety of the senses). Therefore it is added, *They are numerous by specific modification of qualities, and so are external diversities:* that is, the several objects of these eleven

---

* रूपग्रहणलिङ्गं चक्षुः शब्दग्रहणलिङ्गं श्रोत्रमित्यादि ।

organs, or sound, touch, form, flavour, and odour, which are the objects of five; speech, manipulation, motion, excretion, and generation, the objects of other five; and reflexion, the object of mind; these all proceed from specific modification of qualities. From the variety (or special difference) of such modifications of the qualities the multifariousness of the organs proceeds, as well as the diversity of external objects: consequently this variety is not the work of *Íswara*, nor of egotism, nor of intellect, nor of nature, nor of soul; but from modification of the qualities, produced by spontaneity. It does not proceed designedly (it is not the result of a will to act), because the qualities are non-sentient (unconscious or irrational). How then does it take place? This, as will be afterwards explained, is in like manner as the secretion of milk is for the growth of the calf, so the proceedings of nature take place for the liberation of soul, without soul's being cognizant of them; so the unconscious qualities become modified by the existence of the eleven organs, and their varieties are thence derived. Hence the eye is placed in its elevated orbit for the purpose of looking up to heaven; and in like manner the nose, the ear, the tongue are commodiously situated for the apprehension of their respective objects: the organs of action are also distributed conveniently for the discharge of their several duties of their own nature, through the modification of the qualities, not as their objects; as it is elsewhere said, "Qualities abide in qualities; that which is the function of the qualities is their object." External diversities, therefore, are to be regarded as made by the qualities: this is the meaning of the text. Of which nature is the cause.

The several functions of the organs are next specified.

COMMENT.

After defining mind as an instrument both of sensation and of action, this verse explains how it is that there are various organs and objects of sense; and it is said to depend in both cases upon specific modifications of the qualities of nature.

Mind is an instrument both of sensation and of action. Its function is *sankalpa*, a word that more commonly means 'resolve, purpose, expectation;' as in the *Hitopadésa,* 'the crow,' *Laghupatanaka,* says, 'All has been heard by me; and this is my resolve, that we must be friends *.' And MENU: 'Desire is the root of expectation; sacrifice is its product †:' or, as KULLÚKA BHAṬṬA explains it, '*Sankalpa* is understanding to this effect, that by a certain ceremony a desired consequence is effected ‡.' In both passages the notion of 'conclusion from foregone premises' is conveyed, and that seems to be its meaning here. Thus VÁCHESPATI explains it: 'The mind carefully considers a substance perceived by an organ of sense, (and determines) this is simple, that is not so; or discriminates them by their condition of predicate and predicable ‖.' Again, it is said, "First, knowledge or perception is simple (inconsiderate), like the knowledge of a child, a dumb man, or the like: it is produced by the mere thing; but when, after this, the thing, as distinguished by its properties, by its genus, and the like, is recognised by the understanding, and intellect is in accordance with perception, that period (or interval) of determination is the operation of the mind." Here, then, *sankalpa* is the process of reflection, the consideration of the object of simple perception, so as to form a definite idea, which mind transmits, through individuality and intellect, to soul. In this way mind is an organ both of perception and action; perceiving the objects presented by the senses, and forming them into a positive idea. It is further identified with both classes of organs by originating from the same source, egotism affected by goodness; and consequently it consists of the same material §.

The second portion of the stanza conveys a doctrine that is not very intelligible. The variety of the senses and of the objects of the senses is

---

* श्रुतं मया सर्व्वं तथापि चैतावान् संकल्पस्त्वया सह सौहृद्यमवश्यं करणीयं । † संकल्पमूलः कामो वै यज्ञाः संकल्पसम्भवाः । ‡ अनेन कर्म्मणा इदमिष्टं फलं साध्यत इत्येव विषया बुद्धिः संकल्पः । ‖ आलोचितमिन्द्रियेण वस्त्विदमिति सम्मुग्धमिदमेवं नैवमिति सम्यक् कल्पयति विशेषणविशेष्यभावेन विवेचयतीति । § सात्विकाहंकारोपादानत्वं च साधर्म्यं ।

said to arise spontaneously in them, from specific modification of the three qualities. VÁCHESPATI understands the allusion to external objects to be merely illustrative; that is, the internal organs are diversified by modification of the qualities, in the same manner that external objects are varied by the same modification*:' and the translation follows this explanation. In the *Bháshya* a different reading in the original occurred, which would require the passage to be rendered, 'and *from* variety of external objects †:' thus ascribing the diversity of the organs, not only to modification of the qualities, but to the diversity of external objects, which require suitable, and therefore various organs for their apprehension. The reading is, however, clearly incompatible with his argument, although GAURAPÁDA is somewhat obscure; but the variety is noticed and admitted by the author of the *Chandriká* ‡.

The *S. Pravachana Bháshya* considers the multifariousness spoken of in the Sútra, which conveys apparently a similar doctrine to that of the *Káriká*, as restricted to mind: 'Multifariousness is from modification of qualities, as the variety of human condition (is from various association): that is, as the very same individual assumes different characters, according to the influence of his associations; becoming a lover with a mistress, a sage with sages, a different person with others; so mind, from its connection with the eye or any other organ, becomes identified with it, and consequently is diversified according to the function of sight and the rest of the organs with which it is severally associated ‖.' The association of mind with the organs is intimated by the Védas, as in the text, 'My mind was elsewhere, I did not hear §.' The very illustration used by Locke:

---

* बाह्यभेदाश्चेति दृष्टान्तार्थं यथा बाह्यभेदास्तथैतदपीत्यर्थः । † बाह्यभेदाच्च । ‡ बाह्यभेदाच्चेतिपाठे तु ग्राह्यभेदादपीन्द्रियभेद आवश्यको बोध्य इत्यर्थः । ‖ गुणपरिणामभेदान्नानात्वमवस्थावत् । यथैक एव नरः संगवशान्नानात्वं भजते कामिनीसंगात् कामुको विरक्तसंगाद्विरक्तोऽन्यसंगाच्चान्य एव मनोऽपि चक्षुरादिसंगात् चक्षुराद्येकीभावेन दर्शनादिवृत्तिविशिष्टतया नाना भवति । § अन्यत्रमना अभूवं नाश्रौषमिति ।

"A man whose mind is intently employed in the contemplation of some objects, takes no notice of impressions made by sounding bodies upon the organ of hearing: therefore it is evident that perception is only when the mind receives the impression," says the English philosopher; and the Hindu infers, that 'the mind must cooperate with the organs of sense, even for perception, as they would otherwise be incapable of performing their functions *.'

The materiality of mind, considered as distinct from consciousness, intelligence, and soul, and as neither more nor less than an internal sense, a *sensorium*, is much less absurd than the same character of it when considered as part of, or identical with, soul, as was the doctrine of the Epicureans, whose description of mind, as an organ merely, agrees well enough with the Hindu notion:

Primum; animum dico mentem quam sæpe dicamus
Esse hominis partem nihilo minus ac manus ac pes
Atque oculei, partes animantes totius exstant. LUCRETIUS, III. 94.

XXVIII.

THE function of five, in respect to colour and the rest, is observation only. Speech, handling, treading, excretion, and generation are the functions of five (other organs).

BHÁSHYA.

The term 'only' (*mátra*) is to be understood in the sense of specialty, or the exclusion of what is not specified; as in the sentence, "Alms only are received;" that is, nothing else is received. Thus the eyes are observant of colour (form), not of flavour and the rest; and so of the

* चक्षुरादीनां मनः संयोगं विना व्यापाराक्षमत्वादनुमीयते ।

other senses. And in this way the function of the eye is colour (vision); of the tongue, taste; of the nose, smell; of the ear, sound (hearing); of the skin, touch: these are the functions of the intellectual organs. *Speech and the rest* (are the functions) of the five organs of action; or, speech is the function of the voice (*larynx*, &c.); handling, of the hands; treading, of the feet; dejection of excrement separated from food, of the rectum; and generation of offspring, of the sexual organs: 'function or object' being required for each term by the grammatical construction of the sentence.

The functions of intellect, egotism, and mind are next described.

COMMENT.

The text particularizes the functions of the organs of sense severally.

The general term for the office of the senses is *álochana* *, literally 'seeing, beholding, perceiving, observing.' According to ancient authorities it is said to comprise both the first undeliberative, and the second deliberative knowledge; or, in short, what is understood by 'perception †.' The commentator on the *S. Pravachana*, who gives this explanation, observes, however, that some consider deliberative perception to be the property of the mind only, whilst simple or undeliberative perception is that of the external senses; and this appears to be the doctrine of the Sánkhyas: the senses receive simple impressions from without of their own nature; whether those impressions are *perceived*, depends upon the cooperation of the internal sense, or mind. The term for 'function' is *vritti*, explained by *vyápára*, 'active exercise or application;' also by *sámarthyam*, 'ability, adequacy;' and *phala*, 'fruit, result.' GAURAPÁDA

---

* आलोचनं।   † आलोचनञ्च पूर्व्वाचार्य्यैर्व्याख्यातं। अस्तिचालोचनं ज्ञानं प्रथमं निर्विकल्पकं। परंपुनस्तथा वस्तुधर्म्मैर्जात्यादिभिस्तथेति। तथाच निर्विकल्पकसविकल्पकरूपद्विविधमपि ऐन्द्रियकज्ञानमालोचनमंगमिति।

has *vishaya*, 'object;' and it may be said, that the function and object of a sense is the same thing, sight being both the function and the object of the eye. There is some difficulty in translating some of the terms satisfactorily, although there is none in understanding what is meant by them. Thus *rúpa*, 'form,' or, as rendered in the text, 'colour,' is the object and office of the eye; it is therefore equivalent both to visible substance and sight. So of *śabda*, 'sound;' it is both hearing and that which is heard. *Sperśa*, 'touch,' is the faculty and the substance to which contact may be applied. In *rasa*, 'taste,' and *gandha*, 'smell,' we have the double equivalents, as both words in English, as well as in Sanscrit, express both the sense and the sensible property. In English, 'voice' is a function; but here, at least, *vách** is also the instrument of speech. In the other organs of action the function is more readily rendered; but the difficulty in any case is only that of language, and the sense is sufficiently explicit.

XXIX.

Of the three (internal instruments) the functions are their respective characteristics: these are peculiar to each. The common function of the three instruments is breath and the rest of the five vital airs.

BHÁSHYA.

The natural properties, which are the several characteristics, are the *respective characteristics* (as previously defined). *Ascertainment is intellect* (ver. 23): that also is the function of intellect. *Consciousness is egotism* (ver. 24): consciousness is both its characteristic and its function. *Mind ponders* (ver. 27): such is its definition; and reflection, therefore, is the function of mind. Of these three, intellect, egotism, and mind, their respective characteristics are their specific functions. The functions of the intellectual organs, as before explained, are also specific (the same is

* वाच् ।

the case with the organs of action). But now their common function is described. *The common function of the instruments.*—The function of the instruments in common is *breath and the rest of the five vital airs;* the airs called *prána, apána, samána, udána,* and *vyána.* These are the five airs which are the common function of all the organs of sense. The air, for instance, called *prána* is that which is perceptible in the mouth and nostrils, and its circulation is the common function of the thirteen kinds (of instruments): that is, where there is breath, the organs acquire (are connected with) soul (they become living). Breath, like a bird in a cage, gives motion (vitality) to the whole. It is called *prána,* 'breath' or 'life,' from 'breathing.' From carrying downwards (*apanayana*), the air *apána* is so named; the circulation of which, also, is the common function of the organs. *Samána* is so named from conducting equally (*samanayana*) the food, &c. (through the frame). It is situated in the central part of the body, and its circulation is the common function of the instruments. The air *udána* is denominated from ascending, or from drawing or guiding best (*un-nayana*). It is perceptible in the space between the navel and the head, and the circulation that it has is the common function of the organs. Lastly, the air by which internal division and diffusion through the whole body is effected is called *vyána,* from its pervading (*vyápti*) the body like the etherial element. The circulation of that, also, is the common function of the assemblage of the organs. In this manner these vital airs, as the common function of the instruments, are explained; that is, the common function of the thirteen kinds (of organs).

COMMENT.

Besides the peculiar functions of the three internal instruments, mind, egotism, and intellect, which as the same with their definitions have already been specified, they have a common office in the evolution or circulation of the internal aerial humours which constitute vitality.

The translation limits this community of function to the three internal instruments only, or to intellect, egotism, and mind; and such is the interpretation of VÁCHESPATI MISRA: 'The five airs, or life, is the function of the three (internal) instruments, from being present where they are, and absent where they are not*." So the *S. Pravachana Bh.* explains the Sútra *Sámánya karana vritti* †; which is also the phrase of the *Káriká*, 'the function of the three internal instruments ‡.' Gaurapáda, however, understands vitality to be the common function of all the organs, external and internal; or thirteen instruments, ten of the former, and three of the latter kind. The expression of the text also is general, and applicable either to all the organs, or to any of them, as variously understood. The two meanings are not irreconcilable, although, strictly speaking, the sense followed in the translation is most correct; for although vitality is the common function of all the senses, yet it is essentially so of the internal senses only: it might continue with the privation of any or all of the external senses, but could not, as Váchespati states, subsist without the internal organs, as it depends upon their existence for its own. So also the *S. Pravachana Bháshya* calls the vital airs not only the 'functions,' but 'modifications, of the internal instruments ‖.' These vital airs are not to be confounded with *váyu*, or 'elemental air,' for the Védas are authority for their different origin: 'From him is born vital air, mind, and all the senses, heaven, wind, light, water, and the all-sustaining earth §.' 'The attribution of aerial operation to modification of the internal instruments arises from their being susceptible of a sort of motion similar to that of air, and from their being governed by the same deity ¶.' The vital airs are, in fact, the vital functions of breathing, circulation, and digestion. That these functions, resulting from organization, should be supposed to partake of the nature of aerial humours, originates very possibly from some misapprehension of the phænomena of breathing, flatulence, and arterial pulsation. The term used by Gaurapáda to designate their

---

* त्रयाणामपिकरणानां पञ्चवायवो जीवनं वृत्तिस्तद्भावे भावात्तदभावे चाभावात् । † सामान्यकरणवृत्तिः । ‡ अन्तः करणत्रयस्यवृत्तिः । ‖ परिणामभेदाः । § एतस्माज्जायते प्राणो मनः सर्व्वेन्द्रियाणिच । खं वायुज्योतिरापश्च पृथिवी विश्वधारिणी । ¶ अन्तः करणपरिणामेऽपि वायुतुल्यसंचारविशेषाद्वायुदेवताधिकाराच्च वायुव्यवहारोपपत्तिरिति ।

action occurs *syandana*, 'moving, circulation,' in the copy; but *spandana*, 'throbbing, pulsation,' were perhaps a preferable reading. The offices assigned to them are evidently connected with notions either of circulation or a pulse. Thus *Prána* is breath, expiration and inspiration. *Apána* is flatulence, *crepitus*. *Samána* is eructation, supposed to be essential to digestion. *Udána* is the pulsation of the arteries in the head, the neck, and temples; and *Vyána* is the pulsation of the rest of the superficial arteries, and occasional puffiness of external parts, indicating air in the skin. The situations assigned to the five airs by the *S. Tatwa Kaumudí* are much less consistent and intelligible. Thus *Prána* is there said to be the function of the tip of the nostrils, head, navel, and great toes; *Apána*, of the back of the neck, the back, the feet, and the organs of excretion and generation; *Samána*, of the heart, the navel, and the joints; *Udána*, of the head, throat, palate, forehead, and root of the nose; and *Vyána*, of the skin. With exception of the last, it is not easy to understand how such absurd situations should have been selected. The *S. Bháshya* may be taken as the expression of the earlier notions.

XXX.

Of all four the functions are instantaneous, as well as gradual, in regard to sensible objects. The function of the three (interior) is, in respect of an unseen one, preceded by that of the fourth.

BHÁSHYA.

Of all four the functions are instantaneous.—The four are, intellect, egotism, and mind, in connection with any one of the organs of sense. Of these four the function is instantaneous in regard to perception, or in the ascertainment of perceptible objects. Intellect, egotism, mind, and the eye see form at once, in one instant, (coming instantly to the conclusion) that is a post. The same three, with the tongue, at once appreciate flavour; with the nose, odour: and so with the ear and skin.

Again; their functions are also *gradual in regard to sensible objects.*—Of that aggregate of four the function is also (occasionally) gradual (progressive). Thus, a person going along a road sees an object at a distance, and is in doubt whether it be a post or a man: he then observes some characteristic marks upon it, or a bird perched there; and doubt being thus dissipated by the reflection of the mind, the understanding discriminates that it is a post; and thence egotism interposes, for the sake of certainty, as, verily (or, I am certain) it is a post. In this way the functions of intellect, egotism, mind, and eye are (successively) discharged. And as in the case of a visible object, so it is as to sound and the rest of the objects of perception.

But *in respect of an unseen one, the functions of the three are preceded by that of the fourth.*—*Unseen* implies time past, or future: for instance, in respect to 'form,' the function of the eye has preceded that of intellect, egotism, and mind, as has that of the skin in respect to touch; of the nose in regard to smell; of the ear in relation to sound; and of the tongue in respect to taste. The functions of intellect, egotism, and mind are preceded in order by those of the senses in regard to time future or past, whilst in regard to time present they may be either instantaneous or gradual. Further—

COMMENT.

The consentaneous or successive operation of the three internal and any one of the external organs in the formation of ideas is here described.

The cooperation of the three internal organs and any organ of sense may be instantaneous (*yugapat*), like a flash of lightning, or as at the sight of a tiger, when the recognition of him, knowledge of his ferocity, conclusion of personal peril, and determination to try to escape are the business of one and the same moment: or their operation may be gradual or successive (*kramaśas*), allowing leisure, for instance, for the eye to see, for the mind to consider, for egotism to apply, and for intellect to conclude. Gaurapáda rather disarranges the order of succession, and places the function of egotism last, assigning to it the office of belief or conviction. Váchespati's illustration is more regular: 'Thus, the ear hears the twang of a bowstring; mind reflects that this must be for the flight of an arrow; egotism says, It is aimed at me; and intellect determines, I must run away *.' Whenever the object is unseen, *adrishta*, not present, whether it be past or be to come, there must have been a prior perception of it; that is, as the text is explained by the commentators, there must have been a prior perception of it by an organ of sense. The expression of the text, *tat púrviká vritti*, 'their prior function,' might be thought to refer to a prior notion gained by the conjoint operation of the internal and external organs at some former period. This, however, would be recollection, the seat of which, as well as of judgment or inference, is in *buddhi*, or 'intellect,' alone; as in the *Pátanjala* Sútra, 'Proof, refutation deliberation, sleep, memory; these are said to be the functions of intellect †.' The prior operation, therefore, is merely perception or observation by the external sense, *alochanam* (see ver. 28), conveying simple ideas to the mind. Taking, then, this prior simple idea acquired through an external organ, any further consideration of it is the gradual operation of the three internal instruments. Where the object is present, conviction may be either momentary or successive: the Sánkhyas maintaining the possibility of consentaneous operation of the organs of sense and mind, egotism and intellect, in opposition to the doctrine of the Vaiséshikas, that the formation of ideas is in all cases a graduated process: Where the object is absent, the idea must be formed by the internal organs so far in successive order that they must be consequent upon a former impression received by an external sense; but as concerns themselves, their action may be either simultaneous or successive ‡. The

---

* अथप्रणिहितमनाः कर्णान्ताकृष्टसशरशिञ्जिनीमण्डलीकृतकोदण्डः प्रचण्डतरः पाटच्चरोयमिति निश्चिनोति अथ च मां प्रत्येतीत्यभिमन्यते अथाध्यवस्यत्यपसरामीतः स्थानादिति ।

† प्रमाणविपर्य्ययविकल्पनिन्द्रास्मृतय इति । एतत् सर्व्वं पातञ्जले सूचितं या एता बुद्धिवृत्तय उक्ता इति ।

‡ अन्तः करणत्रयस्य युगपत् क्रमेण च वृत्तिर्दृष्टपूर्व्विका—यथा दृष्टे तथाऽदृष्टेऽपीति योजना ।

illustration which occurs in the *Bháshya* and other commentaries, of the course of reasoning by which the nature of a distant object is determined, is something like that with which, in the Philebus, the formation of opinion is elucidated.

XXXI.

THE instruments perform their respective functions, incited by mutual invitation. The soul's purpose is the motive: an instrument is wrought by none.

BHÁSHYA.

Swam is repeated, implying 'several order:' that is, intellect, egotism, mind, perform their respective functions, the incitement to which is mutual invitation. *Ákúta* implies 'respect and alertness.' They do this for the accomplishment of the *purpose of soul.* Egotism and the rest effecting it through intellect: that is, intellect, knowing the wishes of egotism and the rest, proceeds to its own peculiar function. If it be asked, why it does so? the answer is, *the purpose of the soul is the motive.* Soul's purpose is to be fulfilled: for this object the activity of the qualities occurs, and thence these instruments make manifest the object of the soul. How is it that (being devoid of intelligence) they act? They act of their own accord. *An instrument can be wrought by none.*—The purpose of soul alone causes them to act: this is the meaning of the sentence: an instrument is not made—not roused—to act by any human superior.

It is next specified how many (instruments) intellect and the rest are.

COMMENT.

The circumstances that induce the internal and external organs to perform their respective functions are said to be mutual incitement, and spontaneous disposition to effect the objects of soul.

The organs of sense are said to act by mutual invitation or incitement. Their cooperation in the discharge of their respective functions is compared to that of different soldiers in an army, all engaged in a common assault, but of whom one agrees to take a spear, another a mace, another a bow. It is objected, that the organs being declared non-sentient, incapable of intelligence, cannot be supposed to feel, much less to know, any mutual design or wish, *ákúta** or *abhipráya*†; and the terms are explained to signify the insensible influence which the activity of one exerts upon that of another, if there be no impediment in the way; a sort of sympathetic or consentaneous action. '*Ákúta* here means incitement to activity; that is, at the time when one organ is in action, the activity of another, if no obstruction hinder it‡.' 'With this view the several instruments are directed by a presiding power, which may be termed the adaptation of the mutual fitness of their natures‖.' The motive for this sympathetic action is the purpose of soul, fruition or liberation; which purpose they of their own accord, but unconsciously, operate to fulfil, in the same way as the unconscious breast spontaneously secretes milk for the nourishment of the infant; according to the Sútra, 'As the cow for the calf:' that is, as the milk of the cow of its own accord exudes for the use of the calf, and awaits not the effort of another, so the organs of their own accord perform their office for the sake of their master, soul §. *S. Pravachana Bh.* They must act of their own nature; it is not in the power of any one to compel them to act. GAURAPÁDA's expression is, 'Not by any sovereign man¶:' perhaps some particle, such as *vá*, may have been omitted in the copy, making the sense, 'Neither by a deity nor a mortal;' or the phrase may imply, that they are not compelled to action even by soul, as a divinity; but fulfil soul's purposes through an innate property, undirected by any external agent.

---

* आकूतं। † अभिप्रायः। ‡ आकूतमत्र प्रवृत्त्युन्मुखत्वं तच्चैकस्य व्यापारजननसमय एव तथा चासति बाधकेऽन्यस्यापि। ‖ तेनैषामधिष्ठाता करणानां स्वरूपसामर्थ्योपयोगाभिज्ञेन भवितव्यं। § धेनुवद्वत्साय। यथा वत्सार्थं धेनोः स्वयमेव क्षीरं स्रवति नान्ययत्नमपेक्षते तथैव स्वामिनः पुरुषस्य कृते स्वयमेव करणानि प्रवर्त्तन्त इत्यर्थः। ¶ न केनचिदीश्वरेण पुरुषेण।

XXXII.

Instrument is of thirteen sorts. It compasses, maintains, and manifests: what is to be done by it is tenfold, to be compassed, to be maintained, to be manifested.

BHÁSHYA.

Instrument.—Intellect and the rest are three; the intellectual organs are five; the organs of action are five: all together thirteen. What this performs is next declared: *it compasses, maintains, and manifests;* that is, the organs of action compass and maintain; those of perception manifest. How many kinds of action there are is next specified. Its action, that which is to be done by it, is *tenfold;* of ten kinds, as hearing, touch, &c. by the instruments of perception; speech and the rest by those of action: and thus by the former, manifestation, and by the latter, comprehension and support, are effected.

COMMENT.

The sense of the term *karana,* 'instrument' or 'organ,' is here explained, as a generic denomination for the external and internal organs.

The instruments or organs are thirteen; that is, three internal, intellect, egotism, and mind; and ten external, or the organs of sensation and action. Their respective functions as organs have been explained: their effects as instruments are classed under three heads, 'compassing,' *áharana* *; 'maintaining,' *dhárana* †; and 'manifesting,' *prakáśana* ‡. The first, which means, literally, 'taking, seizing,' and rendered in the text 'compassing,' signifies 'the application of an organ to the object to which it is adapted ||,' and is the especial function of the organs or instruments of action. 'Maintaining,' *dhárana,* 'supporting, upholding,' is, according

---

* आहरणं । † धारणं । ‡ प्रकाशनं । || यथा स्वमुपाददते स्वव्यापारेण व्याप्नुवन्तीति यावत् ।

to the *S. Bháshya*, also the office of the instruments of action; but the authors of the *S. Tatwa Kaumudí* and *S. Chandriká* assign it to the three internal instruments, intellect, egotism, and mind, as being especially the supporters of vitality. '*Buddhi*, *ahankára*, and mind uphold, through their function being designated as the production of the vital airs, &c.*' The elder commentator could not, of course, admit this doctrine; for we have seen (ver. 29) that, according to him, all the senses or instruments contribute to support the vital principle. All the Scholiasts agree in attributing 'manifestation, enlightening,' *prakáśana*, to the intellectual organs. The objects to be effected by the instruments are tenfold, reducible to the same three classes: speech, manipulation, walking, excretion, and generation are to be compassed, to be effected, *áhárya*†, by the actual application of the several organs: sound, taste, touch, smell, form to be manifested, to be made sensible, *prakáśya:* and all of them, together with the vital airs, constituting in fact animal life, are to be *dhâryya*‡, upheld or maintained.

XXXIII.

Internal instruments are three; external ten, to make known objects to those three. The external organs minister at time present: the internal do so at any time.

BHÁSHYA.

Internal instruments.—Intellect, egotism, and mind are three, from the difference between intellect and the others. *External ten.*—The five organs of perception and five of action are the ten external instruments, and they are *to make known objects* for the fruition of intellect, egotism,

---

* बुद्ध्यहंकारमनांसि तु स्ववृत्त्या प्राणादिलक्षणया धारयन्ति ।

† आहार्य्यः ।   ‡ धार्य्यः ।

and mind. *Time present:* that is, the ear hears a present sound, not one that is past, nor one that is to come: the eye sees present form, not that which is past, nor that which is future: the skin touches present substance: the tongue tastes present flavour: the nose smells present odours, nor past nor future. It is the same with the organs of action: the voice articulates actual, not past nor future words: the hand takes hold of a present water-pot, not one that has been or is to be: the feet traverse a present, not a past nor a future walk: and the organs of excretion and generation perform present, not past nor future offices. External organs, therefore, minister at time present. *The internal ones do so for any time.*— Intellect, egotism, and mind regard objects of any period: thus intellect forms an idea, not only of a present water-jar, but of one that has been or will be made: so egotism exercises consciousness of an object past, present, or future: and mind considers the past and future, as well as the present. Internal instrument is, therefore, for all times.

It is next explained which of these instruments apprehends specific, and which unspecific objects.

COMMENT.

The difference between the functions of the external and internal organs, as concerns time, is here explained: the action of the former being confined to time present; that of the latter comprehending also the past and the future.

Internal instrument is so denominated from operating within the body *; the external from being applied to exterior objects, making them known to the internal organization. The term *vishaya*, 'object,' is also explained by *bhogya*, 'that which is to be enjoyed;' and *vyápára*, 'exercise;' and *vishayákhya*, 'that which declares or makes objects known.' It is also defined as 'that which occasions the exercise of the functions of the three internal instruments †.' External sensation is

---

* शरीराभ्यन्तरवृत्तित्वादन्तः करणं । † विषयं व्यापारमाख्याति जनयति ।

necessarily confined to present objects, but mind, consciousness, and intellect apprehend from present objects those which have past, or are to come; as past rain from the swelling of a river; and future rain, in the absence of any other prognostic, from the destruction of the eggs of the ants *. This last phrase alludes probably to the well known destruction of various species of the ant tribe, which in the East takes place immediately before the setting in of the rainy season: they then take wing, and fly abroad in vast multitudes, of which few survive; according to the Hindustani proverb, چبونتي كي جو موت آتي هي تو پر نكلتي 'When the ants are about to die, their wings come forth.' The expression "ants' eggs," *pipílikáńda*, is, however, rather questionable. It occurs in both copies of the *S. Tatwa Kaumudí*.

XXXIV.

Among these organs the five intellectual concern objects specific and unspecific. Speech concerns sound. The rest regard all five objects.

BHÁSHYA.

The intellectual organs concern specific objects: they apprehend objects which have specific properties. The intellectual organs of men distinguish sound, touch, form, taste, smell, along with objects of indifference, pleasure and pain. The organs of the gods apprehend objects which have no specific distinctions. So, amongst the five organs of action, *speech concerns sound.* Speech, whether of gods or of men, articulates words, recites verses, and the like; and this instrument is the same in both orders of beings. *The rest*—all except speech; the hand, the foot, and the organs of excretion and generation—*regard all five objects:* that

---

* यथानदीपूरणोदादभूद्वृष्टिरसत्युपघातके पिप्पीलिकाण्डसंचरणाद्भवि
ष्यतिवृष्टिरिति ।

is, sound and the other four objects of perception belong to all the other organs; for there may be sound, touch, form, taste, and smell in the hands; the foot treads upon the earth, of which sound and the rest may be characteristics; the excretory organ separates that in which the five objects abide; and the generating organs produce the secretion which is equally characterised by the five organs of sense.

COMMENT.

Another distinction is made in the functions of the external instruments, as they regard objects with or without specific characteristics.

Objects are distinguished as having specific characters or effects, *saviśésha* *, and as devoid of them, *nirviśésha* †; and the instruments are discriminated according to their capability of conveying notions of either. The organs of sense in mortals can apprehend only those objects which have specific characters; either sensible, as colour, form, taste, &c.; or moral, as pleasant, painful, or indifferent. The faculties of the gods and of sages can apprehend objects without such characteristic properties, and which exercise no moral effect, producing neither pleasure, pain, nor indifference. The *S. Tatwa Kaumudí* identifies 'specific' with 'gross corporeal' objects ‡, and 'unspecific' with 'subtile and rudimental' objects ‖; the latter of which are cognizable alone by the organs of holy men and deities §. This distinction applies to all the external organs, except the voice, which in men, saints, and gods can articulate sensible, specific, or corporeal words alone; for it is the organ of the voice that is the origin of speech. Speech cannot, like sound, taste, &c., originate with any thing gross or subtile exterior to the speaker; it must proceed from him, through the agency of a gross material instrument, and must therefore be gross or sensible itself. Gross corporeal mechanism cannot be the source of a subtile product, and therefore with every order of beings

---

* सविशेषः। † निर्विशेषः। ‡ स्थूलविषयाः। ‖ सूक्ष्मविषयाः।

§ तथोर्ध्वस्रोतसां योगिनां च श्रोत्रं शब्दतन्मात्रविषयं स्थूलविषयं च। अस्मदादीनां तु स्थूलशब्दविषयमेव।

speech must be specific. 'The rest,' *séshâni* referring to the organ of speech, implies the other organs of action, all of which may regard the five objects of perception; that is, they may comprehend them all; as 'from the combination (or capability) of sound, touch, colour, smell, taste, in objects like a water-jar and others, which may be compassed or taken hold of by the hand, &c.*' *S. Tatwa Kaumudí.*

XXXV.

Since intellect, with the (other two) internal instruments, adverts to every object, therefore those three instruments are warders, and the rest are gates.

BHÁSHYA.

With the internal; that is, intellect, with egotism and mind. *Adverts to;* takes, apprehends; that is, apprehends sound and the rest at all three seasons. *Therefore these three are warders, and the rest are gates.— The rest;* the other instruments; instruments being understood. Further—

COMMENT.

A metaphor is employed to illustrate the functions of the external and internal instruments.

The internal instruments are compared to warders, doorkeepers, or to persons having charge of a door or gate; not opening and closing it merely, but as taking note of all that enter: the external senses being the doors or gateways by which the objects of perception gain admission.

---

* पाण्याद्याहार्याणां घटादीनां पंचशब्दाद्यात्मकत्वादिति ।

XXXVI.

These characteristically differing from each other, and variously affected by qualities, present to the intellect the soul's whole purpose, enlightening it as a lamp.

BHÁSHYA.

These, which are called instruments: they *variously affected by qualities.* How affected? *Like a lamp;* exhibiting objects like a lamp. *Characteristically differing;* dissimilar, having different objects; that is the sense. Objects of the qualities is intended. *Variously affected by qualities;* produced or proceeding from qualities. *Soul's whole purpose.*—The instruments of perception and action, egotism and mind, having illustrated the object of soul (as attainable) through each respectively, *present it to the intellect*, place it in the intellect; and consequently soul obtains pleasure and the rest; that is, every object seated in intellect. Further—

COMMENT.

The process by which ideas are conveyed to soul is here described.

Intellect (*buddhi* or *mahat*) is the instrument or organ which is the medium between the other instruments or organs and soul; that is, all ideas derived from sensation, reflection, or consciousness must be deposited in the chief or great instrument, intellect or understanding, before they can be made known to soul, for whose use and advantage alone they have been assembled. *They are variously affected by the qualities.*—They convey impressions or ideas, with the properties or effects of pleasure, pain, and indifference, accordingly as they are influenced by the qualities of goodness, foulness, and darkness. In fact these organs are identified with the qualities by all the commentators. Gaurapáda says, 'they proceed or are born from them*:' and in the *S. Tatwa Kaumudí* and

* गुणेभ्योजाताः ।

S. Chandriká they are called also 'products or modifications and varieties of the qualities;' thus the former has, 'The external organs, mind, and egotism are affections of qualities; they are changes of condition of the qualities goodness, foulness, and darkness *:' the latter, 'These affections of the qualities are kinds (or varieties) of them †.' It might have been preferable, therefore, to have rendered the expression *gunaviśésha*, 'modifications or affections of the qualities.'

The progressive communication of impression to soul is thus illustrated by VÁCHESPATI: 'As the head men of a village collect the taxes from the villagers, and pay them to the governor of the district; as the local governor pays the amount to the minister; and the minister receives it for the use of the king; so mind, having received ideas from the external organs, transfers them to egotism; and egotism delivers them to intellect, which is the general superintendent, and takes charge of them for the use of the sovereign, soul. The same idea is more concisely expressed in the *S. Pravachana Bh.* '*Sútra:* In the common employment of the organs the chiefship belongs to *buddhi*, as in the world. *Comment:* As the function of the organs is in common, through subservience to the purposes of soul, so the most important is that of intelligence; like the office of the prime minister amongst the chiefs of villages and the rest, who are all alike engaged in the service of the king ‡.' The cooperation of opposites for a common purpose has been once before (p. 54) compared to the light of a lamp, derived from the combination of oil, cotton, and flame.

---

* बाह्येन्द्रियमनोऽहंकाराश्च गुणविशेषाः गुणानां सत्वरजस्तमसां विकाराः । † एते गुणविशेषाः गुणानां भेदाः । ‡ समानकर्म्मयोगे बुद्धेः प्राधान्यं लोकवत् । यद्यपिपुरुषार्थत्वेन समान एव सर्व्वेषां करणानां व्यापारस्तथाऽपि बुद्धेरेव प्राधान्यं लोकवत् लोके हि राजार्थकत्वाविशेषेऽपि ग्रामाध्यक्षादिषु मध्ये मंत्रिण एव प्राधान्यमित्यर्थः ।

XXXVII.

Since it is intellect which accomplishes soul's fruition of all which is to be enjoyed, it is that, again, which discriminates the subtle difference between the chief principle (*pradhána*) and soul.

BHÁSHYA.

All: whatever comes within the reach of the organs, and in all three (past, present, and future) periods. *Fruition:* several or respective enjoyment, through the instrumentality of the organs of perception and action, whether in gods, men, or animals. The internal instrument intellect *accomplishes*, completes or effects; consequently *it is that, again, which discriminates,* makes a distinction between the objects of nature and soul, (or establishes) their difference or severalty. *Subtle:* not to be apprehended by those who have not practised religious austerities, (or such distinctions) as, this is nature, the equipoised condition of the three qualities, goodness, foulness, and darkness; this is intellect; this is egotism; these are the five subtile rudiments; these the eleven organs; these the five gross elements; and this, which is different from them all, is soul. He whose intellect explains all this obtains liberation.

It was said above (ver. 34) that "objects are specific and unspecific:" which these are respectively is next described.

COMMENT.

The function of discriminating between soul and nature is here also assigned to intellect.

The immediate contiguity and communication of intellect with soul, as that of a prime minister and a sovereign, enables it to appreciate the latter; whilst its being the medium of conveyance to external objects familiarizes it with them also; and thus it is enabled to distinguish between both: or, as explained in the *Chandriká,* this discrimination is the necessary consequence of its relative function; for as it conveys ideas of pleasure or pain to soul, and is in this way the cause of its fruition, it is subservient to another, to something of a different nature from its own; and the knowledge of this is discrimination between nature and soul. 'All, sound and the rest, with which the preposition *prati* (implying severalty) is to be connected. The fruition is that of soul. As intellect accomplishes this, consequently although it be as it were a chief principle, yet it is for another's use, not its own; and as hence arises the purpose of liberation, this sense is accordingly intended to be expressed in the phrase, *It is that again which discriminates*, &c. *'

XXXVIII.

THE elementary particles are unspecific: from these five proceed the five elements, which are termed *specific;* for they are soothing, terrific, or stupifying.

BHÁSHYA.

The five subtile elements, which are produced from egotism, or the rudiments sound, touch (substance), form, flavour, and odour, are said to be *unspecific;* they are the objects (of perception) to the gods, characterised by pleasure, producing neither pain nor stupefaction. *From these five proceed the five elements*, called earth, water, fire, air, and ether. These are said to be *specific*. From the rudiment smell, earth proceeds; from the rudiment flavour, water; from form (colour), fire; from touch (substance), air; and from the rudiment sound, proceeds ether. These gross elements *are termed specific*. They are the objects of the senses of men, and are *soothing*, causing pleasure; *terrific*, causing pain; and *stupifying*, causing insensibility; as the ethereal element may give delight to one

---

* सर्वं शब्दादियोग्यं प्रति य उपभोगः पुरुषस्य तं यस्मात्साधयति तस्मात्सा प्रधानापि परार्थैव न स्वार्थेति भावः मोक्षहेतुजनकत्वादपि स तथैवाभिप्रेत्याहसैवपुनरिति ।

person coming forth at once from within a house, so the same may be the source of pain to one affected by cold, or heat, or wind, or rain; and if he be going along a road leading through a forest, in which he loses his way, it may then, from the perplexity of space, occasion stupefaction: so the air (or wind) is agreeable to a person oppressed by heat, disagreeable to one feeling cold; and when tempestuous and loaded with clouds of sand and dust it is stupifying. The same may be said of fire and the rest. There are other specific varieties.

COMMENT.

It was intimated in ver. 34, that objects were both specific and unspecific; and it is here explained, that by the former is meant the various property which the same element possesses at different times, and under different circumstances, in regard to mortals; and by the latter, the uniform and unvaried operation of the subtile rudiments in respect to the gods.

The precise nature of the rudimental elements is not very intelligible, according to their usual identification with what we are accustomed to consider as qualities, not substances, or sound, tangibility, form or colour, flavour, and odour; *śabda*, *sparsa*, *rúpa*, *rasa*, and *gandha*. It seems, however, that we should regard the rudimental elements as the imperceptible subjects of these qualities, from which the grosser and visible elements, ether, air, light, water, and earth, originate. So Vijnána Bhikshu calls them 'subtile substances, the elements which are the holders (sustainers or subjects) of the species of sound, touch, colour, taste, and smell; but in which, as a genus, the three species of pleasurable, painful, and indifferent do not occur: they are not varieties of the gross elements, but in each respectively the elementary property exclusively resides; whence they are said to be *rudiments*. In those elements that elementary property resides alone (without being diversified, as agreeable, &c.); and as there is no distinction between a property and its subject, that which is a rudimental substance is called a rudiment, *tan mátra;* the existence of which as a cause is inferred from that of the gross element as an effect*.' *Tan mátra* is a compound of *tad*, 'that,' and *mátra*, 'alone;' implying, that in which its own peculiar property resides, without any change or variety: so VÁCHESPATI explains the text, 'Sound and the rest; the subtile rudiments; for the properties of agreeable, &c. do not belong to them, they have no quality which is fit for (mortal) fruition. This is the meaning of the word *mátra*†.'—'These rudiments, though not appreciable by human sense, are said to be sensible to sages and to gods, producing to them pleasure only, from the predominance with them of the quality of goodness, and consequently of happiness‡.'

The notion of something more subtile than the elements was not unknown to early Grecian philosophy, and Empedocles taught that they were compounded of some more minute matter, or of elements of the elements, στοιχεία στοιχείων. Plutarch and Stobæus, according to Cudworth, understand by these rudiments of the elements primary atoms; but it may be doubted if they are to be so understood, for, according to Aristotle, Empedocles held that there were four elements, out of which all bodies were composed, and which were not mutually transmutable. In fact the doctrine of Empedocles, which was that of the school of Pythagoras, offers another analogy to the Indian, in the assertion, not of four, but of five elements, according to Plutarch, or the author *De placitis philosophorum*, l. II. c. 6, or ether, fire, earth, water, and air. Intellect. Syst. I. 97. That Empedocles was not of the atomic school is evident from

---

* तन्मात्राणि च यज्जातीये तु शान्तादिविशेषत्रयं न तिष्ठति तज्जातीयानां शब्दस्पर्शरूपरसगन्धानामाधारभूतानि सूक्ष्मद्रव्याणि स्थूलानामविशेषाः । तस्मिंस्तस्मिंस्तु तन्मात्रे तेन तन्मात्रता स्मृता । स्थूलभूतात् कार्य्यात् तत् कारणतया तन्मात्रस्यानुमानेन स्थूलात्पंचतन्मात्रस्य बोध इत्यर्थः । † शब्दादितन्मात्राणि सूक्ष्माणि न चैषां शान्तत्वादिरस्त्युपभोगयोग्यो विशेष इति मात्रशब्दार्थः । ‡ तन्मात्राणि च देवादिमात्रभोग्यत्वेन केवलं सुखात्मकान्येव सुखाधिक्यादिति ।

Lucretius, who specifies him as one of those who greatly misunderstood the principles of things:

> Principiis tamen in rerum fecere ruinas
> Et graviter magnei magno cecidere ibi casu. I. 741–2.

It may be suspected that something like the Hindu notion, that the senses, or their faculties, and the gross elements, partake of a common nature, is expressed in the celebrated, though otherwise not very intelligible verses of the same philosopher:

> *Γαίῃ μὲν γὰρ γαῖαν ὀπώπαμεν, ὕδατι δ' ὕδωρ*
> *Αἰθέρι δ' αἰθέρα δῖαν, ἀτὰρ πυρὶ πῦρ ἀΐδηλον:*

'By the earthy element we perceive earth; by the watery, water; the air of heaven by the aerial element; and devouring fire by the element of fire.'

As opposed to the simple unvaried rudiments, the derivative gross elements, which are sensible to men and animals, are susceptible of three qualities; they may have specific or varied effects, may be diversified as species; they are said, accordingly, to be soothing or agreeable *, terrific or disagreeable †, and stupifying, bewildering ‡; that is, they may be either of these, according to the different circumstances in which the influence of one or other of the three qualities predominates. When goodness prevails, whether it be in themselves or in the object affected, they are *śánta*, 'tranquil or pleasant;' when foulness, they are *ghora*, 'frightful, disagreeable;' and when darkness prevails, they are 'perplexing,' *múrha:* as VÁCHESPATI; 'In the gross elements, ether and the rest, some, through the predominance of goodness, are soothing, pleasant, agreeable, light; some, through the prevalence of foulness, are terrific, painful, restless; whilst others, through the influence of darkness, are stupifying, depressing, heavy ‖.'

---

* शान्ताः । † घोराः । ‡ मूढाः । ‖ आकाशादिस्थूलेषु सत्वप्रधानतया केचिच्छान्ताः सुखाः प्रसन्ना लघवः केचिद्रजःप्रधानतया घोरा दुःखा अनवस्थिता केचित्तमः प्रधानतया मूढा विषण्णा गुरवः ।

XXXIX.

Subtile (bodies), and such as spring from father and mother, together with the great elements, are three sorts of specific objects. Among these, the subtile bodies are lasting; such as issue from father and mother are perishable.

BHÁSHYA.

Subtile: the rudimental elements, that, when aggregated, form the rudimental or subtile body, characterised by intellect (*mahat*) and the rest, and which always exists, and undergoes successive states of being (transmigration): those are subtile (bodies). *Such as spring from father and mother* are the cementers or means of the aggregation of gross bodies, or by the effect of the mixture of blood and seminal secretion in sexual cohabitation, at fit seasons they form the envelopment of the subtile body in the womb; that subtile body then is nourished, through the umbilical cord, by the nutriment derived from the food and drink received by the mother; and the (entire) body, thus commenced with the triple ingredient of the subtile rudiments, the cognate investure, and the gross elements, becomes furnished with back, belly, legs, neck, head, and the rest; is enveloped in its sixfold membranes; is provided with blood, flesh, tendons, semen, marrow, and bones; and is composed of the five gross elements; ether being supplied for its cavities (or extension), air for its growth, fire for its nutriment, water for its aggregation, and earth for its stability: and thus being equipped with all its (component) parts, it comes forth from the maternal womb. In this way there are three kinds (of bodies): which of these is constant, and which temporary, is next described. *The subtile bodies are lasting.—Subtile;* rudimental elements: these are *lasting*, constant; by them body is commenced, and migrates, according to the imperative influence of acts, through the forms of beasts, deer, birds, reptiles, or immovable substances; or, in consequence of virtue, proceeds through the heaven of Indra, and other celestial abodes. So the subtile body migrates until knowledge is attained; when that is attained, the sage, abandoning all body, acquires liberation: these sorts of bodies, or *subtile*, therefore, are called *lasting*. *Such as issue from father and mother are perishable.*—Having left that subtile body, the frame that proceeds from mother and father ceases, even here, at the time that the breath departs; the body born of parents ceases at the time of death, and merges into earth and the other gross elements.

What subtile body is, and how it migrates, is next described.

COMMENT.

Objects were distinguished in the preceding verse according as they were with or without specific or diversified effects: they are here classified according to their forms, their origin, and duration.

A question of some difficulty, however, arises here, as to the objects of the classification. Are they bodies in general? or are they gross bodies only? In the preceding stanza it was stated, that the subtile elements, the *tan mátras*, were unspecific; whilst their effects, the gross elements, were 'specific,' *viśésha*. It is now stated, that there are three kinds of *viśéshas*, 'sorts, species, specific differences;' but it is not explicitly defined *of what* these are the varieties. Mr. Colebrooke, following the principal commentators, renders it 'sorts of objects;' that is, of bodies in general. Professor Lassen, carrying on the sense of *viśésha*, 'specific,' from the preceding stanza, considers the variety here spoken of to concern only gross or perceptible elementary bodies: "Distincta, elementa quæ distincta dicuntur (ver. 38). Distinctorum triplex est divisio in subtilia, a parentibus progenita, crassa" (ver. 39). He admits that the commentators are against this interpretation, but concludes rather that they are in error, than that Íswara Krishna should have employed the word *viśésha* in a double sense.

The interpretation of Prof. Lassen is highly creditable to his critical acumen and judgment, and is possibly correct, although it is scarcely compatible with the notions of subtilty and durability which the text ascribes to this branch of the triad. His view is not, as he supposes, wholly unsupported by the commentators; for Vijnána Bhikshu similarly explains the stanza, as will presently be noticed. The passage is one of some importance, as it regards apparently the history of the Sánkhya doctrines respecting the nature of that subtile body which is the immediate vehicle of soul, as we shall have occasion to notice more particularly, when we come to verse 40. If the meaning of the text be as Prof. Lassen renders it, it furnishes reason to suppose that the author of the *Káriká* had introduced an innovation upon the original doctrine, as will be subsequently indicated.

According to GAURAPÁDA and NÁRÁYANA, the sorts or species intimated in this verse are different from those described in the preceding; the former calls them, as above, 'other varieties *;' and the latter has, referring to ver. 38, 'So many are the specific varieties; but these are not all, there are others †.' VÁCHESPATI's expression, 'A further species of species ‡, might be thought to refer to the gross elements; but, from the explanation that follows, it is evident he does not intend to limit the specific differences to gross elementary bodies. Agreeably to the explanation, then, in which these writers concur, bodies in general are threefold, subtile, generated, and elementary; and consistently with this view they consider 'subtile,' *súkshma*, as equivalent to *tan-mátra*, 'rudimental:' thus GAURAPÁDA has, 'Subtile is the aggregated rudimental elements, forming a rudimento-elemental subtile body ‖:' so also VÁCHESPATI; 'Subtile means subtile bodies; subtile body is one specific object §:' and the *Chandriká*; 'Subtile are what are called rudimental bodies ¶.' Consequently they also conceive the subtile objects spoken of in this verse to be something entirely different from the gross elementary *viśéshas*, or 'species,' of the preceding verse; not merely sub-species or varieties of the same: and it must be admitted that there is some inconsistency in the *Káriká's* speaking of *subtile* bodies being a species of *gross* bodies; of

---

* अन्ये विशेषाः । † एतावन्त एव विशेषा इति न किन्त्वन्येऽपि सन्तीत्याह । ‡ विशेषाणामवान्तरं विशेषमाह । ‖ तन्मात्राणि संगृहीतं तन्मात्रिकं सूक्ष्मशरीरं । § सूक्ष्माः सूक्ष्मदेहाः परिकल्पिताः । सूक्ष्मं शरीरमेको विशेषः । ¶ सूक्ष्मा लिंगशरीराख्याः ।

the *imperceptible* being a variety of the *perceptible*. According to VIJNÁNA BHIKSHU, however, the text merely intends by 'subtile,' *súkshma*, a modification of gross elementary body; a corporeal frame, which is subtile only relatively, or which is more refined than the second kind of body specified in the text, that which is begotten: 'The nature of that body which is the support of rudimental body is explained in the *Káriká*, "subtile, generated," &c.: here is meant, body aggregated of the five elements, the (product or) effect of the rudimental elements, which is subtile relatively to generated body *.' The same notion is again intimated by expressions which will be subsequently cited; and there remains no doubt that this commentator understands by the *súkshma* of the text, 'a subtile variety of gross elementary body,' *distinctorum distinctio*. The other commentators understand by it, 'rudimental bodies,' *elementa indistincta*. Either interpretation is therefore allowable: the latter agrees best with the philosophy, the former with the construction, of the original.

In the second variety of bodies of course specific or sensible bodies only are intended; bodies generated or begotten are made of the gross elements, agreeably to the Sútra, 'Body consists of the five elements †:' they are, however, in some degree distinguished here from the elements; holding, according to GAURAPÁDA, a middle place between them, and rudimental bodies serving to combine them; *upacháyaka* causing *upachaya*, 'proximate aggregation;' the parts of the embryo being derived in the first instance from the parents, and their development being the result of the accession of the elements, for purposes which he describes. There is some incongruity, however, in this explanation, as it makes a distinction where there is no essential difference; organized matter being, in fact, the same with elementary matter. The other commentators, therefore, give a different explanation of the term 'great elements,' restricting

---

* तस्य च कारिकायामुक्तं सूक्ष्मा मातापितृजा इति । अथ तन्मात्रा कार्य्यं मातापितृजशरीरापेक्षया सूक्ष्मं यद्भूतपंचकमिति ।

† पांचभौतिको देहः ।

it to inorganic matter. Thus VÁCHESPATI observes, 'Subtile body is one variety of objects; generated bodies are a second; and the great elements a third: water-jars and the like (inorganic bodies) are comprised in the class of the great elements*.' So also the *Chandriká:* 'Subtile bodies are those called rudimental; generated, are gross bodies; and the great elements are mountains, trees, and the like†.'

In this threefold division of bodies, as explained by the Scholiasts on the *Káriká*, we have, in fact, but two distinctions, subtile and gross; the latter being subdivided into organic and inorganic. The twofold distinction is that which is especially recognised in the Sútras: thus in the *S. Pravachana Bháshya*, the Sútra, 'Thence (the origin) of body‡,' is explained, 'from the twenty-three *tatwas* (or categories) two kinds of bodies, subtile and gross, proceeded‖:' and again, 'Gross body is for the most part generated (some bodies being inorganic), the other (subtile body) is not§.'

The chief object of the stanza is, however, to assert the different duration of these three kinds of bodies; *subtile are permanent:* and here we have an argument in favour of the translation adopted; for no form of gross body could be considered as lasting: as composed of the elements, in however delicate a form, it must resolve into them at the time of death; whilst the subtile bodies, consisting of the subtile elements, endure either till liberation¶, or until the great Pralaya

Dissolvi quo quæque supremo tempore possint.

---

* सूक्ष्मं शरीरमेको विशेषः। मातृपितृजा द्वितीयः। महभूतानि तृतीयः महाभूतवर्गे घटादीनां विषेश इति। † सूक्ष्मा लिंगशरीराख्याः। मातापितृजाः स्थूलदेहाः। प्रभूताः पर्ब्बतवृक्षादयः। ‡ तस्माच्छरीरस्य। ‖ तस्मात्त्रयोविंशतितत्वात् स्थूलसूक्ष्मशरीरद्वयस्यारम्भ इति। § मातापितृजं स्थूलं प्रायश इतरन्नतथा। ¶ आमोक्षावस्थायिनः। ** आमहाप्रलयादवतिष्ठन्ते।

XL.

(Subtile body), primæval, unconfined, material, composed of intellect, with other subtile principles, migrates, else unenjoying; invested with dispositions, mergent.

BHÁSHYA.

Primæval; whilst yet the universe is uncreated: in the first creation of nature, at that season subtile body is produced. *Unconfined;* uncombined either in the state of animals, men, or gods; and from its subtilty wholly unrestrained, or passing into rocks and the like without obstruction; it migrates; it goes. *Permanent:* until knowledge is attained it migrates. *Composed of intellect, with other subtile principles;* having *mahat* and the rest: that is, intellect in the first place, with egotism and mind, to the five subtile rudiments, to the subtile principles, to the rudimental elements. It *migrates;* it traverses the three worlds, as an ant the body of *Siva. Unenjoying;* without enjoyment: that subtile body becoming capable of enjoyment only in consequence of acquiring the property of action, through its aggregation by external generated body. *Invested with dispositions.—Dispositions,* as virtue and the rest; which we shall hereafter explain (see ver. 43). *Invested with;* coloured or affected by. Subtile body is that which, at the period of universal dissolution, possessed of *mahat,* intelligence, and the other subtile principles, merges into the chief one (or nature), and, exempted from further revolution, remains extant there until creation is renewed, being bound in the bondage of the stolidity of nature, and thereby incompetent to the acts of migrating and the like. At the season of re-creation it again revolves, and is hence called *linga,* ‘characteristic’ or ‘mergent,’ or *súkshma,* ‘subtile.’

From what cause the thirteen instruments (intellect, egotism, and the eleven organs) revolve, as has been said, is next explained.

COMMENT.

The condition of subtile body, in regard to commencement, duration, and term, is here described.

The commentators are agreed that the subtile body here spoken of is the *linga*, or the *linga saríra*, 'rudiment,' or 'rudimental body;' ordinarily, though perhaps not quite accurately, confounded: the *linga* consisting, as intimated in the last phrase of the *Bháshya*, of thirteen component parts, intellect, egotism, and the organs of sense and action; whilst the *linga saríra* adds to these a bodily frame, made up of the five rudimental elements. In this form, however, they always coexist, and it is not necessary to consider them as distinct: thus the Sútra of KAPILA states, 'one *linga* of seventeen *;' that is, according to the Scholiast, 'in the beginning, at creation: there is but one rudimental body at the period of creation, consisting of an aggregate of the eleven organs, five rudimental elements, and intellect †.' This was at first embodied in the person of HIRANYAGARBHA, or BRAHMÁ, and afterwards 'multiplied individually, according to variety of actions ‡.' In this enumeration egotism is omitted, being included, according to the commentator, in intellect. 'Unconfined,' *asakta*, means unobstructed, capable of passing into any bodies. The next epithet, *niyata*, translated 'material,' is explained by GAURAPÁDA as above, by *nitya*, 'permanent, lasting;' and VÁCHESPATI attaches to it the same signification, 'It endures till the period of universal dissolution ‖; and the *S. Pr. Bháshya* observes, also, that it ceases, or is destroyed, only at the same season §: a property, of which it may be observed by the way, that it furnishes another reason for identifying the *súkshma*, or 'subtile body,' of the foregoing stanza with the *linga*, or 'rudimental body,' of this verse. The *Chandriká* explains *niyata* differently, 'distinct in different persons ¶.' The composition of subtile body is explicitly described by VÁCHESPATI: 'Subtile body is an assemblage of intellect, egotism, the eleven senses, and the five

* सप्तदशैकं लिंगं ।

† लिंगशरीरं सर्गादौ समष्टिरूपमेकं भवतीत्यर्थः । एकादशेन्द्रियाणि पंचतन्मात्राणि बुद्धिश्चेतिसप्तदश ।

‡ व्यक्तिभेदः कर्म्मविशेषात् ।

‖ आमहाप्रलयादवतिष्ठते ।

§ प्रलये तन्नाशः ।

¶ प्रत्यात्मभिन्नं ।

elements *.' He ascribes, however, to this a specific or 'diversified existence, from its endowment with senses, which are the sources of pleasure, pain, or indifference †.' The commentators agree that subtile body is subject to enjoyment or suffering only through its connection with generated body; understanding apparently thereby, not its abstract capability of either, but the actual condition in which it partakes of them; for it is repeatedly declared that the seat of enjoyment and suffering is *buddhi*, or 'intellect;' through the presence of which as an ingredient in subtile body, it is immediately added, the latter is invested with 'dispositions,' *bhávas;* that is, with the properties of intellect enumerated in ver. 23, virtue, vice, knowledge, ignorance, &c. The term *bháva* was rendered by Mr. Colebrooke in that place by 'sentiments,' but in another (ver. 43) he expressed the same 'dispositions,' which, as far as relates to the mental *bhávas*, appears to be a preferable equivalent. Of the consequences of these dispositions, reward in heaven, or punishment in hell, dead, decomposed animal body is no longer susceptible: 'In a dead body there can be no sense of pleasure or pain; this all admit ‡.' In order, however, to be placed in circumstances leading to such enjoyment or suffering, generated body is necessary; and therefore subtile body migrates, *sansarati*, goes from one body to another continually: hence the world is called *sansára*, 'migration' or 'revolution.' 'Through the influence of intellect the whole of subtile body is affected by dispositions or conditions, in the same manner as a garment is perfumed from contact with a fragrant *champa* flower ‖.' *S. Tatwa Kaumudí*. Subtile body is called *linga* from its consisting of those principles which are so termed, either from their indicating or characterising that nature from which they proceed, or from their being ultimately resolvable into it. Thus the

---

* महदहंकारैकादशेन्द्रियपंचतन्मात्रपर्य्यन्तमेषां समुदायः सूक्ष्मशरीरं ।

† शान्तघोरमूढैरिन्द्रियान्वितत्वाद्विशेषः ।

‡ मृतशरीरे सुखदुःखाद्यभावस्य सर्व्वसम्मतत्वात् ।

‖ अधिवासितं यथा सुरभिचम्पकसंपर्क्काद्वस्त्रं तदामोदवासितं भवति ।

Chandriká has, '*Linga*, from designating, apprising*:' GAURAPÁDA, as above, 'It merges into nature at the season of dissolution:' and VÁCHESPATI, '*Linga* is so termed because it suffers resolution (*laya*), or from its characteristic indication of the source from which it proceeds†.' See also remarks on ver. 10. p. 43.

XLI.

As a painting stands not without a ground, nor a shadow without a stake, &c. so neither does subtile person subsist supportless, without specific (or unspecific) particles.

BHÁSHYA.

As a picture without the support of a wall or the like does not stand; as the shadow does not stand without the stake (the gnomon of a dial); that is, without them does not exist. The term *et cetera* comprises (other illustrations); as, water cannot be without coldness, nor coldness without water; fire without heat; air without touch; ether without extension; earth without smell; so by this illustration it is intimated that it, the rudiment (*linga*), does not subsist without unspecific or rudimental particles. Here also specific elements are implied, or body composed of the five gross elements; for without a body, having specific particles, where can the place of the *linga* be; which, when it abandons one corporeal frame, takes refuge in another. *Supportless;* devoid of support. *Subtile* (person); instrument of thirteen kinds: this is the meaning of the text.

For what purpose (these subtile elements are embodied) is next described.

---

* लिंगनाज् ज्ञापनाल्लिंगं। † लिंगं लयं गच्छतीति लिंगं हेतुमत्त्वेनचास्य लिंगत्वमिति भावः।

COMMENT.

In the preceding verse it was stated that subtile person migrated, or as soon as deprived of one body it took refuge in another. It is now explained why this must be; and that it proceeds from the necessity of something to give to subtile principles asylum and support.

The text accordingly states, that the 'rudiment,' the *linga*, cannot exist without such support; but with regard to the support itself there is some difference of opinion, the passage being variously read and interpreted.

Gaurapáda reads the expression, *aviśéshair viná*, 'without unspecific particles;' by which he states that he means the 'rudimental particles,' the *tan mátras*. He adds, that specific particles, gross elementary bodies, are also necessary; using the terms *aviśésha* and *viśésha* as they were before employed (ver. 38), to represent severally the rudimental and gross elements. Váchespati and Náráyana read the phrase *viśéshair viná*, 'without specific particles;' but they use the term 'specific' apparently in its general acceptation of 'species,' without reference to its technical employment in ver. 38; for they confine its purpose to that of 'subtile bodies.' '*Without specific particles;* without subtile bodies: that is the meaning*.' *S. Tatwa Kaumudí*. '*Without specific particles;* without very subtile bodies: the rudiment (*linga*), being unsupported, does not remain; but being supported by subtile bodies it exists†.' *S. Chandriká*. So far therefore, although the reading be different, the interpretation appears to be the same. The *linga*, or 'rudiment'—for it is to be observed, that it is this which is spoken of by both text and comment, and not the *linga śaríra*, 'rudimental body'—cannot subsist without a bodily frame. Whence that frame is derived, Gaurapáda makes sufficiently clear. The *linga*, or 'rudiment,' consists of but thirteen principles—the unclothed faculties and senses: the rudimental body, by which they are aggregated and

---

* विना विशेषैरिति सूक्ष्मशरीरैरित्यर्थः । † विशेषैरतिसूक्ष्मशरीरैर्विना लिंगं निराश्रयं न तिष्ठति किन्तु सूक्ष्मशरीराश्रितं तिष्ठति ।

defended, is a *tan mátrika* body, composed of the rudimental elements (p. 123). This again, for worldly existence, is enveloped in a bodily frame of gross elementary composition.

It may, however, be suspected that the authors of the *S. Tatwa Kaumudí* and the *Chandriká* have not attended to the distinction, and that they intend by their 'specific or subtile bodies' only one of the 'species,' or *viśéshas*, which may be intimated in ver. 38; a modification of the gross elements enclosing, not the naked 'rudiment,' the *linga*, but the 'rudimental body,' the *linga śarira*. Such, at any rate, is the interpretation of Vijnána Bhikshu, who, commenting on this stanza of the *Káriká*, explains '*specific particles*, those which are called subtile amongst gross; a species or variety of gross elements:' and he says, that 'the definition of subtile body which is given in the preceding stanza, "composed of intellect with other subtile elements" (p. 128), as compared with the expression of the present verse, proves that there is a distinction made between subtile body and the specific variety of the gross elements, which is also called subtile *.'

The question then is not one merely of a difference of interpretation, but it is a difference of doctrine. According to Gaurapáda's explanation, which appears to be the original theory, living bodies consist of two parts, one of a subtile, and one of a gross nature; the latter perishes or decomposes at death; the former may live on through the existence of the world: the latter gives cover to the former, which is the immediate vehicle of soul, and accompanies it constantly, through successive perishable bodies, until soul's liberation, or until a period of universal dissolution restore its component parts to their primitive and common parent. To this body the term of *linga śarira*, 'rudimental body,' is properly applied; it is also called *átiváhika*, that which is swifter than the wind in passing from body to body; and, as Mr. Colebrooke observes, "it seems

* विशेषैः स्थूलसूक्ष्माख्यैः स्थूलावान्तरभेदैरिति यावदस्यां कारिकायां सूक्ष्माख्यानां स्थूलभूतानां लिंगशरीराद्भेदावगमेन महदादिसूक्ष्मपर्य्यन्तमित्यादि पूर्वोदाहृतकारिकायां सूक्ष्मभूतपर्य्यन्तस्य लिंगत्वेनेत्यर्थः ।

to be a compromise between an immaterial soul and the difficulty which a gross understanding finds in grasping the comprehension of individual existence, unattached to matter." Tr. R. As. Soc. I. 32.

But some of the expounders of the Sánkhya doctrines have not thought even the rudimental body sufficiently material for the purpose of independent existence, when separated from gross body; and a third corporeal frame has been devised for its support, to which the present verse of the *Káriká* and the other passages which seem to allude to a subtile form of specific or gross elementary matter relate, according to Vijnána Bhikshu: 'Having abandoned gross body, a support is necessary for the passage of rudimental body to other regions, and another species of body is established *.' This is more particularly explained in the same writer's commentary on a somewhat obscure Sútra immediately preceding: '"In the body, which is the receptacle of the receptacle of that (rudimental body); for the denomination of *body* is applied to one as it is to the other." That is, the receptacle or support of that rudiment, which will be described as composed of the five elements, is supported or contained in body constituted of the six organic ingredients (bones, blood, &c.); to which the name *body* is applied, from the same being applicable to the sense of the word *adhish'hána* (*déha*, "body," being understood apparently in either case "containing" or "comprehending"). The corporeity of the vehicle or receptacle (*adhishṫhána*) arises from its relation to the (aggregate) *linga;* the corporeity of gross body, from its being the receptacle of vehicular body. This is the meaning of the text. We have therefore three (kinds of) body established †.' Quoting a passage which appears opposed to

---

* स्थूलदेहं त्यक्त्वा लोकान्तरगमनाय लिंगदेहस्याधारभूतं शरीरान्तरं सिध्यतीति ।

† तदधिष्ठानाश्रये देहे तद्वादात्तद्वादः ॥ तस्य लिंगस्य यदधिष्ठानमाश्रयो वक्ष्यमाणभूतपंचकं तस्याश्रये षाट्कौशिकदेहे तद्वादो देहवादस्तद्वादात् तस्याधिष्ठानशब्दोक्तस्य देहवादादित्यर्थः लिंगसम्बन्धादधिष्ठानस्य देहत्वमधिष्ठानाश्रयाच्च स्थूलस्य देहत्वमिति पर्य्यवसितार्थः । तथा च शरीरत्रयं सिद्धं ।

this, and to intimate, as Gaurapáda has done, a twofold distinction only of bodies, the same writer observes, 'What is said in writings, upon the authority of the Védas, that there are but two (kinds of) bodies, arises from their identifying the rudimental and vehicular bodies as one, as they are mutually permanent and subtile *.' This is no doubt correct; but it is very unlikely that the elder writers admitted any form of the gross elements to be equally permanent and subtile as the rudiments from which they proceeded. In the institutes of Manu, for instance, although the doctrine there laid down is of a different tenor from that of the Sánkhya system, we have but two kinds of bodies, a subtile and a substantial one, described: 'After death another body, composed of the five rudimental elements, is immediately produced, for wicked men, that may suffer the tortures of the infernal regions †.' *Manu*, XII. 16. We have here, then, a body composed of the five rudimental elements. In the *Bhagavad Gita* it is intimated that soul retains the senses and mind in the intervals of migration: 'At the time that spirit obtains a body, and when it abandons one, it migrates, taking with it those senses, as the wind wafts along with it the perfume of the flowers ‡.'

If Váchespati be correct in his interpretation of the word *purusha*, the Véda makes one kind of subtile body of the size of the thumb: '"Yama drew forth violently the subtile body, as big as the thumb."—The specification of the size merely denotes minuteness; extraction of soul would be absurd; and therefore by *purusha* must be meant "a subtile body," that which reposes in gross body ||.' This, agreeably to the older doctrine, would

---

* यच्छास्त्रेषु शरीरद्वयमेवश्रूयते तल्लिंगशरीराधिष्ठानशरीरयोरन्योन्यनियतत्वेन सूक्ष्मत्वेनचैकताभिप्रायादिति । † पंचभ्य एव मात्राभ्यः प्रेत्य दुष्कृतिनान्नृणाम् । शरीरं यातनार्थीयमन्यदुत्पद्यते ध्रुवं । ‡ शरीरं यदा वाप्नोति यच्चाप्युत्क्रामतीश्वरः । गृहीत्वैतानि संयाति वायुर्गन्धानिवाशयात् । || आगमश्चात्रभवति । अंगुष्ठमात्रं पुरुषं निश्चकर्ष यमो बलादिति । अंगुष्ठमात्रत्वेनसूक्ष्मतामुपलक्षयति । आत्मनो निष्कर्षासंभवेन सूक्ष्ममेवशरीरं पुरुषस्तदपि हि पुरि स्थूले शरीरे शेत इति ।

be rudimental body; according to later refinement, vehicular. It is the latter which, as Mr. Colebrooke mentions (Tr. R. As. Soc. I. 33) in Patanjali's *Yoga sástra*, is conceived to extend, like the flame of a lamp over its wick, to a small distance above the skull; and which, according to M. Cousin, is "la fameuse pensée intracranienne, dont on a cru faire récemment une découverte merveilleuse." *Hist. de la Philosophie*, I. 195.

The notion of some corporeal, however subtile, envelopment of soul—the *εἴδωλον*, *umbra*, *manes*, *simulacrum*, spirit, or ghost—giving to invisible and intangible soul some visible and tangible materiality, "such," as Good (Translation of Lucretius) observes, "as will at least enable the soul to assume some degree of material configuration, and to be capable of corporeal feelings, however spiritualized and refined, even after its separation from the body"—has prevailed in all times and in all ages. Nor was the doctrine confined to the people or the poets: such of the philosophers as maintained the immateriality of soul, attaching to it, until its final purification, some portion of corporeal substance, or some substantial, though subtile investure, or *ὄχημα*, or vehicle. Thus Cudworth (vol. III. 517) states, that 'the ancient assertors of the soul's immortality did not suppose human souls, after death, to be quite stripped stark naked from all body, but that the generality of souls had then a certain spirituous, vaporous, or airy body accompanying them; as also they conceived this spirituous body to hang about the soul also here in this life, before death, as its interior indument or vestment, which also then sticks to it when that other gross earthly part of the body is by death put off as an outer garment." It also appears, that "besides the terrestrial body, and this spirituous body, the ancients held that there is a third kind, of a higher rank, peculiarly belonging to such souls, after death, as are purged and cleansed from corporeal affections, called by them *σῶμα αὐγοειδὲς*, or a luciform body." The authorities quoted by Cudworth for these opinions are new Platonists, or Christian writers of the fourth and fifth centuries; and it seems not unlikely that they borrowed some of their notions from the doctrines of Christianity. They profess, however, to repeat the tenets of Pythagoras and Plato; and Cudworth asserts, that the distinction of two interior vehicles or tunicles of the soul, besides that outer vestment of the terrestrial body, is not a mere figment of the latter Platonists, but a tradition derived down from antiquity. Mosheim, in his translation of Cudworth, has entered, in a note, very fully into an inquiry as to the origin of the opinion of a subtile body investing soul, and concludes, "Vetus hæc opinio aut si mavis superstitio, ab ipsis fere Græcorum heroicis temporibus ducta:" and Brucker, in reference to his observations on this subject, remarks, "Hoc vero magna doctrina et ingenio demonstravit Mosheimius hanc de vehiculo opinionem non demum in juniorum Platonicorum cerebro enatam esse sed fuisse dogma canæ antiquitatis." *Hist. Philos.* I. 714. Although, therefore, less clearly expressed than by the Hindu writers, the early Greek philosophers entertained similar notions of the nature of the subtile body, which was inseparable from soul until the period of its final exemption from transmigration.

XLII.

For the sake of soul's wish, that subtile person exhibits (before it), like a dramatic actor, through relation of means and consequence, with the aid of nature's influence.

BHÁSHYA.

The purpose of soul is to be fulfilled, therefore nature proceeds to action. This (purpose) is twofold, apprehension of sound and the other objects of sense, and apprehension of the difference between qualities and soul. Apprehension of sound and the other objects of sense is enjoyment of sensual gratification, as fragrance and the like in the spheres of *Brahmá* and the rest: apprehension of the difference between the qualities and soul is liberation. Therefore it is said, For the sake of soul's wish subtile person is active. *Through relation of means and consequences.*—*Means* (or antecedents) are virtue and the like: *consequences* are their results, such as their ascending to heaven and so forth, as we shall hereafter explain. *By their relation;* their connection. *With the aid of nature's influence;* of the influence of the chief one, nature. As a king in his own kingdom does what he wishes of his own authority, so by the application of the supreme authority of nature, through the relation of means (or causes) and consequences, subtile body exhibits: that is, nature commands subtile body to assume different conditions, by taking different (gross) bodies. Subtile body is that which is aggregated of subtile atomic rudimental elements, and is possessed of thirteen instruments (or faculties and senses). It assumes various conditions, by its birth, amongst gods, animals and men. How does (it exhibit)? *Like an actor,* who when he enters upon the scene is a god, and when he makes his exit is again a mortal: or again, a buffoon. So the subtile body, through the relation of causes and consequences, having entered the womb, may become an elephant, a woman, or a man.

It was said (ver. 40), "Subtile body migrates, invested with dispositions." What those dispositions are is now described.

COMMENT.

The circumstances on which transmigration depends are here said to be the purpose of soul, enforced by the authority of nature.

Soul's purpose is either fruition or liberation; and to accomplish one or other of these, subtile body passes through various conditions, assuming different exterior forms, as an actor puts on different dresses to personate one while *Ráma,* another while *Yudhishṫhira,* or again, *Vatsa* *. The purpose of soul is enforced by the power, authority, or influence of nature †. *Vibhutwa,* as illustrated by GAURAPÁDA, means 'kingly or supreme authority.' VÁCHESPATI understands it as 'universality' rather, as in the text of the *Purána:* 'This wonderful vicissitude is from the universality of nature ‡;' that is, from its invariable presence and consequent influence. But besides these motives, the purpose of soul and

---

* यथा हि नटस्तद्भूमिकामाधाय रामो वाऽजातशत्रुर्वा वत्सराजो वा भवति। † विभुत्वयोगात्। ‡ वैश्वरूप्यात् प्रधानस्य परिणामोऽयमद्भुतः।

influence of nature, which may be regarded as the remote and proximate causes of transmigration in general, it is still necessary to have what may be regarded as a special, or exciting, or efficient cause; the reason of the particular migration; the cause wherefore, in particular instances, subtile body should ascend from the exterior frame of a man to that of a god, or wherefore it should descend from the exterior frame of a man to that of a brute. This depends, then, upon the relation of certain occasional or instrumental means or causes, *nimittas* *, with their incidental consequences or effects, the *naimittikas* †; as virtue and vice, which lead severally to reward and punishment after death; that is, to regeneration in an exalted or degraded condition. Thus the *Chandriká* explains the terms: '*Nimitta* is virtue and the rest; *naimittika* is the effect, having the *nimitta* for its cause, as gross bodies, &c. By the relation or connection of these two, subtile body, assuming the form of gods or other beings, performs its part ‡.' Professor Lassen has been needlessly perplexed by this verse, and has strangely rendered it as follows: "Corpusculum hocce propter genii causam effectum, ludionis instar se habet ad has modo ad illas originarias et derivatas conditiones pronum, post conjunctionem procreatricis cum potestate sua."

XLIII.

Essential dispositions are innate. Incidental, as virtue and the rest, are considered appurtenant to the instrument. The uterine germ (flesh and blood) and the rest belong to the effect (that is, to the body).

---

* निमित्तं । † नैमित्तिकं । ‡ निमित्तं धर्म्मादि नैमित्तिकं धर्म्मादिकारणकं स्थूलदेहादि तदुभयप्रसंगेन सम्बन्धेन लिंगं सूक्ष्म शरीरं देवादिशरीरं परिगृह्य व्यवहरति ।

BHÁSHYA.

Dispositions (*bhávas*, 'conditions') of being are considered to be threefold, innate, essential, and incidental. The first, or *innate*, are those four which in the first creation were cognate with the divine sage KAPILA, or virtue, knowledge, dispassion, and power. The *essential* are declared; these were four sons of BRAHMÁ, SANAKA, SANANDANA, SANÁTANA, and SANATKUMÁRA; and these four dispositions were produced with them, who were invested with bodies of sixteen years of age (or perpetually juvenile bodies), in consequence of the relation of causes and effects (or in consequence of merit in a former existence): therefore these dispositions are called *essential*. *Incidental* are those derived through the corporeal form of a holy teacher; from which (in the first instance) knowledge is incidentally obtained by such as we are; from knowledge comes dispassion; from dispassion, virtue; and from virtue, power. The form of a teacher is an incidental product (of nature), and therefore these dispositions are termed *incidental:* "Invested by which, subtile body migrates" (ver. 40). These four dispositions are of the quality of goodness; those of darkness are their contraries: as above, "Virtue, &c. are its faculties partaking of goodness; those partaking of darkness are the reverse" (ver. 23). Consequently there are eight dispositions, or virtue, knowledge, dispassion, power, vice, ignorance, passion, weakness. Where do they abide? *They are considered appurtenant to the instrument.* Intellect is an instrument, and to that they are appurtenant; as in ver. 23, "Ascertainment is intellect; virtue, knowledge," &c. *Effect;* body. *The uterine germ and the rest belong to it;* those which are born of the mother, *the germ and the rest*, or the bubble, the flesh, the muscle, and the rest, which are (generated), for the development of the infant, in the union of the blood and the seminal fluid. Thus the conditions of infancy, youth, and old age are produced; the instrumental causes of which are food and beverage; and therefore they are said to be attributes of the effect (or of the body), having, as the instrumental cause, the fruition of the sensual pleasures of eating and the like.

It was said (ver. 42), "Through the relation of means and consequences:" this is next explained.

COMMENT.

We have here an explanation of what is to be understood by the term *dispositions*, used in a former passage (ver. 40).

The translation of *bháva* * adopted by Mr. Colebrooke in this place is 'disposition:' in the passage referred to he had employed, as above remarked, 'sentiment;' but it was there changed, in order to preserve consistency. Neither word perhaps exactly expresses the purport of the original, nor is it easy to find one that will precisely correspond. In some respects 'condition,' mode, or state of being, *conditio*, as rendered by Professor Lassen, is preferable, as better comprehending the different circumstances to which *bháva* is applied; although, as he has occasion subsequently to remark, it does not very well express all the senses in which *bháva* occurs. These circumstances or conditions, according to the obvious meaning of the text, are of two kinds, or intellectual and corporeal. The first comprise virtue, knowledge, dispassion, power, and their contraries; the second, the different periods of life, or embryo, infancy, youth, and senility. They are also to be regarded as respectively cause and effect; virtue, &c. being the efficient cause, or *nimitta;* bodily condition the *naimittika*, or consequence; as VÁCHESPATI explains the object of the stanza, 'which,' according to him, 'distinguishes incidental cause and consequence, the latter being the incidental conditions of body †.'

But besides the division of conditions or dispositions into the two classes of intellectual and corporeal, they are also characterised according to their origin, as *sánsiddhika*, *prákrita*, and *vaikrita*, rendered in the text 'innate, essential, and incidental.' Prof. Lassen translates them *conditiones absolutæ*, *pendentes ab origine*, *pertinentes ad evoluta principia*. Both the two first are innate, and some further distinction is necessary. 'Superhuman' or 'transcendental' would perhaps best explain the first, as they are, according to the commentator, peculiar to saints and sages. According to GAURAPÁDA, they occur only in one instance as the cognate

---

* भावः । † निमित्तं नैमित्तिकं च विभजते । वैकृतिका नैमित्तिकाः ।

conditions of the divine Kapila, the author of the Sánkhya system. The second class, which may be rendered 'natural,' agreeably to his view, which is a little mystical, originated with the four holy and chaste sons of Brahmá. The third class, those which are incidental or constructive, *vaikrita*, belong to mortals, as they are produced in them by instruction. Váchespati recognises but two distinctions, identifying, as in the translation, the innate (*sánsiddhika*) with the essential (*prákrita*) dispositions, they being both *swábhávika*, 'inseparable, inherent,' not the production of tuition, and opposing to it the constructive or incidental (*vaikritika*)*. A similar account of their origin as in the *Bháshya* is given, but under these two heads only: 'Thus in the beginning of creation the first sage, the venerable and great *Muni* Kapila, appeared, spontaneously endowed with virtue, knowledge, dispassion, and power. The incidental and unspontaneous dispositions were produced by the cultivation of the means (of producing them), as (the lessons of) Práchetasa and other great *Rishis*†.' These dispositions or conditions are dependent upon the instrument, that is upon *buddhi*, or 'intellect,' of which they are faculties, as was explained in verse 23. The states or conditions of life depend upon the body, and are the immediate effects of generation and nutriment, the more remote effects of virtue, vice, &c.

XLIV.

By virtue is ascent to a region above; by vice, descent to a region below: by knowledge is deliverance; by the reverse, bondage.

---

* वैकृतिका नैमित्तिका—प्राकृतिका सांसिद्धिकाभावाः स्वाभाविका इति यावत्।

† तथाहि सर्गादावादिविद्वान् अत्र भगवान् कपिलो महामुनिर्धर्म्मज्ञानवैराग्यैश्वर्य्यसम्पन्नः प्रादुर्बभूवेति। वैकृतिकाश्च भावा असांसिद्धिका उपायानुष्ठानोत्पन्ना यथा प्राचेतसप्रभृतीनां महर्षीणां।

BHÁSHYA.

By virtue ascent.—Having made virtue the efficient cause, it leads upwards. By *upwards* eight degrees are intended, or the regions of Brahmá, Prajápati, Soma, Indra, the Gándharbas, the Yákshas, the Rákshasas, and Piśáchas: the subtile body goes thither. Or if vice be the efficient cause, it migrates into an animal, a deer, a bird, a reptile, a vegetable, or a mineral. Again; *by knowledge, deliverance:* knowledge of the twenty-five principles; by that efficient cause, deliverance: the subtile body ceases, and (soul is) called 'supreme spirit' (*paramátmá*). *By the reverse, bondage:* ignorance is the efficient cause, and that (effect) bondage is natural (*prákrita*), incidental (*vaikárika*), or personal (*dákshina*), as will be explained: "He who is bound by natural, incidental, or personal bondage is not loosed by any other (means than knowledge)."

Next, other efficient causes are declared.

XLV.

By dispassion is absorption into nature; by foul passion, migration: by power, unimpediment; by the reverse, the contrary.

BHÁSHYA.

If any one has dispassion without knowledge of principles, then from such dispassion unpreceded by knowledge occurs absorption into nature, or when the individual dies he is resolved into the eight primary elements, or nature, intellect, egotism, and the five rudiments; but there is no liberation, and therefore he migrates anew. So also *by foul passion;* as, I sacrifice, I give gifts, in order to obtain in this world divine or human enjoyment; from such foul passion proceeds worldly migration. *By power, unimpediment.*—Where eightfold power, as minuteness, &c. is the efficient cause, then non-obstruction is the effect. Such power is unimpeded in the sphere of Brahmá, or in any other. *By the reverse, the contrary.*—The contrary of unimpediment is obstruction, which proceeds from want of power, every where obstructed.

Thus sixteen efficient causes and effects have been enumerated: what they comprehend (or amount to) is next described.

COMMENT.

In these two verses the efficient causes of the various conditions of subtile body and their effects, or its conditions, are detailed.

These causes and effects are collectively sixteen, eight of each: the former are positive and negative, as diversified by the qualities of goodness and foulness (ver. 23); and the effects respectively correspond. They are accordingly,

Cause.	*Effect.*
1. Virtue.	2. Elevation in the scale of being.
3. Vice.	4. Degradation in the scale of being.
5. Knowledge.	6. Liberation from existence.
7. Ignorance.	8. Bondage or transmigration.
9. Dispassion.	10. Dissolution of the subtile bodily form.
11. Passion.	12. Migration.
13. Power.	14. Unimpediment.
15. Feebleness.	16. Obstruction.

By 'virtue,' *dherma*, both religious and moral merit are intended. *Ascent*, going upward, is elevation to a more exalted station in another birth; the term *sthána* implying both place and degree. According to Gaurapáda, this ascent is eightfold, and the subtile frame may after death assume a new body amongst the various classes of spirits, Piśáchas, Rákshasas, Yákshas, and Gandherbas; or may attain a place in the heaven of Indra; of Soma, or the moon; of the Prajápatis, or progenitors of mankind; or even in the region of Brahmá. It is a curious, though perhaps an accidental coincidence, that the Syrians and Egyptians enumerated also, according to Plato (Epinomis), eight orders of heavenly beings: their places, however, seem to be the planets exclusively. The author of the *S. T. Kaumudí* understands by *ascent*, or elevation, ascent to the six superterrestrial regions, *Dyu*, or *Bhuvar loka*, the atmosphere; *Swer loka*, the heaven of Indra; *Mahar loka*, *Janaloka*, and *Tapoloka*, worlds of sages and saints; and *Satya loka*, of Brahmá. By *degradation* he understands descent to the subterrene regions, *Pátála*, *Rasátala*, &c. These notions are, however, not incompatible, as rewards and punishments in heaven and hell are but temporary, and subtile body must even afterwards assume terrestrial form, and undergo a series of migrations before escape from the bondage of existence can be finally accomplished.

Bondage is said by the commentators to be of three kinds, intending thereby three different errors or misconceptions of the character of soul and nature; the prevalence of which precludes all hope of final emancipation. 'These errors or bonds are, 1. *Prákritika;* the error or bondage of the materialists, who assert soul in nature (or matter): 2. *Vaikritika;* the error of another class of materialists, who confound soul with any of the products of nature, as the elements, the senses, egotism or intellect: and, 3. *Dákshina;* the error or bondage of those who, ignorant of the real character of soul, and blinded by the hope of advantage, engage in moral and religious observances:' as VÁCHESPATI *. These errors confine the soul to its subtile material frame for various protracted periods; as, for instance, in the case of those who identify soul with sense, for ten *manwantaras*, or above three thousand millions of years (3,084,480,000).

By *dispassion* occurs 'absorption into nature,' *prakriti laya* †; or, as the *Kaumudí* and *Chandriká* express it, 'resolution into the chief one and the rest ‡.' GAURAPÁDA makes the meaning of the phrase sufficiently clear: according to him it signifies the resolution of even the subtile body into

---

* बन्धस्त्रिविधः प्राकृतिको वैकृतो दाक्षिणश्चेति। तत्रप्रकृतावात्मज्ञानाद् ये प्रकृतिमुपासते तेषां प्राकृतो बन्धः। वैकारिको बन्धस्तेषां ये विकारानेव भूतेन्द्रियाहंकारबुद्धीः पुरुषबुद्ध्योपासते। इष्टापूर्त्तेन दाक्षिणः पुरुषतत्वानभिज्ञो हि इष्टापूर्त्तकारी कामोपहतमना बध्यत इति। † प्रकृति लयः। प्रधानादिषु लयः।

its constituent elements: but this is not in this case equivalent to liberation; it is only the term of one series of migrations, soul being immediately reinvested with another person, and commencing a new career of migratory existence until knowledge is attained.

The remainder of the text requires no explanation.

XLVI.

THIS is an intellectual creation, termed *obstruction, disability, acquiescence*, and *perfectness*. By disparity of influence of qualities the sorts of it are fifty.

BHÁSHYA.

This aggregate of sixteen causes and effects is called *an intellectual creation*. *Pratyaya* means *buddhi*, 'intellect.' "Intellect is ascertainment," &c. (ver. 23). This intellectual creation is of four kinds, *obstruction, disability, acquiescence, and perfectness*. In this classification, *doubt* (obstruction) is ignorance; as when any one beholding a post (at a distance) is in doubt whether it is a post or a man. *Disability* is when, even though the object be distinctly seen, the doubt cannot be dissipated. The third kind is called *acquiescence;* as when a person declines to doubt or determine whether the object be a post or not; saying, What have I to do with this. The fourth kind is *perfectness;* as when the delighted observer notices a creeper twining round the object, or a bird perched upon it, and is certain that it is a post. *By disparity of influence of qualities.*—By the unequal (or varied) influence of the qualities of goodness, foulness, and darkness, acting on this fourfold intellectual creation, there are fifty modifications of it: and these kinds in which severally goodness, foulness, or darkness prevails, and the other two are subordinate, are next particularized.

COMMENT.

In this and the five following stanzas the modifications of the causes and consequences, or the conditions of existence produced by the intellectual faculties, as influenced by the three qualities, are detailed and classified.

By 'intellectual creation,' *pratyaya serga* *, is to be understood the various accidents of human life occasioned by the operations of the intellect, or the exercise of its faculties, virtue, knowledge, dispassion, power, and their contraries. *Pratyaya* properly means 'trust,' but is here considered to be synonymous with *buddhi*. It may be understood as implying 'notion;' and *pratyaya serga* is the creation or existence of which we have a notion or belief, in contradistinction to bodily or organic existence, of which we have an idea or sensible perception; the *bhúta serga* †, or 'elemental creation.'

Existence then, dependent on the faculties of the intellect and their consequences, is further distinguished as of four kinds: 1. 'Obstruction,' *viparyaya*, is explained by VÁCHESPATI 'ignorance' (*ajnána*), by GAURAPADA 'doubt' (*sansaya*): 2. 'Disability,' *aśakti*, is imperfection of the instruments or senses: 3. *Tushṫi* is 'acquiescence' or 'indifference:' and, 4. *Siddhi* is 'complete or perfect knowledge.' 'In the three first are comprised the seven intellectual faculties, virtue and the rest (see p. 88), all except knowledge, which is comprehended in perfectness ‡.' *S. Tatwa Kaumudí*. This is the collective or generic division. Each genus is again divided so as to form fifty species, according as they are affected by the three qualities, or the predominance of one, and the depression of another ‖. The species are enumerated in the succeeding verse.

---

* प्रत्ययसर्गः । † भूतसर्गः । ‡ तत्रविपर्य्ययाशक्तितुष्टिषु यथायोगं सप्तानां धर्म्मादीनां ज्ञानवर्ज्जमन्तर्भावः सिद्धौ च ज्ञानस्येति ।

‖ एकैकस्याधिकबलता द्वयोर्वा एकैकस्यन्यूनबलता द्वयोर्वा ।

XLVII.

THERE are five distinctions of obstruction; and, from defect of instruments, twenty-eight of disability: acquiescence is ninefold; perfectness eightfold.

BHÁSHYA.

Five distinctions of obstruction; namely, obscurity, illusion, extreme illusion, gloom, and utter darkness: these will presently be explained. There are *twenty-eight kinds of disability from defect of instruments;* which also we shall describe. *Acquiescence is ninefold,* being the kinds of knowledge partaking of the quality of foulness in an ascetic. *Perfectness is eightfold,* which in holy men consists also of the kinds of knowledge partaking of the quality of goodness. These will all be explained in order; and first of *obstruction.*

COMMENT.

We have here the fifty varieties of intellectual creation, or conditions dependent upon the faculties of intellect, simply enumerated under each head respectively.

The text in each case is limited to the enumeration of the number of the varieties, leaving their designations and descriptions to be supplied by the scholia: accordingly we have in the *Bháshya* the five distinctions of obstruction specified. They are referred to in the text, in the succeeding stanza, for the purpose of enumerating their subdivisions, and it is unnecessary therefore to enter upon the detail here.

XLVIII.

THE distinctions of obscurity are eightfold, as also those of illusion; extreme illusion is tenfold; gloom is eighteenfold, and so is utter darkness.

BHÁSHYA.

Obscurity is eightfold; final dissolution being so distinguished through ignorance; as when a person thinks that soul merges into the eight forms of *prakriti*, or the five rudiments, egotism, intellect, and nature, and thence concludes, I am liberated: this is eightfold obscurity. The same is the number of kinds of *illusion;* in consequence of which, Indra and the gods, being attached to the possession of the eight kinds of superhuman power, such as minuteness and the rest, do not obtain liberation, but upon the loss of their power migrate again: this is called eightfold illusion. *Extreme illusion is of ten kinds*, accordingly as the five objects of sense, sound, touch, form, taste, and smell, are sources of happiness to the gods or to men. In these ten objects (or the five objects of sense twice told) consists extreme illusion. *Gloom is eighteenfold.*—The faculties of superhuman power are eight sources, and the objects of sense, human or divine, are ten, making eighteen; and the feeling that makes men rejoice in the enjoyment of these eighteen, and grieve for the want of them, is gloom. *Utter darkness* has in like manner eighteen varieties, originating with the eightfold superhuman power and the ten objects of perception; but it applies to the profound grief felt by one who dies amidst the abundance of sensual delights in the season of enjoyment, or who falls from the command of superhuman faculties: that is utter darkness. In this manner the five varieties of obstruction, obscurity and the rest, are severally subdivided, making sixty-two varieties.

COMMENT.

The five kinds of obstruction, ignorance, or uncertainty, alluded to in the preceding stanza, are here specified, and their subdivisions enumerated.

'Obstruction,' *viparyaya* *, means, properly, whatever obstructs the soul's object of final liberation: it is consequently any cause of bondage,

* विपर्य्ययः ।

of confinement to worldly existence, or of perpetual migration, and is therefore one of the four elements of the creation of the world; as, if spirit was not so confined, created forms would never have existed. So the Sútra of KAPILA has, 'Bondage is from obstruction *;' but liberation depends on knowledge: bondage therefore arises from ignorance, and ignorance or error is obstruction. GAURAPÁDA accordingly uses *sanśaya* †, 'doubt' or 'error,' as the synonyme of *viparyaya;* and the specification of its sub-species confirms this sense of the term, as they are all hinderances to final emancipation, occasioned by ignorance of the difference between soul and nature, or by an erroneous estimate of the sources of happiness, placing it in sensual pleasure or superhuman might.

The five varieties of obstruction or error are, 'obscurity,' *tamas;* 'illusion,' *moha;* 'extreme illusion,' *mahámoha;* 'gloom,' *támisra;* 'utter darkness,' *andhatámisra.* The distinctions are more subtle than precise, but their general purport is sufficiently obvious; they all imply ignorance of self, and thirst of pleasure and power. Another enumeration, that of the *Yoga*, or *Pátanjala* school, as repeated by VIJNÁNA BHIKSHU, calls the five species, 'ignorance' (*avidyá*), 'egoism' (*asmitá*), 'love' (*rága*), 'hate' (*dwésha*), and 'idle terror' (*abhinivésa*), as fear of death and the like ‡. They are called also in the same system, 'the five afflictions ‖.' These are identified with the species named in the text. *Obscurity* is that ignorance which believes soul to be sealed in primary nature, or one of its first seven products; and is therefore eightfold. *Illusion* is that egoism that exults in the appropriation of the eight superhuman faculties; and is consequently eightfold also. *Extreme illusion*, or love, is addiction to sensual objects, as they are grateful respectively to gods and men: therefore this class of impediments to liberation is tenfold. *Gloom*, or hate, is of eighteen kinds; ten as affecting the ten objects of sense, or the five divine and five human, as before distinguished, and termed by GAURA-

---

* बन्धो विपर्य्ययात् ।

† संशयः ।

‡ अविद्यास्मितारागद्वेषाभिनिवेशाः पञ्च योगोक्ता बन्धहेतुविपर्य्ययस्यावान्तरभेदा इति ।

‖ अविद्यास्मितारागद्वेषाभिनिवेशाः पंचक्लेशा इति पातञ्जले ।

PÁDA, *drishtá**, 'seen,' perceived by men; and *anusravikå*†, 'heard traditionally,' by men, of the gods: and eight connected with the possession of the eight superhuman faculties. The mental conditions here intended are those of fierceness and impatience, with which sensual enjoyments are pursued, or superhuman powers are exercised. *Utter darkness*, or terror, is the fear of death in men; and in gods, the dread of expulsion from heaven by the Asuras: in either case the loss of pleasure and power is the thing lamented; and as their sources are eighteen, so many are the subdivisions of this condition. These distinctions are said to be the work of former teachers; as in the *S. Pravachana Bháshya:* 'The subdivisions are as formerly described: that is, the subdivisions of obstruction, which is said to be of five species, are such as were fully detailed by former teachers, but are in the Sútra but briefly alluded to, for fear of prolixity‡.'

XLIX.

DEPRAVITY of the eleven organs, together with injuries of the intellect, are pronounced to be disability. The injuries of intellect are seventeen, by inversion of acquiescence and perfectness.

BHÁSHYA.

From defect of instruments there are twenty-eight kinds of disability; this has been declared (ver. 47): these are, *depravity of the eleven organs*, or deafness, blindness, paralysis, loss of taste, loss of smell, dumbness, mutilation, lameness, constipation, impotence, and insanity. *Together with injuries of the intellect:* as, together with these, there are twenty-eight kinds of disability, there are seventeen kinds of injuries of the

---

* दृष्टाः । † आनुश्रविकाः । ‡ अवान्तरभेदाः पूर्ब्बवत् । विपर्य्यस्यावान्तरभेदा ये सामान्यतः पंचोक्तास्तेपूर्ब्बवत् पूर्ब्बाचार्य्यैर्यथोक्तास्तथैव विशिष्या अवधार्य्या विस्तरभयान्नेहोच्यन्त इत्यर्थः ।

intellect. *By inversion of acquiescence and perfectness:* that is, there are nine kinds of acquiescence, and eight of perfectness; and with the circumstances that are the reverse of these (seventeen), the eleven above specified, compose the twenty-eight varieties of disability. The kinds of injury of the intellect which are the reverse of (the sorts of) acquiescence and perfectness will be understood from the detail of their varieties.

The nine kinds of acquiescence are next explained.

COMMENT.

The various kinds of the second class of conditions or disability are here enumerated.

'Disability,' *aśakti,* or incapability of the intellect to discharge its peculiar functions *, is the necessary result of imperfection of the senses, or of any of the organs of perception and of action. But besides these, which are sufficiently obvious, such as blindness, deafness, and any other organic defect, there are seventeen affections of the intellect itself equally injurious to its efficiency. These are described as the contraries of the conditions which constitute the classes acquiescence and perfectness. Under the former head are enumerated, dissatisfaction as to notions of nature, means, time, and luck, and addiction to enjoyment of the five objects of sense, or the pleasures of sight, hearing, touching, &c. The contraries of perfectness are, want of knowledge, whether derivable from reflection, from tuition, or from study, endurance of the three kinds of pain, privation of friendly intercourse, and absence of purity or of liberality.

L.

NINE sorts of acquiescence are propounded; four internal, relating to nature, to means, to time, and to luck; five external, relative to abstinence from (enjoyment of) objects.

---

* बुद्धेरशक्तिः स्वव्यापारे ।

BHÁSHYA.

Five internal sorts of acquiescence.—Those which are in the individual are internal. They are said to *relate to nature, to means, to time, and to luck.* The first is, when a person understands what nature is, its being with or without qualities, and thence knows a principle (of existence) to be a product of nature; but knows this only, and is satisfied: he does not obtain liberation: this is acquiescence in regard to *nature.* The second is, when a person, ignorant of the principles (of existence), depends upon external means, such as the triple staff, the water-pot, and other implements (used by ascetics): liberation is not for him: this is acquiescence in regard to *means.* Acquiescence in regard to *time* is when a person satisfies himself that liberation must occur in time, and that it is unnecessary to study first principles: such a one does not obtain liberation. And in the same way acquiescence as relates to *luck* is when a person is content to think that by good luck liberation will be attained. These are four kinds of acquiescence. *Five external, relative to abstinence from (enjoyment of objects).*—The external sorts of acquiescence are five; from abstinence from enjoyment of (five) objects of sense; that is, when a person abstains from gratification through sound, touch, form, flavour, and smell; such abstinence proceeding from observation of (the evils of) acquiring, preserving, waste, attachment (to sensual pleasures), and injuriousness. Acquiring is pain (or trouble), for the sake of increase, by the pasturage of cattle, trade, acceptance of gifts, and servitude. There is pain in the preservation of what has been acquired; and if they be enjoyed, they are wasted; and waste, again, is vexation. When attachment to sensual pleasures prevails, the organs have no repose: this is the fault of such attachment. Without detriment to created things there is no enjoyment (of sensible objects); and this is the defect of injuriousness. From observing then the evil consequences of acquiring and the rest, abstinence from enjoyment of the five objects of sense is practised; and these are the five sorts of external acquiescence. From the variety of these internal and external kinds proceed the nine sorts of acquiescence. Their names are differently enumerated in other works, or *ambhas, salilam, ogha, vrishťi, sutamas, páram, sunetram, nárikam,* and *anuttamámbhasikam:* and from the reverse of these kinds of acquiescence, constituting the varieties of disability, injuries of the intellect arise, named (according to the last mentioned nomenclature) *anambhas, asalilam,* and so on. From the contrariety of these, therefore, are inferred the injuries of the intellect.

Perfectness is next described.

COMMENT.

The different kinds of acquiescence, apathy, or indifference, are specified in this verse.

The kinds of acquiescence, content, or complacency, *tushti*, are of two descriptions; internal or spiritual, *ádhyátmika*, and external or sensible, *bahya*. GAURAPÁDA explains the former, 'being in self or spirit *.' VÁCHESPATI defines them, 'Those kinds of acquiescence are called *internal* which proceed from discrimination of self, as different from nature †.' According to VIJNÁNA BHIKSHU, they are those principles or sentiments which preside over collected or composed soul ‡. Of the different species, the first, or that which relates to nature, acknowledges it as the radical principle of all things, but expects that as every thing is but a modification of nature, so nature will effect all that is necessary, even liberation, for example, and the individual *I* remains passive and complete ‖. Another person, as the means of liberation, adopts a religious or mendicant order, or at least bears the emblems, as the staff, the water-pot, and the like: the term *vividiká* used in the *Bháshya* is of doubtful import, and is perhaps an error. Others suppose that liberation must come in time, or at least by a long continued course of meditation. Others imagine it may come by good luck; and contenting themselves with these notions or practices, omit the only means of being freed from existence, discriminative meditation. The five

---

* आत्मनि भवाः ।

† प्रकृति व्यतिरिक्तमातत्मानमधिकृत्य यस्मात् तास्तुष्टयस्तस्मादाध्यात्मिकाः ।

‡ आत्मानं संघातमधिकृत्य वर्त्तन्ते ।

‖ साक्षात्कारपर्य्यन्तः परिणामः सर्व्वोऽपि प्रकृतेरेव तं (मोक्षं) च प्रकृतिरेव करोत्यहं तु कूटस्थः पूर्ण इति ।

external kinds of acquiescence are self-denial, or abstinence from the five objects of sensual gratification; not from any philosophic appreciation of them, but from dread of the trouble and anxiety which attends the means of procuring and enjoying worldly pleasures; such as acquiring wealth, preserving it, spending it, incessant excitement and injury or cruelty to others. Besides the terms ordinarily significant of these divisions of acquiescence, the Scholiasts specify other words, the usual sense of which is quite different, and which may therefore be regarded as the slang or mystical nomenclature of the followers of the *Yoga*. There is some difference in the precise expressions, but they are of a similar purport in general. The first four, the synonymes of the internal modes of acquiescence, are alike in all the authorities; or, *ambhas* *, 'water;' *salila* †, also 'water;' *ogha* ‡, 'quantity;' and *vrishti* ‖,' 'rain.' GAURAPÁDA then has for the five exterior modes, *sutamas* §, 'great darkness;' *pára* ¶, 'shore;' *sunĕtra* **, 'a beautiful eye;' *nárika* ††, 'feminine;' and *anuttamámbhisika* ‡‡, 'unsurpassed water.' VÁCHESPATI makes them, *páram*, *supáram* ‖‖, 'good shore;' *apáram* §§, 'shoreless;' *anuttamambhas* ¶¶, 'unsurpassed water;' and *uttamámbhas* ***, 'excellent water.' The *Chandriká* has the same, except in the third place, where the term is *párápára* †††, 'both shores;' with which the *S. Prav. Bh.* agrees. No explanation of the words is any where given, nor is any reason assigned for their adoption.

LI.

REASONING, hearing, study, prevention of pain of three sorts, intercourse of friends, and purity (or gift) are perfections (or means thereof). The fore-mentioned three are curbs of perfectness.

---

* अम्भस्। † सलिलं। ‡ ओघः। ‖ वृष्टिः। § सुतमस्
¶ पारं। ** सुनेत्रं। †† नारीकं। ‡‡ अनुत्तमाम्भसिकः।
‖‖ सुपारं। §§ अपारं। ¶¶ अनुत्तमाम्भस्। *** उत्तमाम्भस्।
††† परापारं।

BHÁSHYA.

Reasoning; as when a person always reasons, What here is truth? What is the future? What is final felicity? How may I attain the object (of my existence)? and from reflecting in this manner, the knowledge is acquired that soul is different from nature; that intellect, egotism, the rudiments, the senses, the elements, are several and distinct. In this manner knowledge of the (twenty-five) principles is attained, by which liberation is accomplished. This is the first kind of perfectness, called *reasoning*. Next, from knowledge acquired by *hearing* proceeds knowledge of nature, intellect, egotism, the rudiments, the senses, and the elements; whence liberation ensues: this is perfectness by hearing. When from *study*, or the perusal of the Védas and other (sacred) writings, knowledge of the twenty-five principles is acquired; that is the third kind of perfectness. *Prevention of the three kinds of pain.*—When, for the purpose of preventing the three kinds of pain, internal, external, and superhuman, a holy teacher has been attended, and liberation is derived from his counsel; then this constitutes the fourth kind of perfectness. This is threefold, with reference to the three different sorts of pain, and makes, with the three preceding, six varieties of perfectness. Next, *intercourse of friends;* as when a friend, having acquired knowledge, obtains liberation: this is the seventh kind of perfectness. *Gift;* as when a person assists holy men, by donations of a dwelling, of herbs, of a staff, a wallet, food, or clothing; and (in requital) receives from them knowledge, and thus obtains liberation: this is the eighth sort of perfectness. In other books these eight kinds of perfectness are termed *táram*, *sutáram*, *táratáram*, *pramodam*, *pramoditam*, *pramodamánam*, *ramyakam*, and *sadápramuditam.*——From contrariety to these, the injuries of intellect which occur, or causes of disability, are termed *atáram*, *asutarám*, &c.; thus completing the twenty-eight kinds of disability, as in the text (ver. 49), "Depravity of the eleven organs, together with injuries of the intellect," &c. Thus the contraries of the sorts of acquiescence being nine, and the contraries of the kinds of perfectness being eight, they form seventeen injuries of intellect; and these, with the eleven defects of the organs, constitute twenty-eight kinds of disability, as previously stated.

In this way the various kinds of obstruction, disability, acquiescence, and perfectness, have been affirmatively and negatively described. Again, *the forementioned three are curbs of perfectness.—Forementioned;* that is, obstruction, disability, and acquiescence; they are curbs of perfectness: threefold curbs from their severalty. As an elephant is kept in check when restrained by a goad (or curb), so, impeded by obstruction, disability, and acquiescence, the world suffers ignorance: therefore abandoning them, perfectness alone is to be pursued; for by a person having perfectness knowledge is attained, and thence liberation.

It was stated (ver. 40) that "subtile body migrates, invested with dispositions:" those dispositions were previously said to be virtue and the rest, eight in number, modifications (or faculties) of intellect; which again have been described as modified by obstruction, disability, acquiescence, and perfectness. These (together) constitute intellectual creation, also called dispositional (or conditional): but subtile body is called a rudimental (or personal) creation, extending throughout the fourteen sorts of created things. (See v. 53.) It then becomes a question, whether soul's purpose is accomplished by one kind of creation, or by both? This is next explained.

COMMENT.

The different kinds of perfectness are here specified.

By 'perfectness,' *siddhi**, is here to be understood the means of perfecting or fulfilling the purpose of soul, or the conditions essential to its attainment; the circumstances productive of knowledge; the necessary consequence of which is exemption from future transmigration. '† Reasoning, hearing, study, intercourse of friends, and gift, are secondary kinds of perfectness, as subsidiary to the prevention of the three kinds of pain,

---

* सिद्धिः । † विहन्यमानस्य दुःखस्य त्रित्वात्तद्विघातास्त्रय इति । इमा मुख्यास्तिस्रः सिद्धयस्तदुपायतयात्वितरा गौण्यः पंच सिद्धयः । तास्ता अपि हेतुहेतुमत्तयाव्यवस्थिताः ।

which constitutes a triple principal class: they are respectively distinguished as objects, and the means of effecting those objects.' *S. Tatwa Kaumudí. Reasoning*, according to VÁCHESPATI, is 'investigation of scriptural authority by dialectics which are not contrary to the scriptures:' and *investigation* is defined, 'refutation of dubious doctrine, and establishment of positive conclusions *.' '*Hearing* is oral instruction, or rather the knowledge thence derived, or knowledge derived either from hearing another person read, or from expounding a work †.' *S. Pr. Bh. Intercourse of friends* ‡ is explained in the *S. Tatwa Kaumudí* to signify 'dissatisfaction with solitary inquiry, and discussion with a teacher, a pupil, or a fellow-student ‖.' VIJNÁNA BHIKSHU defines it, 'acquirement of knowledge from a benevolent visitor, who comes to give instruction §.' VÁCHASPATI and NÁRÁYANA agree in rendering *dána* ¶—which GAURAPÁDA explains by 'gift, liberality,' particularly to religious characters —by *śuddhi* **, 'purity;' meaning the purity of discriminative knowledge; deriving it from the root *daip* ††, 'to purify;' and not from *dá* ‡‡, 'to give.' The former cites the authority of PATANJALI for this sense of one kind of perfectness: 'Undisturbedness of discriminative knowledge, that is, purity; which is not attained except through long repeated and uninterrupted practice of veneration. That is also comprehended in discrimination by the term *dána* ‖‖. He also observes that others interpret it '*gift*, by which a sage, being propitiated, imparts

---

* आगमाविरोधन्यायेनागमार्थपरीक्षणं। परीक्षणं च संशयपूर्वपक्षनिराकरणेनोत्तरपक्षव्यवस्थापनं।

† अन्यदीयपाठमाकर्ण्य स्वयंवा शास्त्रमाकल्य यज्ज्ञानं जायते तदिति।

‡ सुहृत्प्राप्तिः।

‖ सुहृदां गुरुशिष्यसब्रह्मचारिणां सम्वादकानां प्राप्तिः।

§ स्वयमुपदेशार्थं गृहागतात् परमकारुणिकाज्ज्ञानलाभः।

¶ दानं।

** शुद्धिः।

†† दैप्, शोधने।

‡‡ दा, दाने।

‖‖ विवेकख्यातेरविप्लवः। अविप्लवः शुद्धिः—सा च नविनादरनैरन्तर्य्यदीर्घकालसेविताभ्यासपरिपाकाद्भवतीति दानेन विवेकख्यात्यां कार्य्येण सोपि संगृहीतः।

knowledge *.' The *S. Prav. Bh.* gives this interpretation only †. The term for 'curb,' *ankuśa* ‡, is the goad or iron hook used to guide an elephant: it is here explained by *nivárana*, 'hindering;' and 'as obstruction, disability, and acquiescence hinder perfectness, they are to be shunned ‖.'

LII.

Without dispositions there would be no subtile person: without person there would be no pause of dispositions: wherefore a twofold creation is presented, one termed *personal*, the other *intellectual*.

BHÁSHYA.

Without dispositions, without intellectual creations, *there would be no subtile person*, no rudimental creation; from the non-assumption of repeated successive bodily forms, without the necessary influence of anterior conditions (or dispositions). *Without person*, without rudimental creation, *there would be no pause of dispositions*; from the indispensability of virtue or vice for the attainment of either subtile or gross body, and from the non-priority of either creation, they being mutually initiative, like the seed and the germ. There is no fault in this, for (the relation) is that of species, it does not imply the mutual relation of individuals. Thence proceeds a twofold creation, one termed *conditional* (or intellectual), the other *rudimental* (or personal). Further—

COMMENT.

It is here explained that a double condition of existence, a twofold creation, necessarily prevails; one proceeding from the intellectual facul-

---

* धनादिदानेनाराधितो ज्ञानी ज्ञानं प्रयच्छति। † दानं च यथा धनादिदानेन परितोषिताज्ज्ञानलाभ इति। ‡ अंकुशः। ‖ सिद्धि परिपन्थित्वाद्विपर्य्ययाशक्तितुष्टयो हेया इत्यर्थः।

ties, the other from the rudimental elements; each being indispensable to the other.

It was stated (ver. 40) that subtile body migrates, invested with dispositions: and it was then explained (ver. 43, et seq.) what those dispositions or conditions were, viz. the conditions of the intellect (described in ver. 23), or virtue, vice, knowledge, ignorance, passion, dispassion, power, and debility. These were said (v. 46) to constitute an intellectual creation, or a series of conditions originating in affections of *buddhi*, or the intellectual principle. But the effects of these dispositions, the consequences of virtue or vice and the rest, can only be manifested in a bodily state, and therefore require necessarily a creation of a different character, personal or rudimental creation, such as subtile body, investing the imperceptible products of nature; intellect and its faculties included. Nor is such a creation indispensable for the existence or exercise of the intellectual conditions or sentiments alone, but it is equally necessary for their occasional cessation: thus virtue, vice, and the rest necessarily imply and occasion bodily condition; bodily condition is productive of acts of vice and virtue; vice and virtue, again, occasion bodily condition; and so on: like the seed and the tree, each mutually generative of the other; the tree bears the seed; from the seed springs the tree, again to put forth seed; and so on for ever; neither being initiative, neither being final. But one result of bodily condition is knowledge; knowledge is liberation, when soul is disengaged: subtile body then resolves into its rudiments, and the dispositions or conditions of the intellect terminate. In this way there are two creations, the *bhávákhya* *, that termed 'conditional' or 'intellectual;' and the *lingákhya* †, that called 'rudimental' or 'personal.' Both these seem to be considered by the text, as well as by GAURAPÁDA and VÁCHESPATI, as varieties of one species of the *Pratyaya sarga*, or 'intellectual creation.' The commentator on the *S. Pravachana* so far agrees with them, but he seems to restrict the two kinds more closely to a creation of intellect, regarding the *linga* as *buddhi* itself, and the *bháva*

---

* भावाख्यः ।   † लिंगाख्यः ।

as its conditions or dispositions. Thus, commenting on this verse of the *Káriká,* he observes, '*Bháva* signifies the modes of the apprehension (or the faculties) of intelligence, as the properties knowledge, virtue, and the rest. *Linga* is the great principle, or intelligence *.' He calls them both *samashti sarga,* 'a collective or generic creation.' By the other commentators, however, the *linga* is also called the *tanmátra,* or 'rudimental creation †:' and it further seems to imply 'gross body;' for 'fruition, which is one of soul's objects, cannot be accomplished without both bodies; without the receptacle that enjoys, and the objects to be enjoyed ‡.' The author of the *Chandriká* has accordingly adopted a totally different version of this passage, understanding by *bhávákhya,* not any reference to intellectual creation, but the creation of sensible objects, the objects to be enjoyed; *lingákhya,* or 'personal creation,' being the enjoyer: 'Without the *bhávas,* or present objects of sense, the *linga,* or aggregate of imperceptible principles, intelligence and the rest, could not be means of fruition; whilst without intelligence and the rest there could be no pause, no cessation, of the means of enjoying sensible objects. This is the purport of the text ‖.' And he defines *linga* to be 'that which is only indicated, which is actually not visible, as intellect and the rest;' and *bháva,* 'that object which is perceived or apprehended by the senses, the class of sensible objects §.'

The succession of the two kinds of creation, as mutually cause and effect, is said by VÁCHESPATI to be eternal, and without a beginning, as

---

* भावो वासनारूपा बुद्धेर्ज्ञानादिगुणा लिंगं महत्तत्वं बुद्धिरिति ।

† लिंगमिति तन्मात्रसर्गमुपलक्षयति । ‡ भोगः पुरुषार्थो न भोग्यान् शब्दादीन् भोगायतनं च शरीरद्वयमन्तरेण सम्भवतीति । ‖ भावैः प्रत्यक्षैर्विषयैर्विना लिंगं महदाद्यतीन्द्रियवृन्दं न भोगसाधनमित्यर्थः। लिंगेन महदादिना विना न भावानां विषयानां निवृत्तिर्नभोगसाधनत्वमयमभिप्रायः । § लिंगाख्यो लिंग्यत एव न तु साक्षात् क्रियत इति लिंगं महदाद्यतीन्द्रियवर्गः । भावाख्यो भूयते प्राप्यतेऽर्थादिन्द्रियेणेति विषयवर्गः ।

even in the commencement of a *kalpa* bodily existence results from the conditions of similar existence in a former *kalpa**.

LIII.

THE divine kind is of eight sorts; the grovelling is fivefold; mankind is single in its class. This, briefly, is the world of living beings.

BHÁSHYA.

Divine, of eight sorts; Bráhma, Prájapatya, Saumya, Aindra, Gándherba, Yáksha, Rákshasha, and Paiśácha. Animals, deer, birds, reptiles, and immovable substances are the five *grovelling* kinds. *Mankind is single.* In this way there are fourteen sorts of creatures, there being three classes in the three worlds. Which is supreme in each is next explained.

COMMENT.

The intellectual or rudimental creation hitherto described has been that of creation generally; we now have an account of specific or individual creation, composed of fourteen classes of beings.

The fourteen classes of beings are, first, eight superhuman, or *Bráhma,* that of BRAHMÁ and other supreme gods; 2. *Prájapatya,* that of progenitors, the Menus, the Rishis, or divine sages; 3. *Saumya,* lunar or planetary; 4. *Aindra,* that of INDRA and divinities of the second order; 5. *Gándherba,* that of the demigods attendant on INDRA, and of similar beings; 6. *Rákshasa,* that of demons, foes of the gods; 7. *Yáksha,* that of the attendants of KUVÉRA; 8. *Paiśácha,* that of mischievous and cruel fiends. These are divine or superhuman beings. The ninth class is that of man, which contains but one species. We have then five classes of

---

* कल्पादावपि प्राचीनकल्पोत्पन्नभावलिंगसंस्कारवशाद्भावलिंगयोरुत्प
त्तिर्नानुपपन्नेति सर्व्वमवदातं ।

inferior beings; or, counting from the preceding, 10. Animals, or domestic animals, *paśu;* 11. Wild animals, as deer and the like, *mriga;* 12. Birds; 13. Reptiles, or creeping things, including fish *sarísripa;* and 14. *Sthávara*, fixed things, such as vegetables and minerals. These constitute the *vyashti serga**, specific or individual creation; or, as denominated in the text, the *bhautika sarga*, the creation of *bhútas*, 'beings;' or elemental creation; the forms of things requiring the combination of the gross elements.

LIV.

Above, there is prevalence of goodness: below, the creation is full of darkness: in the midst, is the predominance of foulness, from Brahmá to a stock.

BHÁSHYA.

Above: in the eight divine regions. *Prevalence of goodness:* the extensiveness or predominance of the quality of goodness. Above is goodness predominant, but there are foulness and darkness also. *Below, the creation is full of darkness.*—In animals and insensible things the whole creation is pervaded by darkness in excess, but there are goodness and foulness. *In the midst*, in man, *foulness predominates*, although goodness and darkness exist; and hence men for the most part suffer pain. Such is the world, *from* Brahmá *to a stock;* from Brahmá to immovable things. Thus non-elemental creation, rudimental creation, conditional and elemental creation, in beings of divine, mortal, brutal, and (immovable) origin, are the sixteen sorts of creation effected by nature.

COMMENT.

The various qualities dominating in the different orders of beings are specified in this stanza.

---

* व्यष्टिसर्गः ।

The coexistence of the several qualities, with the predominance of one or other of them, in different beings, has been previously explained (p. 54), as well as the different orders or states of existent beings; constituting, according to GAURAPÁDA, sixteen forms or kinds of creation: that is, apparently, each of the four classes of beings proceeds from four modifications of nature; or, from the invisible principles, from the subtile rudiments, from the conditions or dispositions of intellect, and from the gross elements.

LV.

THERE does sentient soul experience pain, arising from decay and death, until it be released from its person: wherefore pain is of the essence (of bodily existence).

BHÁSHYA.

There: in the bodies of gods, men, and animals. *Pain* produced by *decay*, and produced by *death*. *Sentient soul:* soul having sensibility. *Experiences:* soul experiences; not nature, nor intellect, nor egotism, nor the rudiments, senses, nor gross elements. How long does it suffer pain? this (the text) discusses. *Until it be released from its person.* As long as it is in subtile body, composed of intellect and the rest, it is discrete (or individualized); and as long as migratory body does not rest, so long, in brief, soul suffers pain, arising from decay and death, in the three worlds. *Until it be released from its person:* until the discontinuance of subtile person. In the cessation of subtile body consists liberation; and when liberation is obtained, there is no more pain. By what means, then, can liberation be effected? Whenever knowledge of the twenty-five principles, the characteristic of which is knowledge of the distinctness of soul and body, is attained; or whenever a person knows that this is nature, this intellect, this egotism, these are the five rudiments, these the eleven senses, these the five elements, and this is soul, separate and dissimilar from them all; then from such knowledge proceeds cessation of subtile person, and thence liberation.

The object of the activity (or development of nature) is next explained.

COMMENT.

The presence of soul in these creations, and for what period, is here specified.

Having defined the different objects which form the twenty-five categories or *tatwas* of the Sánkhya philosophy, the text now comes to the main object of that and of all Hindu systems, the final dissolution of the connection between soul and body. The rest of the *Káriká* is devoted to the illustration of this topic. In this verse it is said that soul experiences pain in the different stages of existence, until its corporeal frame is discontinued; for soul itself is not susceptible of pain, or of decay, or death: the site of these things is nature, but nature is unconscious, insensible; and the consciousness that pain exists is restricted to soul, though soul is not the actual seat of pain; its experience of pain depends upon its connexion with rudimental person, of the material constituents of which, decay, death, and pain are concomitants. 'Pain and the rest are from nature, they are properties of intelligence. How do they become connected with sense? Soul (*purusha*) is that which reposes (*śété*) in body (*puri*): subtile body is immediately connected with it, and becomes thereby connected with sense *.' *S. Tatwa Kaumudí.* When soul is released from body, its susceptibility of pain ceases: pain is therefore of the essence † of its own nature; that is, it is the inseparable concomitant of bodily creation, according to PATANJALI, as quoted in the *S. Chandriká:* 'All is pain to the wise, through the conflict of opposite qualities, and by the sufferings arising from afflicting vicissitudes ‡;' that is, from the

---

* दुःखादयः प्राकृता बुद्धिगुणास्तत् कथमेते चेतनसम्बन्धिनो भवन्तीति। पुरुष इति पुरि लिंगे शेते पुरुषः। लिंगं च तत्सम्बन्धीति चेतनोऽपि तत्सम्बन्धी भवतीत्यर्थः।

† स्वभावेन।

‡ परिणामतापसंस्कारदुःखैर्गुणवृत्तिविरोधाच्च दुःखमेव सर्वं विवेकिनां।

dread of death and the reiteration of birth; to which even the conditions of spirits, sages, and gods are subject. Thus the Sútra of KAPILA: 'The pain of death, decay, and the rest is universal *;' as explained in the *S. Prav. Bháshya:* 'The pain of death, decay, and the rest is the common portion of all beings, whether above or below, from BRAHMÁ to immovable things †.' So also another Sútra: 'It is to be shunned, from the connection of successive birth by the thread of regeneration ‖:' that is, according to the commentator, 'since regeneration is unavoidable, even after ascent to the regions above; and in consequence of the succession of births, that regeneration must be in an inferior condition; even the world above is to be shunned ‖.' GAURAPÁDA and VÁCHESPATI take no notice of the expression, 'Pain is of the essence.' The *S. Chandriká* explains it, 'Creation is essentially of the nature of pain §.' RÁMA KRISHNA calls it, 'Former acts;' the acts of a former life ¶.

LVI.

THIS evolution of nature, from intellect to the special elements, is performed for the deliverance of each soul respectively; done for another's sake as for self.

BHÁSHYA.

This (or 'thus, this,' *ityésha*) implies conclusiveness and limitation (that is, in this way all that has been hitherto described). ***Evolution of nature:*** in the instrumentality or act of nature. Whatever *evolution of*

---

* समानं जरामरणादिजं दुःखं । † ऊर्द्धाधोगतानां ब्रह्मादिस्थावरान्तानां सर्व्वेषामेव जरामरणादिदुःखं साधारणं । ‡ आवृत्तिस्तत्राप्युत्तरयोनियोगाद्धेयः । ‖ तथापि तूर्द्धगतावपि सत्यामावृत्तिरस्ति अत उत्तरोत्तरयोनि योगादधोयोनिसम्बन्धात् सोऽपिलोको हेय इत्यर्थः । § स्वत एव सर्गो दुःखरूपः । ¶ स्वभावं प्राक्तनकर्म्म ।

nature, from intellect to the special elements: that is, (the evolution) of intellect from nature; of egotism from intellect; of the rudiments and senses from egotism; and of the gross elements from the subtile. ***Is performed for the deliverance of each soul respectively.***—This evolution is effected for the liberation of each individual soul which has assumed body, whether brute, human, or divine. How (is it effected)? It is done ***for another's sake as for self:*** as, for instance, a person neglecting his own objects transacts those of a friend, so does nature; soul makes no return to nature. ***As for self;*** not for self: for the sake, in fact, of another is the apprehension of sound and the other objects of sense, or knowledge of the difference between soul and qualities; for souls are to be provided (by nature), in the three worlds, with objects of sense, and at last with liberation: such is the agency of nature; as it is said, "Nature is like a utensil, having fulfilled soul's object it ceases."

It is here objected, Nature is irrational, Soul is rational; then how can nature, like a rational thing, understand that by me, soul is to be provided in the three worlds with the objects of sense, and at last with liberation? This is true; but action and cessation of action are both observed in irrational things; whence it is said—

COMMENT.

The object of nature's activity is here said to be the final liberation of individual soul.

Nature is properly inert, and its activity, its "motion" or evolution, takes place only for the purpose of soul, not for any object of its own. The term is *árambha*, 'commencement,' 'successive origin or beginning,' as detailed in former passages: that is, of intellect from crude nature; of egotism from intellect; and so on. This is the spontaneous act of nature: it is not influenced by any external intelligent principle, such as the Supreme Being or a subordinate agent; as BRAHMÁ, it is without (external) cause *.' 'But it is objected, Nature being eternal, her works

* प्रकृत्यैव कृतो नेश्वरेण न ब्रह्मोपादानेनाप्यकारणः ।

should be so too; and forms once evolved should therefore endure for ever. To this it is replied, The work is done for a special purpose, the liberation of individual soul; and that when this is accomplished, nature ceases with regard to that individual, as a man boiling rice for a meal desists when it is dressed †.' *S. Tatwa Kaumudí.* According to GAURAPÁDA, and to the text of the following stanza, nature so acts spontaneously; but the incompetency of nature, an irrational principle, to institute a course of action for a definite purpose, and the unfitness of rational soul to regulate the acts of an agent whose character it imperfectly apprehends, constitute a principal argument with the theistical Sánkhyas for the necessity of a Providence, to whom the ends of existence are known, and by whom nature is guided, as stated by VÁCHESPATI: 'But whether this (evolution) be for its own purpose or that of another, it is a rational principle that acts. Nature cannot act without rationality, and therefore there must be a reason which directs nature. Embodied souls, though rational, cannot direct nature, as they are ignorant of its character; therefore there is an omniscient Being, the director of nature, which is *Iswara*, or God †.' This is not inconsistent with the previous doctrine, that creation is the evolution of nature: it is so, but under the guidance of a ruling Power. The atheistical Sánkhyas, on the other hand, contend that there is no occasion for a guiding Providence, but that the activity of nature, for the purpose of accomplishing soul's object, is an intuitive necessity, as illustrated in the ensuing passage.

---

* यथौदनकाम ओदनस्य पाके प्रवृत्तिरोदनसिद्धौ निवर्त्तत एवं प्रत्येकं पुरुषान् मोचयितुंप्रवृत्ता प्रकृतिर्यं पुरुषं मोचयति तं प्रति न पुनर्प्रवर्त्तते।

† स्यादेतत् स्वार्थे परार्थे वा चेतनः प्रवर्त्तते। न च प्रकृतिरचेतनैव भवितुमर्हति तस्मादस्ति प्रकृतेरधिष्ठाता चेतनः। न च क्षेत्रज्ञाश्च चेतना अपि प्रकृतिमधिष्ठातुमर्हन्ति तेषां प्रकृतिस्वरूपानभिज्ञत्वात्। तस्मादस्ति सर्व्वार्थदर्शी प्रकृतेरधिष्ठाता चेश्वर इति।

LVII.

As it is a function of milk, an unintelligent (substance), to nourish the calf, so it is the office of the chief (principle) to liberate the soul.

BHÁSHYA.

As grass and water taken by the cow become eliminated into milk, and nourish the calf; and as (the secretion ceases) when the calf is grown; so nature (acts spontaneously) for the liberation of soul. This is the agency of an unintelligent thing.

COMMENT.

The intuitive or spontaneous evolution of nature, for soul's purpose, is here illustrated.

As the breast secretes milk for a purpose of which it is unconscious, and unconsciously stops when that purpose, the nutriment of the young animal, is effected; so nature, though irrational, constructs bodily forms for the fruition and liberation of soul; and when the latter is accomplished, ceases to evolve. The illustration is from KAPILA, as in the Sútra, 'From irrationality the activity of nature is like (the secretion of) milk *.'

LVIII.

As people engage in acts to relieve desires, so does the undiscrete (principle) to liberate the soul.

BHÁSHYA.

As mankind, being influenced by desire, engage in acts of various kinds for its gratification or fulfilment, and desist when the object is

* अचेतनत्वे क्षीरवच्चेष्टितं प्रधानस्य ।

accomplished, so the Chief one, active for the purpose of liberating soul, desists, after having effected the twofold purpose of soul; one, cognizance of enjoyment of the objects of sense; the other, cognizance of the difference between soul and qualities.

COMMENT.

Another illustration is here given of the activity of nature.

According to VÁCHESPATI, this verse is an explanation of the phrase (in ver. 56), 'For another's sake as for self *;' assigning, in fact, an object to nature, the accomplishment of its own wish; *autsukya* being rendered by *ichchhá*, 'wish:' and this wish, which is, 'the liberation of soul, being gratified, nature desists †.'

LIX.

As a dancer, having exhibited herself to the spectator, desists from the dance, so does nature desist, having manifested herself to soul.

BHÁSHYA.

As a dancer (or actress), having exhibited her performances on the stage in dramatic representations, rendered interesting by the display of love and other passions, in situations drawn from history or tradition, and accompanied by music and singing, desists from acting when her part is finished, so nature, having exhibited itself to soul, in the various characters of intellect, egotism, the rudiments, senses, and elements, desists.

What the cause of such cessation is, is next described.

COMMENT.

An illustration is here given of the discontinuance of nature's activity.

Ranga, properly a stage or theatre, is said in the *S. Tatwa Kaumudí*

---

* स्वार्थ इव परार्थे । † सा खल्विष्यमाणप्राप्तौ निवर्त्तते ।

to imply also the audience *. A dancer is equally an actress, *narttaki*, at least was so in ancient times. The dancing girls of Hindustan are rather singers, than either actresses or dancers.

LX.

GENEROUS nature, endued with qualities, does by manifold means accomplish, without benefit (to herself) the wish of ungrateful soul, devoid as he is of qualities.

BHÁSHYA.

By manifold means.—Nature is the benefactress of soul, of unrequiting soul. How? By the characters of men, gods, and animals; by circumstances involving pain, pleasure, and insensibility; by the properties of the objects of sense: in this way having by various means exhibited herself to soul, and shewn that 'I am one; thou art another;' having done this, nature desists. Thus she *accomplishes the wish* of that (soul) which is eternal, *without benefit* (to herself): as a benevolent man gives assistance to all, and seeks no return for himself, so nature pursues or effects the purpose of soul, without deriving from it any advantage.

It was said above (ver. 59), "Having manifested herself, nature desists." It is next shewn what she does, having desisted.

COMMENT.

This verse may be considered as a further explanation of the expression in ver. 56, "Nature labours for the benefit of soul as if for self, but not for any advantage."

'Generous, benevolent †:' 'Not expecting a return; for it is not true generosity to do good to another with the expectation of requital ‡.'

---

* रङ्गस्येति स्थानेन स्थायिनः पारिषदानुपलक्षयति। † उपकारिणी। परार्थं प्रत्युपकारसम्बन्धेनैव प्रवृत्तिरिति न नियमः।

S. Chandriká. ‘Soul being devoid of qualities (ver. 19), is consequently devoid of action, and can therefore do nothing by way of return *.’ Nature ‘accomplishes, goes to,’ *charati* or *ácharati*, or ‘effects,’ *kuruté*. The last word of the verse is differently read.

LXI.

Nothing, in my opinion, is more gentle than nature; once aware of having been seen, she does not again expose herself to the gaze of soul.

BHÁSHYA.

There is nothing in the world more soft (gentle, timid) than nature, in my opinion: for which reason (nature's) opinion consults another's advantage. Wherefore nature says to herself, “I have been beheld by that soul,” and does not again present herself to the view of that soul; that is, she disappears from the presence of soul. That indicates what the text means by *gentle*.

It (the text?) declares *Íswara* (God) to be the cause of the world: thus; “Let this ignorant, brute, godless (soul), for its own pleasure or pain, go to heaven or hell, sent (thither) by *Íswara*.” Others say, spontaneity is cause: “By what (or whom) the swan is created white, the peacock of many colours;” that is, they are so naturally (or spontaneously). Here, therefore, the Sánkhya teachers have said, How can beings endowed with qualities proceed from *Íswara*, who is devoid of qualities? or how from soul, equally devoid of qualities? Therefore (the causality) of nature is rendered probable. Thus; from white threads white cloth is fabricated; from black threads black cloth: and in the same manner, from nature, endowed with the three qualities, the three worlds, endowed with the three qualities also, are produced. This is determined. *Íswara* is without qualities: the origin of the three worlds endowed with qualities, from

---

* पुरुषस्य गुणातीतस्यात एवानुपकारिण उपकारासमर्थस्य ।

him, would therefore be an inconsistency. By this (same reason) soul also cannot be cause. According to some, time is cause: "Time is the five elements; time destroys the world; time watches, when all things sleep; time is not to be surpassed." There are but three categories, the discrete principle, the undiscrete principle, and soul; and by one of them time must be comprehended. Time, then, is a discrete principle; for nature, from its universal creative power, is the cause of time; spontaneity merges into it (nature): and time, therefore, is not cause; neither is spontaneity. Nature alone, therefore, is cause; and there is no cause of nature. *She does not again expose herself to the gaze of soul.* Therefore it is my opinion that there is no cause more gentle, more enjoyable, than nature, such as *Íswara* and the rest.

It is said familiarly in the stanzas of the text, "Soul is liberated; soul migrates:" on this it is observed—

COMMENT.

Nature being once properly understood by soul ceases to act.

Nature being once fully seen—that is, known or understood—by soul: disappears, goes no more into its sight; it ceases to be, with respect to that individual soul. Why is this? Because it is the most soft, the most gentle or timid, *sukumáratara*, of all things. The term *kumára*, properly implying 'soft' or 'young,' is explained by the Scholiasts to signify 'bashful, modest, unable to bear the gaze of soul *.' VÁCHESPATI. *Sukumáratara salajja* †, NÁRÁYANA and RÁMA KRISHNA. In the *S. Bháshya* it is rendered by *subhogyatara* ‡, 'more fit to be enjoyed;' but this refers less to the metaphorical illustration, than to the doctrine, of the text, and might be rendered, 'more plastic;' there being nothing so suitable as nature (matter) for the cause or origin of sensible objects. The *S. Tatwa Kaumudí* amplifies and explains the illustration: 'Nature is like a woman of virtue and family: such a one, of retired habits and modest looks, may be, by

---

* सुकुमारतरमतिपेशलता पुरुषदर्शनासहिष्णुता। † सुकुमारतरं सलज्जं। ‡ सुभोग्यतरं।

some inadvertence, surprised in disabille by a strange man, but she takes good care that another shall not behold her off her guard. Nature being once fully seen by discrimination, has too much matronly decorum to allow herself to be looked at a second time *.' The *S. Chandriká* has a similar exposition †. The *S. Pravachana Bh.* cites this verse in explanation of the Sútra, "Upon the detection of her faults, there is no further approach of nature (to soul); like a woman of family ‡:' that is, 'When nature finds that soul has discovered it is to her that the distress, &c. of migration are owing, she is put to shame by the detection, and ventures no more near soul; as a woman of family keeps aloof from a husband by whom she knows her faults to have been found out. And this is considered as an additional reason for the discontinuance of the activity of nature ‖.' *This is my opinion* § refers to what has preceded, *there is nothing more gentle*, as is shewn by the term *iti;* also by the *Bháshya* of GAURAPÁDA. It is clear, therefore, that the expression refers to the author; such is his opinion; that is, he does not here dogmatise, and say that nature is actually more timid or soft than any thing else—for the phrase is merely a figure of speech, a metaphorical illustration—but that it seems so to him; the words having the force of 'methinks, it seems:' 'Nature,

---

* असूर्य्यम्पश्या हि कुलबधूरतिमन्दाक्षमन्थरा प्रमादाद्विगलितसिचया ञ्चला चेदालोक्यते परपुरुषेण तदसौ तथा प्रयतत अप्रमत्तां यथैनां पुरुषान्तराणि न पश्यन्तीति । एवं प्रकृतिरपि कुलबधूतोऽप्यधिका दृष्टा विवेकेन न पुनर्द्रक्ष्यत इत्यर्थः ।

† प्रकृतिः परमात्मना पुरुषेण यदा ज्ञानचक्षुषा दृष्टा सा पीडायमाना कुलस्त्रीवत् पुनर्द्दर्शनं नोपैति ।

‡ दोषबोधेऽपि नोपसर्पणं प्रधानस्य । कुलबधूवत् ।

‖ पुरुषेण प्रकृतेः परिणामित्वदुःखात्मकत्वादिदोषदर्शनादधिलज्जितायाः प्रकृतेः पुनर्नपुरुषं प्रत्युपसर्पणं कुलबधूवत् यथा स्वामिना मे दोषो दृष्ट इत्यवधारणे लज्जिता कुलबधूर्न स्वामिनमुपसर्प्पति तद्वदित्यर्थः । निवृत्तौ हेत्वन्तरमिति ।

§ इति मे मतिः ।

it seems to me, or methinks, is the most soft, timid, retiring, of all things, and cannot bear to be stared at rudely: once seen, therefore, as she is, she takes care, like a truly modest matron, to be seen no more.' Such is the obvious purport of the text, which is merely a further illustration of the idea conveyed in ver. 59. GAURAPÁDA has gone out of his way rather to discuss the character of a first cause; giving to *sukumáratara* a peculiar import, that of 'enjoyable, perceptible;' which nature eminently is, and is therefore, according to him, the most appropriate source of all perceptible objects, or, in other words, of creation.

LXII.

VERILY not any soul is bound, nor is released, nor migrates; but nature alone, in relation to various beings, is bound, is released, and migrates.

BHÁSHYA.

Therefore, from that cause, soul is not bound, nor indeed is loosed, nor migrates; for, because, nature, *in relation to various beings*—in relation (or connection) with celestial, human, or brute forms, in the character of intellect, egotism, the rudiments, senses, and gross elements—is bound, is liberated, or migrates. For soul is of its own nature loosed, and goes every where, and how therefore should it migrate? migration being for the purpose of obtaining something not previously obtained. The phrases, therefore, Soul is bound, Soul is loosed or migrates, originate in ignorance of the nature of migration. From knowledge, the end of soul and existence, the real nature of soul is attained. That being manifest, soul is single, pure, free, fixed in its own nature. Consequently if there is no bondage there can be no liberation of soul. It is therefore said (see next verse), "Nature binds and liberates herself;" for where subtile body, composed of the rudiments, and having a triple cause, exists, such body is bound with triple bonds; as it is said, "He who is bound by the bonds of nature," of nature's products or of works, "cannot by any other be loosed" (see Comment, ver. 45). Such a subtile body is affected by virtue, vice, &c.

Nature is bound, is loosed, and migrates. *How* is next described.

COMMENT.

The subjection of nature, not of soul, to the accidents of bondage, liberation, and migration is asserted in this verse.

The doctrine here laid down seems at variance with what has preceded, and with the usual purport of the notions that attach the accidents of bondage and liberation to soul. Apparently, however, the difference is one of words only.

Soul is incapable of action, consequently is not liable to change. It cannot be bound, as the consequence of acts which it does not perform; and as it is never in bondage, it cannot be set free. The application of these terms to soul, therefore, is to be understood in a relative, not in a positive sense; and their positive signification is properly restricted to nature. It is nature that is bound, nature that is liberated, nature that undergoes change or migration. When nature attaches herself to soul, when she separates from it, the converse is equally true, soul is attached to, or is separated from, nature; and is consequently said to be bound, to be set free, to undergo change. But soul is passive in all these things; it is nature that is active, that binds, loosens, or changes form. GAURAPÁDA's explanation of these subtleties is not very clear, but such appears to be his understanding of the text. So also VÁCHESPATI: 'Soul is without qualities, and exempt from vicissitude. How then can it be liberated? To soul, not liable to change, there could apply none of the circumstances termed *bondage*, arising from acts, sufferings, or consciousness: nor could worldly change or migration, another name for which is *death*, affect soul, incapable of action *.' The same commentator adds, 'These circum-

* पुरुषश्चेदगुणोऽपरिणामी कथमस्य मोक्षः। सवासनक्लेशकर्म्माशयानां च बन्धसञ्ज्ञितानां पुरुषेऽपरिणामिन्यसम्भवात् अत एव अस्य पुरुषस्य न संसारः प्रेत्यभावापरनामास्ति निष्क्रियत्वात्।

stances, which are in truth the acts and conditions of nature, are ascribed to and affect soul as the superior, in the same manner that victory and defeat are attributed and relate to a king, although actually occurring to his generals; for they are his servants, and the gain or loss is his, not theirs *.' So NÁRÁYANA explains the text: 'Binding is the confinement of nature, in the various forms of intellect, &c.; and bondage and liberation are attributed to soul only through the contiguity of intellect, to which they belong, and not to soul †.' It is from ignorance only that bondage and liberation are ascribed to soul; as by the Sútra ‡, as explained by the Scholiast, 'Binding and liberation, or endurance of, and exemption from pain, are not (conditions) of soul in reality or absolutely, but (are considered as such) from ignorance; for the binding and liberation mentioned are (conditions) of nature ‖.' So also the Sútra §, 'From actual pain suffered by nature proceed binding and liberation, and from its attachments; that is, from its being affected by virtue and the rest, which are the causes of pain; like an animal; that is, as an animal may be bound or loosed, when entangled in a rope ¶.' The distinction, after all, is little more than nominal, except as it is the necessary consequence of the inactivity attributed to the soul.

---

* प्रकृतेरेव तु नानाश्रया सती बध्यते च संसरति च मुच्यते च बन्धमोक्षसंसाराः पुरुष उपचर्य्यन्ते यथा जयपराजयौ भृत्यगतावपि स्वामिन्युपचर्य्येते तदाश्रयेण भृत्यानां तद्भागित्वात्तत्फलस्य शोकलाभादेः स्वामिसम्बन्धात् ।

† प्रकृतिरेव नानाश्रया बुद्ध्यादिद्वारा तादृशी तथा च बन्धादिकं बुद्धिनिष्ठमेव पुरुषे तत्सम्पर्कात् तद्गतमारोप्यत एव केवलं न तु तदप्यस्तीति भावः ।

‡ नैकान्ततो बन्धमोक्षौ पुरुषस्याविवेकादृते ।

‖ दुःखयोगवियोगरूपौ बन्धमोक्षौ पुरुषस्य नैकान्ततस्तत्वतः किन्त्वविवेकात् परमार्थतस्तु यथोक्तौ बन्धमोक्षौ प्रकृतेरेव ।

§ प्रकृतेरांजस्यात् ससंगत्वात् पशुवत् ।

¶ प्रकृतेरेवांजस्येन तत्वतो दुःखेन बन्धमोक्षौ ससंगत्वाद्दुःखसाधनैर्धर्म्मादिभिर्लिप्तत्वात् पशुवद्यथा पशूरज्वालिप्ततया बन्धमोक्षभागी तद्वदित्यर्थः ।

LXIII.

By seven modes nature binds herself by herself: by one, she releases (herself), for the soul's wish.

BHÁSHYA.

By seven modes.—These seven have been specified, as virtue, dispassion, power, vice, ignorance, passion, and weakness. These are the seven modes (or conditions) of nature by which she binds herself, of herself. And that same nature, having ascertained that soul's object is to be accomplished, liberates herself by one mode, or by knowledge.

How is that knowledge produced?

COMMENT.

Nature is bound by seven modes, and liberated by one.

Nature binds herself by acts of whatever kind, especially by the faculties of intellect, enumerated above (ver. 23). She binds herself of her own accord. She frees herself by one mode, by the acquisition of philosophical knowledge. 'Nature binds herself (in her own work), like a silkworm in its cocoon*.' *Sútra.* *Átman* is here uniformly explained by *swa*, 'own self.'

LXIV.

So, through study of principles, the conclusive, incontrovertible, one only knowledge is attained, that neither I AM, nor is aught mine, nor do I exist.

BHÁSHYA.

So, by the order explained, the *study of the twenty-five principles*, knowledge of soul, or the discriminative knowledge, 'this is nature, this

---

* आत्मानं बध्नाति प्रधानं कोषकारवत् ।

is soul, these are the rudiments, senses, and elements,' is acquired. *Neither I am:* I am not. *Not mine:* not my body; that is, I am one (thing), body is another. *Nor do I exist:* that is, exempt from egotism. This is *conclusive, incontrovertible:* free from doubt. *Viparyaya* means 'doubt,' with the negative prefixed, 'absence of doubt;' and *viśuddha,* 'pure;' pure through absence of doubt. *Single.*—There is no other (true knowledge). In this way the cause of liberation is produced, is manifested (individually). *Knowledge* means knowledge of the twenty-five principles, or of soul.

Knowledge being attained, what does soul?

COMMENT.

The knowledge that is essential to liberation is here described.

It is acquired through study of the twenty-five principles, *tatwábhyása;* familiarity with them; frequent recurrence to them: it is finite or conclusive, *apariśésha;* it leaves nothing to be learned: it is perfect, as being without doubt, *aviparyayaviśuddha:* and single, the one thing needful, *kévala.* What sort of knowledge is this? or what is the result it teaches? The absence of individuality; the notion of the abstract existence of soul. *Neither I am, nor is aught mine, nor do I exist:* that is, there is no activity, nor property, nor individual agency. *I am not* precludes action only *. Indeed *As,* the root, together with *bhú* and *kri,* are said to signify action in general †. *Násmi* therefore signifies, not 'I *am* not,' but 'I *do* not.' The *S. Tatwa Kaumudí* then proceeds: 'Thus all acts whatever, whether external or internal, ascertainment, consciousness, reflection, perception, and all others, are denied as acts of soul: consequently, there being no active functions in soul, it follows that neither do I (as an individual agent) exist. *Aham* here denotes "agent;" as, I know, I sacrifice, I give, I enjoy—or so on, implying uniformly the notion of an agent—nor is aught mine: an agent implies mastership; if there be no agent

---

* नास्मीत्यात्मनि क्रियामात्रं निषेधति । † कृभ्वस्तयः क्रियासामान्यवचना इति ।

there can be no abstract mastership (or possession) *.' The same authority gives also a different reading of the first expression, *násmi*, explaining it *ná asmi*, 'I am male;' or *purusha*, 'unproductive of progeny,' of acts †. The *S. Prav. Bh.*, commenting on this verse of the *Káriká*, has, 'Neither I am, denies the agency of soul; nor (is aught mine), denies its attachment (to any objects); nor do I exist, denies its appropriation (of faculties) ‡.' The Sútra is to the same effect: 'From relinquishment (consequent on) study of principles; this is not, this is not ||:' that is, of all the objects proceeding from *prakriti*, not one is soul. The phraseology is ascribed to the Védas, and a similar passage is thence cited: 'Hence comes the conclusion, it is not, it is not (soul), it is not (soul is not), from it: such is not so; it is different, it is supreme, it is that very thing (that it is). It is not, it is not, (means) soul. Such is (the phrase), It is not §,' &c. And the *Chandriká* explains the terms similarly: '*I am not* means I am not agent; therefore I am distinct from the principle of intelligence. *Not mine is pain:* exemption from being the seat of pain and the rest is thence determined. *Nor do I exist:* by this, difference from egotism is expressed ¶.' Ráma Krishna repeats the words of the

---

* तथा चाध्यवसायाभिमानसंकल्पालोचनानि चान्तराणि बाह्याश्चसर्व्वे व्यापारा आत्मनि प्रतिषिद्धानि बोद्धव्यानि यतश्चात्मनि व्यापारावेशो नास्त्यतो नाहम्। अहमितिकर्त्तृपदं। अहं जानाम्यहं जुहोम्यहं ददेऽहं भुञ्ज इति सर्व्वत्र कर्त्तुः परामर्शात्। अत एव न मे। कर्त्ताहि स्वामितां लभते तदभावात् कुतो भाविकी स्वामितेत्यर्थः। † अथवा नास्मीति पुरुषोस्मि न प्रसवधर्म्मा। ‡ नास्मीत्यात्मनः कर्त्तृत्वनिषेधो न मे इति संगनिषेधः नाहं तादात्म्यनिषेधः। || तत्त्वाभ्यासान्नेति नेति त्यागात्। § तथा च श्रुतिः। अथादेशो नेति नेति नह्येतस्मादिति नेत्यन्यत्परमस्ति स एष नेति नेत्यात्मा नेत्यादिरिति। ¶ नास्मीत्यस्य न कर्त्तास्मीत्यर्थस्तेन बुद्धिभिन्नोहमिति प्राप्तं न मे दुःखमितिशेषस्तेन दुःखाद्यारोपाभावो लब्धो नाहमित्यनेनाहंकारभेदग्रहः।

Chandriká. By these expressions therefore, however quaint or questionable, we are not to understand negation of soul. This would be a direct contradiction to its specification as one of the categories of the system, one of the twenty-five essential and existent principles. It is merely intended as a negation of the soul's having any active participation, any individual interest or property, in human pains, possessions, or feelings. *I am, I do, I suffer*, mean that material nature, or some of her products, (substantially,) is, does, or suffers; and not soul, which is unalterable and indifferent, susceptible of neither pleasure nor pain, and only reflecting them, as it were, or seemingly sharing them, from the proximity of nature, by whom they are really experienced*: for soul, according to the Védas, is absolutely existent, eternal, wise, true, free, unaffected by passion, universal †. This verse, therefore, does not amount, as M. Cousin has supposed, to "le nihilisme absolu, dernier fruit du scepticisme."

LXV.

Possessed of this (self-knowledge), soul contemplates at leisure and at ease nature, (thereby) debarred from prolific change, and consequently precluded from those seven forms.

BHÁSHYA.

By that pure (absolute), single knowledge soul beholds nature, like a spectator, *at leisure and composed;* as a spectator seated at a play beholds an actress. *Composed:* who stays (or is involved) in self; or staying or abiding in one's own place. How is *Prakriti; debarred from prolific change?* Not producing intellect, egotism, and the other effects. *Consequently precluded from those seven forms:* desisting from the seven forms

---

* प्रतिबिम्बरूपेण पुरुषेऽपि सुखदुःखे स्तः। † सन्मात्रो नित्यः शुद्धो बुद्धः सत्यो मुक्तो निरञ्जनो विभुः।

or modes by which she binds herself, or virtue, vice, and the rest, and which are no longer required for the use of soul, both whose objects (fruition and liberation) are effected.

COMMENT.

Soul, possessed of the knowledge described in the preceding stanza, or divested of all individuality, becomes indifferent to, and independent of, nature, which therefore ceases to act.

Soul contemplates nature, like a spectator, *prékshaka*, one who beholds a dancer or actress; at leisure, *avasthita*, or without action, *nishkriya;* and at ease, *sustha.* This is also read *swastha,* 'calm, collected in self*;' or *nirákula,* 'unagitated.' Nature consequently has nothing more to do. The objects of soul, fruition and liberation, having been effected, by knowledge, the other faculties of intellect are needless.

LXVI.

He desists, because he has seen her; she does so, because she has been seen. In their (mere) union there is no motive for creation.

BHÁSHYA.

One present at a play, as a spectator, (ceases to behold;) so one, single, pure soul desists. One (nature), knowing I have been seen by him, stops, ceases. Nature is the one, chief cause of the three worlds; there is no second. Although form have terminated, yet from specific difference there is, even in the cessation of (the cooperation of) nature and soul, union, as a generic characteristic. For, if there be not union, whence is creation? *There being union of these two;* that is, of nature and soul; there being union from their universal diffusion: yet *there is*

---

* स्वस्थः स्वस्मिन् तिष्ठति ।

no further occasion for the world; from the object of creation being terminated. The necessity for nature is twofold; apprehension of the objects of sense, as sound, &c.; and apprehension of the difference between qualities and soul: when both these have been effected there is no further use for creation; that is, of further creation (of future regeneration); as in the case of a settlement of accounts between debtor and creditor, consequent on accepting what is given, when such a union is effected there is no further connection of object: so there is no further occasion for nature and soul.

If upon soul's acquiring knowledge liberation takes place, why does not my liberation (immediately) occur? To this it is observed—

COMMENT.

The final separation of soul from nature is here indicated, as no further purpose is answered by their continued union.

The first part of this stanza repeats the illustrations given in preceding verses (61 and 65): "Nature, having been fully seen or understood, ceases to act.—Soul, having seen or understood, ceases to consider;" becomes regardless, *upékshaka.* Consequently there can be no future reunion, no future creation. For mere union of soul and nature is not the cause of the development of the latter, constituting worldly existence: the motive is, the fulfilment of the objects of soul. The activity of nature is the consequence of her subserviency to soul's purposes; and when they are accomplished, all motive for action, all inducement to repeat worldly creation, ceases. 'The two objects of soul, fruition and discrimination, are the excitements to the activity of nature; if they do not exist, they do not stimulate nature. In the text the term *motive* implies that by which nature is excited in creation (to evolve the world): which cannot be in the nonentity of the objects of soul*.' VÁCHESPATI. So also NÁ-

* पुरुषार्थौ च भोगविवेकौ प्रकृत्यारम्भप्रयोजकावित्यपुरुषार्थौ सन्तौ न प्रकृतिं प्रयोजयतः। अच प्रयुज्यते सर्गे प्रकृतिरनेनेति प्रयोजनं तदपुरुषार्थत्वे नास्तीति।

RÁYANA: 'In the (mere) union of these two there is no motive for the production of the world *.' With the accomplishment, therefore, of the objects of soul, individual existence must cease for ever.

LXVII.

By attainment of perfect knowledge, virtue and the rest become causeless; yet soul remains a while invested with body, as the potter's wheel continues whirling from the effect of the impulse previously given to it.

BHÁSHYA.

Though *perfect knowledge*, that is, knowledge of the twenty-five principles, be attained, yet, from the effect of previous impulse, the sage continues in a bodily condition. How? *Like the whirling of a wheel;* as a potter, having set his wheel whirling, puts on it a lump of clay, fabricates a vessel, and takes it off, and leaves the wheel continuing to turn round. It does so *from the effect of previous impulse.*—From the attainment of perfect knowledge, virtue and the rest have no influence upon one who is possessed of such knowledge. These seven kinds of bonds are consumed by perfect knowledge: as seeds that have been scorched by fire are not able to germinate, so virtue and the rest are not able to fetter soul. These then, virtue and the rest, not being (in the case of the *yogí*) the causes (of continued bodily existence), body continues from the effects of previous impulse. Why is there not from knowledge destruction of present virtue and vice? Although they may be present, yet they perish the next moment, and knowledge destroys all future acts, as well as those which a man does in his present body by following instituted observances. With the cessation of the impulse the body perishes, and then liberation occurs.

What liberation, is next specified.

---

* तयोः संयोगेऽपि सर्गस्य जनने प्रयोजनं नास्तीति ।

COMMENT.

A reason is assigned why pure soul is not at once set free from body. This stanza may be considered partly as an illustration of the preceding, explaining the continued union of soul and body even after knowledge is attained. It is also a kind of apology for the human forms of KAPILA and other teachers of the Sánkhya doctrines, who, although in possession of perfect knowledge, lived and died as men. The sage, or *Yogí*, is no longer susceptible of the accidents of virtue, vice, passion, dispassion, and the rest, which are the proximate causes of bodily existence; and his continuance in the bodily form arises from the effects of virtue, &c. lasting after the cause has ceased; like the whirl of a wheel after the impulse that set it going has been withdrawn. 'As, when the potter's work is done, the wheel, in consequence of the impulse or *momentum* given to it, continues revolving, but stops when the period under such influence has expired; so virtue and vice, incident to body initiative and mature, constitute impulse*.' The effects of former acts of virtue and vice, then, cease when the impulse derived from them is worn out; and the possession of knowledge prevents all future acts. GAURAPÁDA apparently suggests a difficulty with respect to acts done in the present body; such as the observance of the Yoga, or performance of prescribed rites. These acts may be performed by a sage possessing perfect knowledge, and should therefore produce certain consequences. They lead, however, to no results; for as far as they are themselves concerned, they are but of brief duration, perishing as soon as performed; and with regard to any future effects, they are anticipated, prevented, or destroyed, by the possession of knowledge. Such seems to be the purport of the passage, but it is not very perspicuous.

---

* यथोपरतेऽपि कुलालव्यापारे चक्रं वेगाख्यसंस्कारवशाद्भ्रमन् स्तिष्ठति कालपरिपाकवशान्नूपरते संस्कारे निष्क्रियं भवति । शरीरस्थितौ च प्रारब्धपरिपाकौ धर्म्माधर्म्मौ संस्कारः ।

LXVIII.

When separation of the informed soul from its corporeal frame at length takes place, and nature in respect of it ceases, then is absolute and final deliverance accomplished.

BHÁSHYA.

When bodily separation is accomplished, by destruction of the effects of virtue, vice, and the rest. ***In respect of it***, having accomplished its object, ***nature ceases:*** then ***absolute***, certain—***final***, unimpeded—***deliverance***, liberation, consequent upon the condition of singleness. Soul obtains singleness (separation), which is both absolute and final.

COMMENT.

This verse refers to the first stanza, and announces the accomplishment of what was there stated to be the object of inquiry, absolute and final liberation.

When the consequences of acts cease, and body, both gross and subtile, dissolves, nature, in respect to individual soul, no longer exists; and soul is one, single, free, *kévala*, or obtains the condition called *kaivalyam*. This, according to Váchespati and Náráyana, means 'exemption from the three kinds of pain *.' Gaurapáda gives no definition of the term, except that it is the abstract of *kévala* †. What the condition of pure separated soul may be in its liberated state, the Sánkhya philosophy does not seem to hold it necessary to inquire.

---

* दुःखत्रयविगमं दुःखविनाशं ।

† केवल भावात् कैवल्यं ।

LXIX.

This abstruse knowledge, adapted to the liberation of soul, wherein the origin, duration, and termination of beings are considered, has been thoroughly expounded by the mighty saint.

BHÁSHYA.

Soul's object is liberation : for that (purpose) this *abstruse*, secret, *knowledge* (has been expounded) *by the mighty saint*, by the divine sage Kapila. *Wherein*, in which knowledge, *the origin, duration, and termination*, the manifestation, continuance, and disappearance, *of beings*, of the products (or developments) of nature, *are considered*, are discussed. From which investigation perfect knowledge, which is the same as knowledge of the twenty-five principles, is produced.

This is the *Bháshya* of Gaurapáda on the Sánkhya doctrines, propounded, for the sake of liberation from migration, by the *Muni* Kapila; in which there are these seventy stanzas.

COMMENT.

This verse specifies by whom the doctrines of the text were originally taught.

The commentary of Gaurapáda closes here in the only copy of the MSS. procurable; and consequently omits all notice of Íswara Krishna, to whom a subsequent stanza of the text attributes the *Káriká*. In the *Bháshya* it is said that the work commented on is the Sánkhya declared by Kapila; but that the *Káriká* is not the work of Kapila, the other Scholiasts agree. It is also different from the Sútras of that teacher, as given in the *Sánkhya Pravachana,* although it follows their purport, and sometimes uses the same or similar expressions. Gaurapáda may therefore probably only mean to intimate that its substance is conformable to the doctrines of the Sútras, not that it is the work of the *Muni*. These doctrines, he adds, are contained in seventy stanzas; of which, however, our copy has but sixty-nine. The verses of the *Káriká*, as usually met with, are seventy-two; but there also reference occurs to seventy verses, as comprising apparently the doctrinal and traditional part of the text, derived from older authorities. Either GAURAPÁDA thought it unnecessary to explain the concluding three verses of the *Káriká*, or there is some omission in the copy, or they do not belong to the work. The concluding verse is evidently inaccurate, the metre of the third line of the stanza being defective.

The KAPILA to whom the Sánkhya philosophy is attributed is variously described by different authorities. In a verse quoted by GAURAPÁDA, in his comment upon the first stanza of the text, he is enumerated amongst the sons of BRAHMÁ. VIJNYÁNA BHIKSHU asserts him to have been an incarnation of VISHNU *. He refers also to the opinion of a Védanta writer, that KAPILA was an incarnation of AGNI, or 'fire,' upon the authority of the Smriti †; but denies their identity. There does not appear to be any good authority for the notion. *Kapila* is a synonyme of fire, as it is of a brown, dusky, or tawny colour; and this may have given rise to the idea of AGNI and the sage being the same. The identification with VISHNU rests on better grounds. The popular belief of the Vaishnavas is, that there have been twenty-four *Avatárás* of VISHNU, and KAPILA is one of them. The earliest authority for this specification is no doubt the *Rámáyana*, in which VÁSUDEVA or VISHNU is said by BRAHMÁ to assume the form of KAPILA, to protect the earth against the violence of the sons of SAGARA, searching for the lost steed intended for their father's *aswamedha*. '‡BRAHMÁ having heard the words of the gods, who were bewildered with the dread of destruction, replied to them, and said, VÁSUDEVA

---

* तदिदं शास्त्रं कपिलमूर्त्या भगवान् विष्णुरखिललोकहिताय प्रकाशितवान्। † अग्निः स कपिलो नाम सांख्यशास्त्र प्रवर्त्तक इति स्मृतेः।

‡ देवतानां वचः श्रुत्वा भगवान् वै पितामहः
प्रत्युवाच सुसंत्रस्तान् कृतान्तबलमोहितान्
यस्येयं वसुधा कृत्स्ना वासुदेवस्य धीमतः
महिषी माधवस्येष्टा स एष भगवान् प्रभुः
कापिलं रूपमास्थाय धारयत्यनिशं धरां।

is the Lord, he is *Mádhava,* of whom the whole earth is the cherished bride; he, assuming the form of KAPILA, sustains continually the world.' So also the *Mahábhárata:* 'Then spake incensed, KAPILA, the best of sages; that VÁSUDEVA, indeed, whom the holy *Munis* call KAPILA *.' According to the *Bhágavat,* he was the fifth incarnation of VISHNU: 'The fifth *Avatára* was named KAPILA, the chief of saints, who revealed to ÁSURI the Sánkhya explanation of first principles, which has been impaired by time †.' Book I. s. 12. The latter half of the third book describes him also as an *Avatár* of VÁSUDEVA, but as the son of DEVAHÚTI, the daughter of SÁYAMBHUVA *Menu,* married to the *Prajapati* KERDDAMA.

LXX.

THIS great purifying (doctrine) the sage compassionately imparted to ÁSURI, ÁSURI taught it to PANCHASIKHA, by whom it was extensively propagated.

COMMENT.

Purifying; that which purifies from the defects which are the cause of pain; *pávana* or *pavitra.* *Great,* chief, principal, *agryam, mukhyam.* This verse anticipates an objection that may be made to the authority of the text; as it may be said, Although the words of KAPILA must command attention, of what weight are the lessons of an uninspired teacher? The answer is, that they are the same which were originally taught by KAPILA himself to his pupil ÁSURI. According to the passage cited by

---

* ततः क्रुद्धो महाराज कपिलो मुनिसत्तमः
वासुदेवेति यं प्राहुः कपिलं मुनिपुंगवाः ॥

† पञ्चमः कपिलो नाम सिद्धेशः कालविप्लुतं
प्रोवाचासुरये सांख्यं तत्वग्रामविनिर्णयं ॥

Gaurapáda, in his notes on the first stanza (p. 1), Ásuri is also a son of Brahmá. He is mentioned elsewhere as the pupil of Kapila, and preceptor of Panchasikha, but there are no details of his history. Of Panchasikha there is some account in the *Mahábhárat*, on occasion of his visiting Janaka, king of *Mithilá*, and imparting to him the Sánkhya philosophy. He is there also said to be named likewise Kapila*; which the commentator explains to mean that he was like Kapila, being the disciple of his disciple †, as the text proceeds to call him; 'He, the long-lived, whom they term the first disciple of Ásuri ‡.' He is also called Kapileya, from his being, it is said, the son of a Bráhmaní named Kapilá. 'Ásuri went to the sphere in which that which is *Brahme*, the mystic-named, and multiform, and eternal, is beheld. His disciple was Panchasikha, nourished with human milk: for there was a certain Brahman matron, named Kapilá, of whom he became the son, and at whose bosom he was fed; thence he obtained the denomination of Kápileya, and divine imperishable knowledge ||.'

LXXI.

Received by tradition of pupils, it has been compendiously written in *Árya* metre by the piously disposed Íswara Krishna, having thoroughly investigated demonstrated truth.

---

* यमाहुः कपिलं सांख्याः परमर्षिंप्रजापतिं । † सः कपिलस्तस्य शिष्यात्तत्तुल्यत्वं । ‡ आसुरेः प्रथमं शिष्यं यमाहुश्चिरजीविनं ।

|| यत्तदेकाक्षरं ब्रह्म नानारूपं प्रदृश्यते
आसुरिर्मण्डले तस्मिन् प्रतिपेदे तदव्ययं
तस्य पंचशिखः शिष्यो मानुष्यपयसाभृतः
ब्राह्मणी कपिलानाम काचिदासीत्कुटुम्बिनी
तस्याः पुत्रत्वमागम्य स्त्रियाः स पिबति स्तनौ
ततः स कापिलेयत्वं लेभे बुद्धिं च नैष्ठिकीं ।

COMMENT.

'Succession or tradition of pupils,' *śishyaparamparā:* each pupil becoming teacher in his turn, as is the case with the Pandits to the present day. It rarely, if ever, happens that any branch of Sanscrit literature is acquired by independent study: every science is studied under some teacher of eminence, who can, not unfrequently, trace his traditionary instruction upwards for several generations. The interval between PANCHASIKHA and ÍSWARA KRISHNA is not particularized, but was probably considerable, as no allusion to the author of the *Káriká* occurs in the older writings. If his commentator GAURAPÁDA be, as is not unlikely, the preceptor of SANKARA ÁCHÁRYA, ÍSWARA KRISHNA must date anterior to the eighth century.

LXXII.

THE subjects which are treated in seventy couplets are those of the whole science, comprising sixty topics, exclusive of illustrative tales, and omitting controversial questions.

COMMENT.

We have here in the text reference to seventy stanzas, as comprising the doctrinal part of the Sánkhya. In fact, however, there are but sixty-nine, unless the verse containing the notice of KAPILA be included in the enumeration; and in that case it might be asked, why should not the next stanza at least, making mention of the reputed author, be also comprehended, when there would be seventy-one verses. The Scholiasts offer no explanation of this difficulty.

The sixty topics alluded to in the text are, according to the *Rája Várttika*, as cited by VÁCHESPATI, 1. the existence of soul; 2. the existence of nature; 3. the singleness, 4. the objectiveness, and 5. the subservience, of nature; and 6. the multifariousness, 7. the distinctness, and 8. the inertness, of soul; 9. the duration of subtile, and 10. that of gross, body. These are the ten radical categories. To them are to be added, the five kinds of obstruction, nine of acquiescence, twenty-eight of disability, and eight of perfectness; making altogether sixty. Another enumeration specifies the sixty categories or objects: 1. soul; 2. nature; 3. intellect; 4. egotism; 5—7. the three qualities; 8. the class of the five rudiments; 9. that of the eleven senses or organs; 10. that of the five elements. These are the ten radical *padárthas*, or categories. The remaining fifty are the same as those previously enumerated. In consequence of comprehending all these topics, the *Káriká* is a system, a *śástra;* not a partial tract or treatise, or *prakarana**; although it omits the illustrative anecdotes and controversial arguments. The *Káriká* must consequently refer to the collection of Kapila's aphorisms, called *Sánkhya Pravachana.* This work is divided into six chapters, or *adhyáyas;* in the three first of which are contained all the dogmas of the system furnishing the materials of the *Káriká;* the fourth chapter is made up of short tales or anecdotes, *ákhyáyikás,* illustrative of the Sánkhya tenets; and the fifth is appropriated to the refutation, *paraváda,* of the doctrines of different schools. Exclusive of these two subjects, Íswara Krishna professes, therefore, to give the substance of the *S. Pravachana,* or of the Sútras of Kapila assembled in that collection.

The *Ákhyáyikás* are in general very brief and uninteresting. The Sútras, in fact, supply only a subject for a story, which the Scholiasts may expand much after their own fancies. Thus the Sútra, 'From instruction in truth, like the king's son †.' On which Vijnána Bhikshu narrates, that 'there was a king's son, who, being expelled in infancy from his native city, was brought up by a forester, and growing up to maturity in that state imagined himself to belong to the barbarous race with which he lived. One of his father's ministers having discovered him, revealed to him what he was, and the misconception of his character was removed, and he knew himself to be a prince. So soul, from

* सकलशास्त्रार्थकथनान्नेदं प्रकरणमपितु शास्त्रमेवेति सिद्धं ।

† राजपुत्रवत्तत्त्वोपदेशात् ।

the circumstances in which it is placed, mistakes its own character, until the truth is revealed to it by some holy teacher, and then it knows itself to be *Brahme* *.'

The controversial portion of the original Sútras is as brief as the narrative, and, from the nature of the subject, much more obscure. The argument is suggested, rather than advanced, and it remains for the Scholiast to amplify and explain it. A specimen of the mode in which this is effected will best exemplify the darkness and difficulty of this part of our subject. Some modern followers of the Védanta assert that liberation is the attainment of (pure) felicity. To this it is replied: 'Manifestation of felicity is not liberation, from its not being a property †.' Thus explained by the Scholiast: 'The condition of happiness, or that of attainment (or manifestation), is not a property of soul. The nature (of soul) is eternal, and is neither an object to be attained, nor the means of attainment. Therefore the attainment of happiness cannot be liberation. This is the meaning (of the Sútra ‡).' 'Attainment of happiness in the region of Brahmá and the rest is a secondary (or inferior) sort of liberation; as to maintain the contrary would be in opposition to the text of the Véda, which says that a wise man abandons both joy and sorrow ||.'

---

* अत्रेयमाख्यायिका कश्चिद्राजपुत्रो जन्मपुरान्निःसारितः शवरेण केनचित् पोषितोहं शवर इत्यभिमन्यमानस्तं द्विजं ज्ञात्वा कश्चिदमात्यः प्रबोधयति न त्वं शवरोऽपि राजपुत्रस्तथा राजासीति स च झटित्येव चाण्डालाभिमानं त्यक्त्वा सात्विकमेव राजभावमालम्बते राजाहमस्मीति। एवमेवादिपुरुषात् परिपूर्णचिन्मात्रत्वेनाभिमत्य नित्यशुद्धादिरूपब्रह्मभावमेवालम्बते ब्रह्माहमस्मीति।

† नानन्दाभिव्यक्तिर्मुक्तिर्निर्धर्म्मत्वात्।

‡ आत्मनि आनन्दरूपोऽभिव्यक्तिरूपश्च धर्म्मो नास्ति स्वरूपं च नित्यमेवेति न साधनसाध्यमतो नानन्दाभिव्यक्तिर्मोक्ष इत्यर्थः।

|| आनन्दाभिव्यक्तिश्च ब्रह्मलोकादौ गौणी मुक्तिरेवेति भावः। अन्यथा विद्वान् हर्षशोकौजहातीति श्रुतिविरोधात्।

'Further; if attainment be a faculty of soul, what sort of faculty is it? Is it constant or temporary. In the first case, there may be, even in the state of accomplishment, still the existence of the object of soul: in the last, inasmuch as there is perishableness of all that is engendered (or, that which has a beginning must have an end), then eternal liberation is subject to termination: therefore the attainment (or manifestation) of felicity is not chief or real liberation; and the assertion that it is so, is a false conclusion of the modern Védántis: this is undeniable*.'

---

* किंचाभिव्यक्तेरात्मधर्म्मत्वे पि सा किं नित्या अनित्या वा आद्ये सिद्धत्वे वा पुरुषार्थत्वं। अन्त्ये जन्यभावस्य विनाशितया मोक्षस्य नाशापत्तिस्तस्मादानन्दाभिव्यक्तिर्मुख्यमोक्ष इति नवीन वेदान्तिनामपसिद्धान्त एवेति धिक्।

श्रीमदीश्वरकृष्णेन

विरचितः

सांख्यकारिकाख्यग्रन्थः

श्रीगौडपादकृतभाष्यसहितः

श्रीमतां पूर्व्वदेशीयभाषालिखितग्रन्थावतारप्रपादकानां
सामाजिकानामनुमत्या

उक्षतरणाभिधाननगरे विद्यामन्दिरसंस्थानमुद्रायन्त्रालये मुद्रितः

संवत्सरे १८३७

सांख्यकारिका

दुःखत्रयाभिघाताज्जिज्ञासा तदभिघातके हेतौ
दृष्टे सापार्था चेन्नैकान्तात्यन्ततोऽभावात् ।१।

सांख्यकारिका भाष्यं

कपिलाय नमस्तस्मै येनाविद्योदधौ जगति मग्ने
कारुण्यात् सांख्यमयी नौरिव विहिता प्रतरणाय ।
अल्पग्रन्थं स्पष्टं प्रमाणसिद्धान्तहेतुभिर्युक्तं
शास्त्रं शिष्यहिताय समासतोऽहं प्रवक्ष्यामि ॥

दुःखत्रयेति । अस्या आर्याया उपोद्घातः क्रियते ॥ इह भगवान् ब्रह्मसुतः कपिलो नाम तद्यथा । सनकश्च सनन्दनश्च तृतीयश्च सनातनः

आसुरिः कपिलश्चैव वोढुः पञ्चशिखस्तथा ।
इत्येते ब्रह्मणः पुत्राः सप्त प्रोक्ता महर्षयः ॥

कपिलस्य सहोत्पन्ना धर्मो ज्ञानं वैराग्यमैश्वर्यञ्चेति । एवं स उत्पन्नः सन्नन्धतमसि मज्जज्जगदालोक्य संसारपारम्पर्येण सत्कारुण्यो जिज्ञासमानाय आसुरिसगोत्राय ब्राह्मणायेदं पञ्चविंशतितत्वानां ज्ञानमुक्तवान् यस्य ज्ञानाद्दुःखक्षयो भवति ।

पञ्चविंशतितत्वज्ञो यत्र तत्राश्रमे वसेत्
जटी मुण्डी शिखी वापि मुच्यते नात्र संशयः ।

तदिदमाहुः । दुःखत्रयाभिघाताज्जिज्ञासेति । तत्र दुःखत्रयं । आध्यात्मिकं । आधिभौतिकं । आधिदैविकंचेति ॥ तत्राध्यात्मिकं द्विविधं शारीरं मानसं चेति । शारीरं वातपित्तश्लेष्मविपर्ययकृतं ज्वरातीसारादि । मानसं प्रियवियोगाप्रियसंयोगादि ॥ आधिभौतिकं चतुर्विधं भूतग्रामनिमित्तं मनुष्यपशुमृगपक्षिसरीसृपदंशमशकयूकामत्कुणमत्स्यमकरग्राहस्थावरेभ्यो ज

रायुजाण्डजस्वेदजोद्भिज्जेभ्यः सकाशादुपजायते ॥ आधिदैविकं । देवाना मिदं दैविकं । दिवः प्रभवतीति वा दैवं तदधिकृत्य यदुपजायते शीतो ष्णवातवर्षाशनिपातादिकं ॥ एवं यथा दुःखत्रयाभिघाताज्जिज्ञासा कार्य्या च । तदभिघातके हेतौ । तस्य दुःखत्रयस्य अभिघातको योऽसौ हेतु स्तत्रेति ॥ दृष्टे सापार्थाचेत् । दृष्टे हेतौ दुःखत्रयाभिघातके सा जिज्ञा साऽपार्था चेद्यदि । तत्राध्यात्मिकस्य द्विविधस्यापि आयुर्वेदशास्त्रक्रियया प्रियसमागमाप्रियपरिहारकटुतिक्तकषायादिक्काथादिभिर्दृष्ट एव आध्यात्मि कोपायः । आधिभौतिकस्य रक्षादिनाऽभिघातो दृष्टः । दृष्टे साऽपार्था चेदेवं मन्यसे न । एकान्तात्यन्ततोऽभावात् । यत एकान्ततोऽवश्यं अत्यन्ततो नित्यं दृष्टेन हेतुनाऽभिघातो न भवति तस्मादन्यत्र एकान्तात्यन्ताभिघातके हेतौ जिज्ञासा विविदिषा कार्य्येति ।

दृष्टवदानुश्रविकः सह्यविशुद्धिक्षयातिशययुक्तः
तद्विपरीतः श्रेयान् व्यक्ताव्यक्तज्ञविज्ञानात् ।२।

यदि दृष्टान्यत्रजिज्ञासा कार्य्या ततोऽपि नैव यत आनुश्रविको हेतुः दुःख त्रयाभिघातकः । अनुश्रवतीत्यनुश्रवस्तत्रभवः आनुश्रविकः स च आगमा त्सिद्धः । यथा

अपाम सोमममृता अभूमागन्मज्योतिरविदाम देवान्
किन्नूनमस्मान् कृणवदरातिः किमु धूर्त्तिरमृतमर्त्त्यस्य ॥

कदाचिदिन्द्रादीनां देवानां कल्प आसीत् । कथं वयममृता अभूमेति विचार्य्यामुंयस्माद्वयमपाम सोमं पीतवन्तः सोमं तस्मादमृता अभूम अमरा भूतवन्त इत्यर्थः किंच अगन्म ज्योतिः गतवतो लब्धवतो ज्योतिः स्वर्गमिति । अविदाम देवान् दिव्यान् विदितवन्तः । एवं च किन्नून मस्मान् कृणवदरातिः नूनं निश्चितं किं अरातिः शत्रुरस्मान् कृणवत्

करोतीति किमु धूर्त्तिरमृतमर्त्त्यस्य धूर्त्तिर्जरा हिंसा वा किं करिष्यति अमृत मर्त्यस्य ॥ अन्यच्चवेदे श्रूयते आत्यन्तिकं फलं पशुवधेन । सर्व्वाल्लोकां जयति मृत्युं तरति पाप्मानं तरति ब्रह्महत्यां तरति यो योऽश्वमेधेन यजत इति । एकान्तात्यन्तिके एव वेदोक्ते अपार्थिवजिज्ञासा इति न । उच्यते । दृष्टवदानुश्रविक इति दृष्टेन तुल्यो दृष्टवत् । कोऽसौ आनुश्रविकः कस्मात्स यस्मादविशुद्धिक्षयातिशययुक्तः । अविशुद्धियुक्तः पशुघातात् तथाचोक्तं

षट् शतानि नियुज्यन्ते पशूनां मध्यमेऽहनि
अश्वमेधस्य वचनादूनानि पशुभिस्त्रिभिः ॥

यद्यपि श्रुतिस्मृतिविहितो धर्म्मस्तथापि मिश्रीभावादविशुद्धियुक्तइति। यथा

बहूनीन्द्रसहस्राणि देवानां च युगे युगे
कालेन समतीतानि कालो हि दुरतिक्रमः ॥

एवमिन्द्रादिनाशात्क्षययुक्तः । तथाऽतिशयो विशेषस्तेन युक्तः । विशेष गुणदर्शनादितरस्य दुःखं स्यादिति । एवमानुश्रविकोऽपि हेतुर्दृष्टवत् ॥ क स्तर्हि श्रेयानितिचेत्। उच्यते। तद्विपरीतः श्रेयान् ताभ्यां दृष्टानुश्रविका भ्यां विपरीतः श्रेयान् प्रशस्यतर इति । अविशुद्धिक्षयातिशयायुक्तत्वात् । स कथमित्याह। व्यक्ताव्यक्तज्ञविज्ञानात् तत्र व्यक्तं महदादिबुद्धिरहंकारः पञ्च तन्मात्राणि एकादशेन्द्रियाणि पञ्चमहाभूतानि । अव्यक्तं प्रधानं । ज्ञःपु रुषः । एवमेतानि पञ्चविंशति तत्वानि व्यक्ताव्यक्तज्ञानि कथ्यन्ते एतद्विज्ञा नाच्छ्रेय इत्युक्तं च पञ्चविंशति तत्वज्ञ इति ॥ अथ व्यक्ताव्यक्तज्ञानां को वि शेष इत्युच्यते ।

मूलप्रकृतिरविकृतिर्महदाद्याः प्रकृतिविकृतयः सप्त
षोडशकस्तुविकारो न प्रकृतिर्न विकृतिः पुरुषः ।३।

मूलप्रकृतिः प्रधानं । प्रकृतिविकृतिसप्तकस्य मूलभूतत्वात् । मूलं च सा प्रकृतिश्च मूलप्रकृतिरविकृतिः । अन्यस्मान्नोत्पद्यते तेन प्रकृतिः कस्यचि

विकारो न भवति । महदाद्याः प्रकृतिविकृतयः सप्त । महाभूतादिति बुद्धिः बुद्ध्याद्याः सप्त बुद्धि १ अहंकारः २ पञ्चतन्मात्राणि ५ एतानि सप्तप्रकृति विकृतयः । तद्यथा । प्रधानाद्बुद्धिरुत्पद्यते तेनविकृतिः प्रधानस्य विकार इति । सैवाहंकारमुत्पादयति अतः प्रकृतिः । अहंकारोऽपि बुद्धेरुत्पद्यत इति विकृतिः स च पञ्चतन्मात्राण्युत्पादयतीति प्रकृतिः । तत्र शब्दतन्मात्रमहंकारादुत्पद्यत इति विकृतिस्तस्मादाकाशमुत्पद्यत इति प्रकृतिः । तथा स्पर्शतन्मात्रमहंकारादुत्पद्यत इति विकृतिस्तदेवं वायुमुत्पादयतीति प्रकृतिः । गन्धतन्मात्रमहंकारादुत्पद्यत इति विकृतिस्तदेवं पृथिवीमुत्पादयतीतिप्रकृतिः । रूपतन्मात्रमहंकारादुत्पद्यत इति विकृतिस्तदेवं तेज उत्पादयतीतिप्रकृतिः । रसतन्मात्रमहंकारादुत्पद्यत इति विकृतिस्तदेव आप उत्पादयतीति प्रकृतिः । एवं महदाद्याः सप्त प्रकृतयो विकृतयश्च ॥ षोडशकश्च विकारः पञ्चबुद्धेन्द्रियाणि पञ्चकर्मेन्द्रियाणि एकादशं मनः पञ्चमहाभूतानि एष षोडशको गणो विकृतिरेव। विकारो विकृतिः ॥ न प्रकृतिर्न विकृतिः पुरुषः ॥ एवमेषां व्यक्ताव्यक्तज्ञानां त्रयाणां पदार्थानां कैः कियद्भिः प्रमाणैः केन कस्य वा प्रमाणेन सिद्धिर्भवति । इह लोके प्रमेय वस्तु प्रमाणेन साध्यते यथा प्रस्थादिभिर्व्रीहयस्तुलया चन्दनादि । तस्मात् प्रमाणमभिधेयं ।

दृष्टमनुमानमाप्तवचनं च सर्वप्रमाणसिद्धत्वात्
त्रिविधं प्रमाणमिष्टं प्रमेयसिद्धिः प्रमाणाद्धि । ४ ।

दृष्टं यथा श्रोत्रं त्वक् चक्षुर्जिह्वा घ्राणमिति पञ्चबुद्धेन्द्रियाणि शब्दस्पर्शरूपरसगन्धा एषां पञ्चानां पञ्चैवविषया यथासंख्यं शब्दं श्रोत्रं गृह्णाति त्वक् स्पर्शं चक्षु रूपं जिह्वा रसं घ्राणं गन्धमिति । एतद्दृष्टमित्युच्यते प्रमाणं । प्रत्यक्षेणानुमानेन वा योऽर्थो न गृह्यते स आप्तवचनाद् ग्राह्यः । यथेन्द्रो देव

राजः उत्तराः कुरवः स्वर्गेऽप्सरस इत्यादि। प्रत्यक्षानुमानाभ्यामप्यामव चनाद्गृह्यते। अपि चोक्तं।

> आगमो ह्याप्तवचनमाप्तं दोषक्षयाद्विदुः
>
> क्षीणदोषोऽनृतं वाक्यं न ब्रूयाद्धेत्वसम्भवात्
>
> स्वकर्म्मण्यभियुक्तो यः सङ्गद्वेषविवर्ज्जितः
>
> पूजितस्तद्विधैर्नित्यमाप्तो ज्ञेयः स तादृशः॥

एतेषु प्रमाणेषु सर्व्वप्रमाणानि सिद्धानि भवन्ति। षट् प्रमाणानि जैमिनिः। अथ कानि तान्यप्रमाणानि। अर्थापत्तिः सम्भवः अभावः प्रतिभा ऐतिह्यं उपमानं चेति षट् प्रमाणानि। तत्रार्थापत्ति र्द्विविधा दृष्टा श्रुता च। तत्रदृष्टा। एकस्मिन् पक्षे आत्मभावो गृहीतश्चेदन्यस्मिन्नप्यात्मभावो गृह्यत एव। श्रुता यथा। दिवा देवदत्तो न भुंक्ते अथ च पीनो दृश्यते अतोऽवगम्यते रात्रौ भुंक्त इति॥ सम्भवो यथा। प्रस्थ इत्युक्ते चत्वारः कुडवाः सम्भाव्यन्ते। अभावो नाम। प्रागितरेतरात्यन्तसर्व्वाभावलक्षणः। प्रागभावो यथा देवदत्तः कौमारयौवनादिषु। इतरेतराभावः पटे घटाभावः। अत्यन्ताभावः खरविषाणवन्ध्यासुतखपुष्पवदिति। सर्व्वाभावः प्रध्वंसाभावोदग्धपटवदिति। यथा शुष्कधान्यदर्शनाद्वृष्टेरभावोऽवगम्यते। एवमभावोऽनेकधा॥ प्रतिभा यथा। दक्षिणेन विन्ध्यस्य सह्यस्य च यदुत्तरं। पृथिव्यामासमुद्रायां स प्रदेशो मनोरमः। एवमुक्ते तस्मिन् प्रदेशे शोभनाःगुणाः सन्तीति प्रतिभोत्पद्यते प्रतिजान्वाससंज्ञानमिति॥ ऐतिह्यं यथा। ब्रवीति लोको यथात्र वटे यक्षिणी प्रवसतीति एव ऐतिह्यं॥ उपमानं यथा। गौरिव गवयः समुद्र इव तडागं। एतानि षट् प्रमाणानि त्रिषु दृष्टादिष्वन्तर्भूतानि। तत्रानुमाने तावदर्थापत्तिरन्तर्भूता। सम्भवाभावप्रतिभैतिह्योपमाश्चाप्तवचने। तस्मात्त्रिष्वेव सर्व्वप्रमाणसिद्धत्वात् त्रिविधं प्रमाणमिष्टं तदाह तेन त्रिविधेन प्रमाणेन प्रमाणसिद्धिर्भवतीति वाक्यशेषः। प्रमेयसिद्धिः प्रमाणाद्धि। प्रमेयं प्रधानं वुद्धिरहंकारः पञ्चतन्मात्राणि एकादशेन्द्रियाणि पञ्च महाभूतानि पुरुष इति एतानिपञ्चविंशति तत्वानि व्यक्ताव्यक्तज्ञान्युच्यन्ते।

तत्र किञ्चित् प्रत्यक्षेण साध्यं किञ्चिदनुमानेन किञ्चिदागमेनेति त्रिविधं प्रमाणमुक्तं तस्य किं लक्षणमेतदाह ।

प्रतिविषयाध्यवसायो दृष्टं त्रिविधमनुमानमाख्यातं
तल्लिङ्गलिङ्गिपूर्वकमाप्तश्रुतिराप्तवचनन्तु ।५।

प्रतिविषयेषु श्रोत्रादीनां शब्दादिविषयेषु अध्यवसायो दृष्टं प्रत्यक्षमित्यर्थः । त्रिविधमनुमानमाख्यातं शेषवत् पूर्ववत् सामान्यतो दृष्टं चेति । पूर्वमस्यास्तीति पूर्ववद् यथा मेघोन्नत्या वृष्टिं साधयति पूर्ववृष्टित्वात् । शेषवद्यथा समुद्रादेकं जलपलं लवणमासाद्य शेषस्याप्यस्ति लवणभाव इति । सामान्यतो दृष्टं । देशान्तराद्देशान्तरं प्राप्तं दृष्टं । गतिमच्चन्द्रतारकं चैत्रवत् । यथा चैत्रनामानं देशान्तराद्देशान्तरं प्राप्तमवलोक्य गतिमानयमिति तद्वच्चन्द्रतारकमिति तथा पुष्पिताम्रदर्शनादन्यत्रपुष्पिताम्रा इति सामान्यतो दृष्टेन साधयति । एतत्सामान्यदृष्टं ॥ किञ्च तल्लिङ्गलिङ्गिपूर्वकमिति तदनुमानं लिङ्गपूर्वकं यत्रलिङ्गेन लिङ्गी अनुमीयते यथा दण्डेन यतिः । लिङ्गिपूर्वकं च यत्र लिङ्गिना लिङ्गमनुमीयते यथा दृष्ट्वा यतिमस्येदं त्रिदण्डमिति ॥ आप्तश्रुतिराप्तवचनं च । आप्ता आचार्य्या ब्रह्मादयः । श्रुतिर्वेदः । आप्तश्चश्रुतिश्च आप्तश्रुती तदुक्तमाप्तवचनमिति ॥ एवं त्रिविधं प्रमाणमुक्तं तत्र केन प्रमाणेन किं साध्यमुच्यते ।

सामान्यतस्तुदृष्टादतीन्द्रियाणां प्रतीतिरनुमानात्
तस्मादपिचासिद्धं परोक्षमाप्तागमात् सिद्धं ।६।

सामान्यतो दृष्टादनुमानादतीन्द्रियाणामिन्द्रियाण्यतीत्यवर्त्तमानानां सिद्धिः

प्रधानपुरुषावतीन्द्रियौ सामान्यतो दृष्टेनानुमानेन साध्येते यस्मान्महदादि लिङ्गं त्रिगुणं। यस्येदं त्रिगुणं कार्य्यं तत्प्रधानमिति। यतश्चाचेतनं चेतनमिवाभाति अतोऽन्योऽधिष्ठाता पुरुष इति। व्यक्तं प्रत्यक्षसाध्यं। तस्मादपि चासिद्धं परोक्षमाप्तागमात् सिद्धं यथेन्द्रो देवराजः उत्तराःकुरवः स्वर्गेऽप्सरस इति परोक्षमाप्तवचनात् सिद्धं॥ अथ कश्चिदाह प्रधानः पुरुषो वा नोपलभ्यते यच्च नोपलभ्यते लोके तन्नास्ति तस्मात्तावपि न स्तः। यथा द्वितीयं शिरस्तृतीयो बाहुरिति। तदुच्यते। अथ सतामप्यर्थानामष्टधोपलब्धि र्न भवति तद्यथा।

अतिदूरात् सामीप्यादिन्द्रियघातान्मनोऽनवस्थानात्
सौक्ष्म्याद्व्यवधानादभिभवात् समानाभिहाराच्च ।७।

इह सतामप्यर्थानामतिदूरादनुपलब्धिर्दृष्टा। यथा देशान्तरस्थानां चैत्र मैत्र विष्णुमित्राणां। सामीप्याद्यथा चक्षुषोऽञ्जनानुपलब्धिः। इन्द्रियाभिघाताद्यथा बधिरान्धयोः शब्दरूपानुपलब्धिः। मनोऽनवस्थानाद्यथा व्यग्रचित्तः सम्यक्कथितमपि नावधारयतिः। सौक्ष्म्याद्यथा धूमोष्मजलनीहारपरमाणवो गगनगता नोपलभ्यन्ते। व्यवधानाद्यथा कुड्येन पिहितं वस्तु नोपलभ्यते। अभिभवाद्यथा सूर्य्यतेजसाभिभूता ग्रहनक्षत्रतारकादयो नोपलभ्यन्ते। समानाभिहाराद्यथा मुद्गराशौ मुद्गः क्षिप्तः कुवलयामलकमध्ये कुवलयामलके क्षिप्ते कपोतमध्ये कपोतो नोपलभ्यते समानद्रव्यमध्याहृतत्वात्। एवमष्टधानुपलब्धिः सतामर्थानामिह दृष्टा। एवं चास्ति किमभ्युपगम्यते प्रधानपुरुषयोरप्येतयोर्वानुपलब्धिः केनहेतुना केन चोपलब्धिस्तदुच्यते।

सौक्ष्म्यात्तदनुपलब्धिर्नाभावात् कार्य्यतस्तदुपलब्धिः
महदादि तच्चकार्य्यं प्रकृतिविरूपं सरूपं च । ८ ।

सौक्ष्म्यात्तदनुपलब्धिः प्रधानस्येत्यर्थः । प्रधानं सौक्ष्म्यान्नोपलभ्यते यथा काशे धूमोष्मजलनीहारपरमाणवः सन्तोऽपि नोपलभ्यन्ते । कथं तर्हि तदुपलब्धिः । कार्य्यतस्तदुपलब्धिः । कार्य्यं दृष्ट्वा कारणमनुमीयते । अस्ति प्रधानं कारणं यस्येदं कार्य्यं । बुद्धिरहंकारपञ्चतन्मात्राणि एकादशेन्द्रियाणि पञ्चमहाभूतानि एव तत्कार्य्यं । तच्चकार्य्यं प्रकृति विरूपं । प्रकृतिः प्रधानं तस्य विरूपं प्रकृतेरसदृशं सरूपं च समानरूपं च यथा लोकेऽपि पितु स्तुल्य इव पुत्रो भवत्यतुल्यश्च । येनहेतुना तुल्यमतुल्यन्तदुपरिष्टाद्वक्ष्यामः । यदिदं महदादिकार्य्यं तत्किं प्रधाने सदुताहोस्विदसदाचार्य्यविप्रतिपत्तेरयंसं शयः । यतोऽत्र सांख्यदर्शने सत्कार्य्यं बौद्धादीनामसत्कार्य्यं । यदि सदस न्नभवत्यथासत्सन्नभवतीतिविप्रतिषेधस्तत्राह ।

असदकरणादुपादानग्रहणात् सर्व्वसम्भवाभावात्
शक्तस्य शक्यकरणात् कारणभावाच्च सत्कार्य्यं । ९ ।

असदकरणान्नसदसदसतोऽकरणं तस्मात्सत्कार्य्यं इहलोकेऽसत्करणं नास्ति यथा सिकताभ्यस्तैलोत्पत्तिस्तस्मात्सतः करणादस्ति प्रागुत्पत्तेः । प्रधानेव्य क्तमतः सत्कार्य्यं । किं चान्यदुपादानग्रहणादुपादानं कारणं तस्यग्रहणा दिहलोके यो येनार्थी स तदुपादानग्रहणं करोति दध्यर्थी क्षीरस्य न तु जलस्य तस्मात् सत्कार्य्यं । इतश्च सर्व्वसम्भवाभावात् सर्व्वस्य सर्व्वत्रसम्भवो नास्ति यथा सुवर्णस्य रजतादौ तृणपांशुसिकतासु तस्मात् सर्व्वसम्भवाभा वात् सत्कार्य्यं । इतश्च शक्तस्य शक्यकरणात् । इह कुलालः शक्तो मृद्दण्ड

चक्रचीवररज्जुनीरादिकरणोपकरणं वा शक्यमेव घटं मृत्पिण्डादुत्पादयति तस्मात् सत्कार्य्यं । इतश्च कारणभावाच्च सत्कार्य्यं । कारणं यल्लक्षणं तल्लक्षणमेव कार्य्यमेव यथा यवेभ्योऽपि यवाः व्रीहीभ्यो व्रीहयः यदाऽसत्कार्य्यं स्यात्ततः कोद्रवेभ्यः शालयः स्युर्न च सन्तीति तस्मात् सत्कार्य्यं । एवं पञ्चभिर्हेतुभिः प्रधाने महदादिलिङ्गमस्ति तस्मात्सत उत्पत्तिर्नासत इति ॥ प्रकृतिविरूपं सरूपं च यदुक्तं तत् कथमित्युच्यते ।

हेतुमदनित्यमव्यापि सक्रियमनेकमाश्रितं लिङ्गं
सावयवं परतन्त्रं व्यक्तं विपरीतमव्यक्तं । १० ।

व्यक्तं महदादिकार्य्यं हेतुमदिति हेतुरस्यास्ति हेतुमत् । उपादानं हेतुः कारणं निमित्तमिति पर्य्यायाः । व्यक्तस्य प्रधानं हेतुरस्ति अतो हेतुमद्व्यक्तं भूतपर्य्यन्तं हेतुमद्बुद्धितत्वं प्रधानेन हेतुमानहंकारो बुद्ध्या पञ्चतन्मात्राणि एकादशेन्द्रियाणि हेतुमन्त्यहंकारेण । आकाशं शब्दतन्मात्रेण हेतुमत् । वायुः स्पर्शतन्मात्रेण हेतुमान् । तेजो रूपतन्मात्रेण हेतुमत् । आपो रसतन्मात्रेण हेतुमत्यः । पृथिवी गन्धतन्मात्रेण हेतुमती । एवं भूतपर्य्यन्तं व्यक्तं हेतुमत् ॥ किं चान्यदनित्यं यस्मादन्यस्मादुत्पद्यते यथा मृत्पिण्डादुत्पद्यते घटः स चानित्यः ॥ किं चाव्याप्यसर्व्वगमित्यर्थः यथा प्रधानपुरुषौ सर्व्वगतौ नैव व्यक्तं ॥ किंचान्यत् सक्रियं संसारकाले संसरति त्रयोदशविधेन करणेन संयुक्तं सूक्ष्मं शरीरमाश्रित्य संसरति तस्मात् सक्रियं ॥ किंचान्यदनेकं बुद्धिरहंकारः पञ्चतन्मात्राण्येकादशेन्द्रियाणि च पञ्चमहाभूतानि तन्मात्राश्रितानि॥ किंच लिङ्गं लययुक्तं लयकाले पञ्चमहाभूतानि तन्मात्रेषु लीयन्ते तान्येकादशेन्द्रियैः सहाहंकारे स च बुद्धौ सा च प्रधाने लयं यातीति ॥ तथा सावयवं अवयवाः शब्दस्पर्शरसरूपगन्धाः तैः सह ॥ किंच परतन्त्रं नात्मनः प्रभवति यथा प्रधानतन्त्रा बुद्धिः बुद्धितन्त्रोऽहंकारः अहंकारतन्त्राणि

तन्मात्राणीन्द्रियाणि च तन्मात्रतन्त्राणि पञ्चमहाभूतानिच। एवं परतन्त्रं परायत्तं व्याख्यातं व्यक्तं॥ अथोऽव्यक्तं व्याख्यामः। विपरीतमव्यक्तं। एतैरेव गुणैर्यथोक्तैर्विपरीतमव्यक्तं हेतुमद्व्यक्तमुक्तं। नहिप्रधानात् परं किञ्चिदस्ति यतः प्रधानस्यानुत्पत्तिः तस्मादहेतुमदव्यक्तं। तथानित्यं च व्यक्तं नित्यमव्यक्तमनुत्पाद्यत्वात् नहि भूतानि कुतश्चिदुत्पद्यन्तेति प्रधानं॥ किं चाव्यापि व्यक्तं व्यापि प्रधानं सर्व्वगतत्वात्॥ सक्रियं व्यक्तमक्रियमव्यक्तं सर्व्वगतत्वादेव॥ तथाऽनेकं व्यक्तमेकं प्रधानं कारणत्वात् त्रयाणां लोकानां प्रधानमेकं कारणं तस्मादेकं प्रधानं॥ तथाश्रितं व्यक्तमनाश्रितमव्यक्तमकार्य्यत्वान्नहि प्रधानात्किंचिदस्ति परं यस्य प्रधानं कार्य्यं स्यात्॥ तथा व्यक्तं लिङ्गमलिङ्गमव्यक्तं नित्यत्वान्महदादि लिङ्गं प्रलयकाले परस्परं प्रलीयते नैवं प्रधानं तस्मादलिङ्गं प्रधानं॥ तथा सावयवं व्यक्तं निरवयवमव्यक्तं नहि शब्दस्पर्शरसरूपगन्धाः प्रधाने सन्ति॥ तथा परतन्त्रं व्यक्तं स्वतन्त्रमव्यक्तं प्रभवत्यात्मनः॥ एवं व्यक्ताव्यक्तयोर्वैधर्म्यमुक्तं साधर्म्यमुच्यते यदुक्तं सरूपं च।

त्रिगुणमविवेकि विषयः सामान्यमचेतनं प्रसवधर्म्मि
व्यक्तं तथा प्रधानं तद्विपरीतस्तथा च पुमान्॥ ११॥

त्रिगुणं व्यक्तं सत्वरजस्तमांसि त्रयो गुणा यस्येति। अविवेकि व्यक्तं नविवेकोऽस्यास्तीति। इदं व्यक्तमिमे गुणा इति न विवेककर्त्तुं याति अयं गौरयमश्व इति यथा ये गुणास्तद्व्यक्तं यद्व्यक्तं ते च गुणा इति। तथा विषयो व्यक्तं भोज्यमित्यर्थः सर्व्वपुरुषाणां विषयभूतत्वात्। तथा सामान्यं व्यक्तं मूल्यदासीवत् सर्व्वसाधारणत्वात्॥ अचेतनं व्यक्तं सुखदुःखमोहान्न चेतयतीत्यर्थः॥ तथा प्रसवधर्म्मि व्यक्तं तद्यथा बुद्धेरहंकारः प्रसूयते तस्मात् पञ्चतन्मात्राणि एकादशेन्द्रियाणि च प्रसूयन्ते तन्मात्रेभ्यः पञ्चमहाभूतानि॥ एव

मेते व्यक्तधर्म्माः प्रसवधर्म्मान्ता उक्ता एवमेभिरव्यक्तं सरूपं यथा व्यक्तं तथा प्रधानमिति। तत्रत्रिगुणं व्यक्तमव्यक्तमपि त्रिगुणं यस्यैतन्महदादि कार्य्यं त्रिगुणं। इह यदात्मकं कारणं तदात्मकं कार्य्यमिति यथा कृष्णतन्तुकृतः कृष्ण एव पटो भवति॥ तथाविवेकि व्यक्तं प्रधानमपि गुणैर्नभिद्यते अन्येगुणा अन्यत् प्रधानमेव विवेक्तुं न याति तदविवेकि प्रधानं॥ तथा विषयो व्यक्तं प्रधानमपि सर्व्वपुरुषविषयभूतत्वाद्विषय इति॥ तथा सामान्यं व्यक्तं प्रधानमपि सर्व्वसाधारणत्वात्॥ तथाऽचेतनं व्यक्तं प्रधानमपि सुखदुःखमोहान्नचेतयतीति कथमनुमीयत इह ह्यचेतनान्मृत्पिण्डादचेतनो घट उत्पद्यते॥ एवं प्रधानमपि व्याख्यातं॥ इदानीन्तद्विपरीतस्तथा पुमानित्येतद्व्याख्यायते। तद्विपरीतस्ताभ्यां व्यक्ताव्यक्ताभ्यां विपरीतः पुमान्। तद्यथा त्रिगुणं व्यक्तमव्यक्तं चागुणः पुरुषः। अविवेकि व्यक्तमव्यक्तं च विवेकी पुरुषः। तथा विषयो व्यक्तमव्यक्तं चाविषयः पुरुषः। तथा सामान्यं व्यक्तमव्यक्तं चासामान्यः पुरुषः। अचेतनं व्यक्तमव्यक्तं च चेतनः पुरुषः सुखदुःखमोहांश्चेतयति संजानीते तस्माच्चेतनः पुरुष इति। प्रसवधर्म्मि व्यक्तं प्रधानंचाप्रसवधर्म्मी पुरुषो नहि किञ्चित् पुरुषात् प्रसूयते। तस्मादुक्तं तद्विपरीतः पुमानिति॥ तदुक्तं तथा च पुमानिति। तत् पूर्व्वस्यामार्य्यायां प्रधानमहेतुमद्यथा व्याख्यातं तथा च पुमान् तद्यथा हेतुमदनित्यमित्यादि व्यक्तं तद्विपरीतमव्यक्तं तत्रहेतुमद्व्यक्तमहेतुमत् प्रधानं तथा च पुमानहेतुमाननुत्पाद्यत्वात्। अनित्यं व्यक्तं नित्यं प्रधानं तथा च नित्यः पुमान्। अक्रियः सर्व्वगतत्वादेव। अनेकं व्यक्तमेकमव्यक्तं तथा पुमानप्येकः। आश्रितं व्यक्तमनाश्रितमव्यक्तं तथा च पुमाननाश्रितः। लिङ्गं व्यक्तमलिङ्गं प्रधानं तथा च पुमानप्यलिङ्गः। न क्वचिल्लीयत इति। सावयवं व्यक्तं निरवयवमव्यक्तं तथा च पुमान् निरवयवः। नहि पुरुषे शब्दादयोऽवयवाः सन्ति। किंच परतन्त्रं व्यक्तं स्वतन्त्रमव्यक्तं तथा च पुमानपि स्वतन्त्रः। आत्मनः प्रभवतीत्यर्थः। एवमेतदव्यक्तपुरुषयोः साधर्म्यं व्याख्यातं पूर्व्वस्यामार्य्यायां। व्यक्तप्रधानयोः साधर्म्यं पुरुषस्य वैधर्म्यं च त्रिगुणमविवे

कीत्यादि प्रकृत्यार्य्यायां व्याख्यातं । तत्रयदुक्तं त्रिगुणमिति व्यक्तमव्यक्तं च तत् के ते गुणा इति तत् स्वरूपप्रतिपादनायेदमाह ।

प्रीत्यप्रीतिविषादात्मकाः प्रकाशप्रवृत्तिनियमार्थाः
अन्योऽन्याभिभवाश्रयजननमिथुनवृत्तयश्चगुणाः ।१२।

प्रीत्यात्मका अप्रीत्यात्मकाः विषादात्मकाश्चगुणाः सत्वरजस्तमांसीत्यर्थः । तत्र प्रीत्यात्मकं सत्वं प्रीतिः सुखं तदात्मकमिति । अप्रीत्यात्मकं रजः । विषादात्मकं तमः । विषादो मोहः । तथा प्रकाशप्रवृत्ति नियमार्थाः । अर्थः शब्दः सामर्थ्यवाची प्रकाशार्थं सत्वं प्रकाशसमर्थमित्यर्थः । प्रवृत्त्यर्थं रजो नियमार्थं तमः स्थितौ समर्थमित्यर्थः प्रकाशक्रियास्थितिशीला गुणा इति। तथाऽन्योऽन्याभिवाश्रयजननमिथुनवृत्तयश्च । अन्योऽन्याभिमवाः अन्योऽन्याश्रयाः अन्योऽन्यजननाः अन्योऽन्यमिथुनाः अन्योऽन्यवृत्तयश्च ते तथोक्ताः । अन्योऽन्याभिभवा इति अन्योऽन्यं परस्परमभिभवन्तीति प्रीत्यप्रीत्यादिभिर्धर्म्मैराविर्भवन्ति यथा यदा सत्वमुत्कटं भवति तदा रजस्तमसी अभिभूय स्वगुणैः प्रीतिप्रकाशात्मकेनावतिष्ठते यदा रजस्तदा सत्वतमसी अप्रीतिप्रवृत्तिधर्म्मेण यदा तमस्तदा सत्वरजसी विषादस्थित्यात्मकेन इति । तथाऽन्योऽन्याश्रयाश्च द्व्यणुकवद्गुणाः । अन्योऽन्यजननाः यथा मृत्पिण्डो घटं जनयति । तथाऽन्योऽन्यमिथुनाश्च यथा स्त्रीपुंसौ अन्योऽन्यमिथुनौ तथा गुणाः । उक्तं च

रजसो मिथुनं सत्वं सत्वस्य मिथुनं रजः
उभयोः सत्वरजसोर्मिथुनं तम उच्यते

परस्परसहाया इत्यर्थः । अन्योऽन्यवृत्तयश्च परस्परं वर्त्तन्ते गुणाः गुणेषु वर्त्तन्त इति वचनात् । यथा सुरूपा सुशीला स्त्री सर्व्वसुखहेतुः सपत्नीनां सैव दुःखहेतुः सैव रागिणां मोहं जनयति एव सत्वंरजस्तमसोर्वृत्तिहेतु

यथा राजा सदोद्युक्तः प्रजापालने दुष्टनिग्रहे शिष्टानां सुखमुत्पादयति दुष्टानां दुःखं मोहं च एवं रजस्सत्वमसो वृत्तिं जनयति । तथा तमः स्वरूपेणा वरणात्मकेन सत्वरजसो वृत्तिं जनयति यथा मेघाः खमावृत्य जगतः सुखमुत्पादयन्ति ते वृष्ट्या कर्षुकाणां कर्षणोद्योगं जनयन्ति विरहिणां मोहमेवमन्योऽन्यवृत्तयो गुणाः । किंचान्यत् ।

सत्वं लघु प्रकाशकमिष्टमुपष्टम्भकं चलं च रजः
गुरु वरणकमेव तमः प्रदीपवच्चार्थतो वृत्तिः । १३ ।

सत्वं लघु प्रकाशकंच यदा सत्वमुत्कटं भवति तदा लघून्यङ्गानि बुद्धिप्रकाशश्च प्रसन्नतेन्द्रियाणां भवति । उपष्टम्भकं चलं च रजः उपष्टभ्नातीत्युपष्टम्भकमुद्योतकं यथा वृषो वृषदर्शने उत्कटमुपष्टम्भं करोति एव रजो वृत्तिः । तथा रजश्च चलं दृष्टं रजोवृत्तिश्चलचित्तो भवति । गुरुवरणकमेव तमः यदा तम उत्कटं भवति तदा गुरूण्यङ्गान्यावृतानीन्द्रियाणि भवन्ति स्वार्थासमर्थानि । अत्राह यदि गुणाः परस्परं विरुद्धाः स्वमतेनैव कमर्थं निष्पादयन्ति तर्हि कथं प्रदीपवच्चार्थतो वृत्तिः प्रदीपेन तुल्यं प्रदीपवदर्थतः साधना वृत्तिरिष्टा यथा प्रदीपः परस्परविरुद्धतैलाग्निवर्त्तिसंयोगादर्थप्रकाशं जनयति एवं सत्वरजस्तमांसि परस्परं विरुद्धान्यर्थं निष्पादयन्ति । अन्तरप्रश्नो भवति त्रिगुणमविवेकिविषय इत्यादि प्रधानं व्यक्तं च व्याख्यातं तत्र प्रधानमुपलभ्यमानं महदादि च त्रिगुणमविवेक्यादीति च कथमवगम्यते तत्राह ।

अविवेक्यादिः सिद्धस्त्रैगुण्यात्तद्विपर्य्ययाभावात्
कारणगुणात्मकत्वात् कार्य्यस्याव्यक्तमपिसिद्धं । १४ ।

योऽयमविवेक्यादिर्गुणः स त्रैगुण्यान्महदादौऽव्यक्तेनायं सिद्ध्यति । अत्रो च्यते तद्विपर्य्ययाभावात्तस्य विपर्य्ययस्तद्विपर्य्ययस्तस्याभावस्तद्विपर्य्ययाभाव स्तस्मात् सिद्धमव्यक्तं । यथा यत्रैवतन्तवस्तत्रैव पटः अन्ये तन्तवोऽन्यः पटो न कुतस्तद्विपर्य्ययाभावात् । एवं व्यक्ताव्यक्तसम्पन्नो भवति दूरं प्रधानमा सन्नं व्यक्तं यो व्यक्तं पश्यति स प्रधानमपिपश्यति तद्विपर्य्ययाभावात् । इत श्चाव्यक्तं सिद्धं कारणगुणात्मकत्वात् कार्य्यस्य । लोके यदात्मकं कारणं तदा त्मकं कार्य्यमपि तथा कृष्णेभ्यस्तन्तुभ्यः कृष्ण एव पटो भवति । एवं महदा दिलिङ्गमविवेकिविषयः सामान्यमचेतनं प्रसवधर्म्मि यदात्मकं लिङ्गं तदा त्मकमव्यक्तमपि सिद्धं । त्रैगुण्यादविवेक्यादिर्व्यक्ते सिद्धस्तद्विपर्य्ययाभावात् एवं कारणगुणात्मकत्वात् कार्य्यस्याव्यक्तमपि सिद्धमित्येतन्मिथ्या लोके यन्नोपलभ्यते तन्नास्ति एवं प्रधानमप्यस्ति किं तु नोपलभ्यते ।

भेदानां परिमाणात् समन्वयाच्छक्तितः प्रवृत्तेश्च
कारणकार्य्यविभागादविभागाद्वैश्वरूपस्य । १५ ।

कारणमस्त्यव्यक्तमितिक्रियाकारकसम्बन्धः । भेदानां परिमाणाल्लोके यत्र क र्त्तास्ति तस्य परिमाणं दृष्टं यथा कुलालः परिमितैर्मृत्पिण्डैः परिमितानेव घटान् करोति एवं महदपि महदादिलिङ्गं परिमितं भेदतः प्रधानकार्य्य मेका बुद्धिरेकोऽहंकारः पञ्च तन्मात्राणि एकादशेन्द्रियाणि पञ्चमहाभूता नीत्येवं भेदानां परिमाणादस्ति प्रधानं कारणं यद्व्यक्तं परिमितमुत्पादयति । यदि प्रधानं न स्यात्तदा निःपरिमाणमिदं व्यक्तमपि न स्यात् परिमाण

स्वभेदानामस्ति प्रधानं यस्माद्व्यक्तमुत्पन्नं । तथा समन्वयादिहलोके प्रसिद्धिर्दृष्टा यथा व्रतधारिणं वटुं दृष्ट्वा समन्वयति नूनमस्य पितरौ ब्राह्मणाविति एवमिदं त्रिगुणं महदादिलिङ्गं दृष्ट्वा साधयामोऽस्य यत् कारणं भविष्यतीति अतः समन्वयादस्तिप्रधानं । तथा शक्तितः प्रवृत्तेश्च इह यो यस्मिन् शक्तः स तस्मिन्नेवार्थे प्रवर्त्तते यथा कुलालो घटस्य करणे समर्थो घटमेव करोति न पटं रथं वा । तथास्ति प्रधानं कारणं कुतः कारणकार्य्यविभागात् । करोतीतिकारणं । क्रियत इति कार्य्यं । कारणस्य कार्य्यस्य च विभागो यथा घटो दधिमधूदकपयसां धारणे समर्थो न तथा तत्कारणं मृत्पिण्डः । मृत्पिण्डो वा घटं निष्पादयति न चैवं घटो मृत्पिण्डं । एवं महदादिलिङ्गं दृष्ट्वानुमीयते । अस्ति विभक्तं तत् कारणं यस्य विभाग इदं व्यक्तमिति । इतश्च अविभागाद्वैश्वरूपस्य विश्वं जगत् तस्य रूपं व्यक्तिः । विश्वरूपस्य भावो वैश्वरूपं तस्याविभागादस्तिप्रधानं यस्मात्त्रैलोक्यस्य पञ्चानां पृथिव्यादीनां महाभूतानां परस्परं विभागो नास्ति महाभूतेष्वन्तर्भूतास्त्रयो लोकाः इति पृथिव्यापस्तेजोवायुराकाशमिति एतानि पञ्चमहाभूतानि प्रलयकाले सृष्टिक्रमेणैवाविभागं यान्ति तन्मात्रेषु परिणामिषु तन्मात्राण्येकादशेन्द्रियाणि चाहंकारे अहंकारो बुद्धौ बुद्धिः प्रधाने एवं त्रयो लोकाः प्रलयकाले प्रकृतावविभागं गच्छन्ति तस्मादविभागात् क्षीरदधिवद्व्यक्ताव्यक्तयोरस्त्यव्यक्तं कारणं । अतश्च ।

कारणमस्त्यव्यक्तं प्रवर्त्तते त्रिगुणतः समुदयाच्च
परिणामतः सलिलवत् प्रतिप्रतिगुणाश्रयविशेषात् । १६ ।

अव्यक्तं प्रख्यातं कारणमस्ति यस्मान्महदादिलिङ्गं प्रवर्त्तते । त्रिगुणतः त्रिगुणात् सत्वरजस्तमोगुणा यस्मिन् तत्त्रिगुणं तत्किमुक्तं भवति सत्वरजस्तमसां साम्यावस्था प्रधानं । तथा समुदयात् यथा गंगास्रोतांसि त्रीणि रुद्र

मूर्द्धनि पतितानि एकं श्रोतो जनयंति एव त्रिगुणमव्यक्तमेकं व्यक्तं जनयति तथा वा तन्तवः समुदिताः पटं जनयन्ति एवमव्यक्तं गुणसमुदयान्म हदादि जनयतीति त्रिगुणतः समुदयाच्च व्यक्तं जगत् प्रवर्त्तते। यस्मादेकस्मात् प्रधानाद्व्यक्तं तस्मादेकरूपेणभवितव्यं। नैषदोषः परिणामतः सलिलवत् प्रतिप्रतिगुणाश्रयविशेषादेकस्मात् प्रधानात् त्रयो लोकाः समुत्पन्नास्तुल्यभावा न भवन्ति देवाः सुखेनयुक्ता मनुष्या दुःखेन तिर्य्यञ्चो मोहेन एकस्मात् प्रधानात् प्रवृत्तं व्यक्तं प्रतिप्रतिगुणाश्रयविशेषात् परिणामतः सलिलवद्भवति। प्रतिप्रतीति वीप्सा। गुणानामाश्रयो गुणाश्रयस्तद्विशेषस्तं गुणाश्रयविशेषं प्रतिनिधाय प्रतिप्रतिगुणाश्रयविशेषं परिणामात् प्रवर्त्तते व्यक्तं यथा आकाशादेकरसं सलिलं पतितं नानारूपात्संश्लेषाद्भिद्यते तद्रसान्तरैरेवमेकस्मात् प्रधानात् प्रवृत्तास्त्रयो लोका नैकस्वभावा भवन्ति देवेषु सत्वमुत्कटं रजस्तमसी उदासीने तेन तेऽत्यंन्तसुखिनो मनुष्येषु रज उत्कटं भवति सत्वतमसी उदासीने तेन तेऽत्यन्तदुःखिनस्तिर्य्यक्षु तम उत्कटं भवति सत्वरजसी उदासीने तेन तेऽत्यन्तमूढाः॥ एवमार्याद्वयेन प्रधानस्यास्तित्वमयमुपगम्यते इतश्चोत्तरं पुरुषास्तित्वप्रतिपादनार्थमाह।

सङ्घातपरार्थत्वात् त्रिगुणादिविपर्य्ययादधिष्ठानात्
पुरुषोऽस्तिभोक्तृभावात् कैवल्यार्थं प्रवृत्तेश्च ।१७।

यदुक्तं व्यक्ताव्यक्तविज्ञानान्मोक्षः प्राप्यत इति तत्रव्यक्तादनन्तरमव्यक्तं पञ्चभिः कारणैरधिगतमव्यक्तवत् पुरुषोऽपि सूक्ष्मस्तस्याऽधुनानुमितास्तित्वं प्रति क्रियते। अस्ति पुरुषः कस्मात् संघातपरार्थत्वात्। योऽयं महदादि संघातः सपुरुषार्थ इत्यनुमीयते अचेतनत्वात् पर्य्यङ्कवत्। यथा पर्य्यङ्कः प्रत्येकं गात्रोत्पलकपादवटतूलीप्रछादनपटोपधानसङ्घातः परार्थो नहि स्वार्थः पर्य्यङ्कस्य नहि किञ्चिदपि गात्रोत्पलाद्यवयवानां परस्परं कृत्यमस्ति।

अतोऽवगम्यतेऽस्ति पुरुषो यः पर्य्यंङ्के शेते यस्यार्थे पर्य्यङ्कस्तत्परार्थमिदं शरीरं पञ्चानां महाभूतानां सङ्घातो वर्त्ततेऽस्ति पुरुषो यस्येदं भोग्यशरीरं भोग्यं महदादिसङ्घातरूपं समुत्पन्नमिति। इतश्चात्माऽस्ति त्रिगुणादिविपर्य्ययात्। यदुक्तं पूर्व्वस्यामार्य्यायां त्रिगुणमविवेकिविषय इत्यादि। तस्माद्वि पर्य्ययाद्येनोक्तं तद्विपरीतस्तथा पुमान्। अधिष्ठानाद्यथेह लङ्घनप्लवनधावनसमर्थैरश्वैर्युक्तो रथः सारथिनाऽधिष्ठितः प्रवर्त्तते तथात्माऽधिष्ठानाच्छरीरमिति। तथा चोक्तं षष्टितन्त्रे पुरुषाधिष्ठितं प्रधानं प्रवर्त्तते। अतोऽस्यात्मा भोक्तृत्वात्। यथा मधुराम्ललवणकटुतिक्तकषायषड्रसोपवृंहितस्य संयुक्तस्यान्नस्य साध्यते एवं महदादिलिङ्गस्य भोक्तृत्वाभावादस्ति स आत्मा यस्येदं भोग्यं शरीरमिति। इतश्च कैवल्यार्थं प्रवृत्तेश्च केवलस्य भावः कैवल्यं तन्निमित्तं या च प्रवृत्तिस्तस्याः स्वकैवल्यार्थं प्रवृत्तेः सकाशादनुमीयते अस्त्यात्मेति यतो सर्व्वो विद्वानविद्वांश्च संसारसन्तानक्षयमिच्छति। एवमेभिर्हेतुभिरस्त्यात्मा शरीराद्व्यतिरिक्तः। अथ सः किमेकः सर्व्वशरीरेऽधिष्ठाता मणिरसनात्मकसूत्रवत् आहोस्विद्बहव आत्मानः प्रतिशरीरमधिष्ठातार इत्यत्रोच्यते।

जननमरणकरणानां प्रतिनियमादयुगपत् प्रवृत्तेश्च
पुरुषबहुत्वं सिद्धं त्रैगुण्यविपर्य्ययाच्चैव ।१८।

जन्म च मरणं च करणानि च जन्ममरणकरणानि तेषां प्रतिनियमात् प्रत्येकनियमादित्यर्थः। यद्येक एव आत्मा स्यात्तत एकस्य जन्मनि सर्व्व एव जायेरन् एकस्य मरणे सर्व्वेऽपि म्रियेरन् एकस्य करणवैकल्ये बाधिर्य्यान्धत्व मूकत्वकुणित्वखंजत्वलक्षणे सर्व्वेऽपि बधिरान्धकुणिखंजाःस्युर्न चैवं भवति तस्माज्जन्ममरणकरणानां प्रतिनियमात् पुरुषबहुत्वं सिद्धं। इतश्चायुगपत् प्रवृत्तेश्च युगपदेककालं न युगपदयुगपत् प्रवर्त्तनं यस्मादयुगपद्धर्म्मादिषु प्रवृत्तिर्दृश्यते एके धर्म्मे प्रवृत्ता अन्येऽधर्म्मे वैराग्येऽन्ये ज्ञानेऽन्ये प्रवृत्ताः

तस्मादयुगपत् प्रवृत्तेश्च बहव इति सिद्धं ॥ किञ्चान्यत्त्रैगुण्यविपर्य्ययाच्चैव त्रिगुणभावविपर्य्ययाच्च पुरुषबहुत्वं सिद्धं। यथा सामान्ये जन्मनि एकः सात्विकः सुखी। अन्यो राजसो दुःखी। अन्यस्तामसो मोहवान्। एवं त्रैगुण्यविपर्य्ययाद्बहुत्वं सिद्धमिति। अकर्त्ता पुरुष इत्येतदुच्यते।

तस्माच्च विपर्य्यासात् सिद्धं साक्षित्वमस्य पुरुषस्य
कैवल्यं माध्यस्थ्यं द्रष्टृत्वमकर्त्तृभावश्च ।१९।

तस्माच्च विपर्य्यासात्तस्माच्च यथोक्तत्रैगुण्यविपर्य्यासाद्विपर्य्ययान्निर्गुणः पुरुषो विवेकी भोक्तेत्यादिगुणानां पुरुषस्य यो विपर्य्यास उक्तस्तस्मात् सत्वरजस्तमःसु कर्त्तृभूतेषु साक्षित्वं सिद्धं पुरुषस्येति योऽयमधिकृतो बहुत्वं प्रति। गुणा एव कर्त्तारः प्रवर्त्तन्ते साक्षी न प्रवर्त्तते नापि निवर्त्तत एव। किं चान्यत् कैवल्यं केवलभावः कैवल्यमन्यत्वमित्यर्थः। त्रिगुणेभ्यः केवलः। अन्यन्माध्यस्थ्यं मध्यस्थभावः परिव्राजकवत् मध्यस्थः पुरुषः। यथा कश्चित् परिव्राजको ग्रामीणेषु कर्षणार्थेषु प्रवृत्तेषु केवलो मध्यस्थः पुरुषोऽप्येवं गुणेषु वर्त्तमानेषु न प्रवर्त्तते। तस्माद्द्रष्टृत्वमकर्त्तृभावश्च यस्मान्मध्यस्थस्तस्माद्द्रष्टा तस्मादकर्त्ता पुरुषस्तेषां कर्म्मणामिति सत्वरजस्तमांसि त्रयो गुणाः कर्म्मकर्त्तृभावेन प्रवर्त्तन्ते न पुरुष एवं पुरुषस्यास्तित्वं च सिद्धं। यस्मादकर्त्ता पुरुषस्तत्कथमध्यवसायं करोति धर्म्मं करिष्याम्यधर्म्मं न करिष्यामीत्यतः कर्त्ता भवति न च कर्त्ता पुरुष एवमुभयथा दोषः स्यादिति। अत उच्यते।

तस्मात्तत् संयोगादचेतनं चेतनावदिव लिङ्गं
गुणकर्तृत्वे च तथा कर्तेव भवतीत्युदासीनः ।२०।

इह पुरुषश्चेतनाकृत् तेन चेतनावभासं युक्तं महदादिलिङ्गं चेतनावदिवभवति यथा लोके घटः शीतसंयुक्तः शीतः उष्णसंयुक्त उष्ण एवं महदादि लिङ्गं तस्य संयोगात् पुरुषसंयोगाच्चेतनावदिवभवति तस्माद्गुणा अध्यवसायं कुर्वन्ति न पुरुषः । यद्यपि लोके पुरुषः कर्तागंतेत्यादि प्रयुज्यते तथाप्यकर्ता पुरुषः कथं गुणकर्तृत्वे च तथा कर्तेव भवत्युदासीनः गुणानां कर्तृत्वे सति उदासीनोऽपि पुरुषः कर्तेव भवति न कर्ता । अत्र दृष्टान्तो भवति यथाऽचौरश्चौरैः सह गृहीतश्चौर इत्यवगम्यत एवं त्रयो गुणाः कर्तारस्तैः संयुक्तः पुरुषोऽकर्ताऽपि कर्ता भवति कर्तृसंयोगात् । एवं व्यक्ताव्यक्तज्ञानां विभागो विख्यातो यद्विभागान्मोक्षप्राप्तिरिति । अथैतयोः प्रधानपुरुषयोः किं हेतुः संघात उच्यते ।

पुरुषस्य दर्शनार्थं कैवल्यार्थं तथा प्रधानस्य
पङ्ग्वन्धवदुभयोरपि संयोगस्तत् कृतः सर्गः ।२१।

पुरुषस्य प्रधानेन सह संयोगो दर्शनार्थं प्रकृतिं महदादिकार्य्यभूतपर्य्यन्तां पुरुषः पश्यति एतदर्थं प्रधानस्यापि पुरुषेण संयोगः। कैवल्यार्थं स च संयोगः पंगून्धवदुभयोरपि द्रष्टव्यः यथा एकः पंगुरेकश्चान्ध एतौद्वावपि गच्छन्तौ महतासामर्थ्येनाटव्यां सार्थस्य स्तेनकृतादुपप्लवात् स्वबन्धुपरित्यक्तौ दैवादितश्चेतश्चस्वगत्या च तौ संयोगमुपयातौ पुनस्तयोः स्ववचसो विश्वस्तत्वेन संयोगो गमनार्थं दर्शनार्थं च भवत्यन्धेन पंगुः स्कन्धमारोपितः एव शरीरारूढपंगुदर्शितेन मार्गेणान्धो याति पंगुश्चान्धस्कन्धारूढः । एवं पुरुषे दर्श

नशक्तिरस्ति पंगुवन्नक्रिया प्रधाने क्रियाशक्तिरस्त्यन्धवन्नदर्शनशक्तिः। यथा वानयोः पंग्वन्धयोः कृतार्थयोर्विभागो भविष्यतीप्सितस्थानप्राप्तयोरेवं प्रधानमपि पुरुषस्य मोक्षं कृत्वा निवर्त्तते पुरुषोऽपि प्रधानं दृष्ट्वा कैवल्यं गच्छति तयोः कृतार्थयोर्विभागो भविष्यति। किं चान्यत् तत्कृतः सर्गस्तेन संयोगेन कृतस्तत्कृतः सर्गस्सृष्टिः। यथा स्त्रीपुरुषसंयोगात् सुतोत्पत्तिस्तथा प्रधानपुरुषसंयोगात् सर्गस्योत्पत्तिः। इदानीं सर्व्वविभागदर्शनार्थमाह।

प्रकृतेर्महान्स्ततोऽहंकारस्तस्माद्गणश्चषोडशकः
तस्मादपि षोडशकात् पञ्चभ्यः पञ्चभूतानि ।२२।

प्रकृतिः प्रधानं ब्रह्म अव्यक्तं बहुधानकं मायेति पर्य्यायाः। अलिङ्गस्य प्रकृतेः सकाशान्महानुत्पद्यते महान् बुद्धिरासुरी मतिः ख्यातिर्ज्ञानं प्रज्ञापर्य्यायैरुत्पद्यते तस्माच्चमहतोऽहंकार उत्पद्यतेऽहंकारो भूतादिर्वैकृतस्तैजसोभिमान इति पर्य्यायाः तस्माद्गणश्चषोडशकः तस्मादहंकाराच्छोडशकःषोडशस्वरूपेणगण उत्पद्यते। स यथा। पञ्चतन्मात्राणि शब्दतन्मात्रं स्पर्शतन्मात्रं रूपतन्मात्रं रसतन्मात्रं गन्धतन्मात्रमिति। तन्मात्रसूक्ष्मपर्य्यायवाच्यानि। तत एकादशेन्द्रियाणि श्रोत्रं त्वक् चक्षुषी जिह्वा घ्राणमिति पञ्च बुद्धीन्द्रियाणि। वाक् पाणिपादपायूपस्थाः पञ्चकर्म्मेन्द्रियाण्युभयात्मकमेकादशं मन एषः षोडशको गणोऽहंकारादुत्पद्यते। किंच पञ्चभ्यः पञ्चभूतानि तस्माच्छोडशकाद्गणात् पञ्चभ्यस्तन्मात्रेभ्यः सकाशात् पञ्च वै महाभूतान्युत्पद्यन्ते। यदुक्तं शब्दतन्मात्रादाकाशं स्पर्शतन्मात्राद्वायुः रूपतन्मात्रात्तेजः रसतन्मात्रादापः गन्धतन्मात्रात् पृथिवी एवं पञ्चभ्यः परमाणुभ्यः पञ्चमहाभूतान्युत्पद्यन्ते। यदुक्तं व्यक्ताव्यक्तज्ञविज्ञानान्मोक्ष इति तत्र महदादिभूतान्तं त्रयोविंशतिभेदं व्याख्यातमव्यक्तमपि भेदानां परिमाणादित्यादिना व्याख्यातं पुरुषोऽपि संघातपरार्थत्वादित्यादिभिर्हेतुभिर्व्याख्यातः। एवमेतानि पञ्चविंशति तत्त्वा

नि यस्त्रैलोक्यं व्याप्तं जानाति तस्य भावोऽस्तित्वं तत्वं यथोक्तं । पञ्चविंशति तत्वज्ञो यत्रतत्राश्रमेरतः । जटी मुण्डी शिखी वाऽपि मुच्यते नात्र संशयः । तानि यथा प्रकृतिः पुरुषो बुद्धिरहंकारः पञ्चतन्मात्रा एकादशेन्द्रियाणि पञ्चमहाभूतानि इत्येतानि पञ्चविंशति तत्वानि । तत्रोक्तं प्रकृतेर्महानुत्पद्यते तस्य महतः किं लक्षणमित्येतदाह ।

अध्यवसायो बुद्धिर्धर्म्मो ज्ञानं विराग ऐश्वर्य्यं
सात्विकमेतद्रूपं तामसमस्माद्विपर्य्यस्तं । २३ ।

अध्यवसायो बुद्धिलक्षणं । अध्यवसनमध्यवसायः यथा बीजे भविष्यवृत्तिकोऽङ्कुरस्तद्वदध्यवसायोऽयंघटोऽयंपट इत्येवं स्यति या सा बुद्धिरितिलक्ष्यते सा च बुद्धिरष्टाङ्गिका सात्विकतामसरूपभेदात् तत्र बुद्धेः सात्विकं रूपं चतुर्विधं भवति धर्म्मो ज्ञानं वैराग्यमैश्वर्य्यं चेति तत्र धर्म्मो नाम दया दान यम नियमलक्षणास्तत्रयमानियमाश्च पातञ्जलेऽभिहिता अहिंसा सत्यास्तेय ब्रह्मचर्य्यापरिग्रहा यमाः शौचसंतोषतपः स्वाध्यायेश्वरप्रणिधानियमाः । ज्ञानं प्रकाशोऽवगमो भानमिति पर्य्यायास्तच्चद्विविधं बाह्यमाभ्यन्तरं चेति । तत्र बाह्यं नाम वेदाः शिक्षा कल्पो व्याकरणं निरुक्तं छन्दोज्योतिषाख्यषडङ्गसहिताः पुराणानि न्यायमीमांसाधर्म्मशास्त्राणि चेति । आभ्यन्तरं प्रकृतिपुरुषज्ञानमियं प्रकृतिः सत्वरजस्तमसां साम्यावस्थाऽयं पुरुषः सिद्धो निर्गुणोव्यापी चेतन इति । तत्र बाह्यज्ञानेन लोकपंक्तिर्लोकानुराग इत्यर्थः । आभ्यन्तरेण ज्ञानेन मोक्ष इत्यर्थः । वैराग्यमपि द्विविधं बाह्यमाभ्यन्तरंच बाह्यं दृष्टविषयवैतृष्ण्यमर्जनरक्षणक्षयसंगहिंसादोषदर्शनात् विरक्तस्याभ्यन्तरं प्रधानमप्यत्रस्वप्नेन्द्रजालसदृशमिति विरक्तस्य मोक्षेप्सोर्यदुत्पद्यते तदाभ्यन्तरं वैराग्यं । ऐश्वर्य्यमीश्वरभावस्तच्चाष्टगुणमणिमा महिमा गरिमा लघिमा प्राप्तिः प्राकाम्यमीशित्वं वशित्वं यत्रकामावसायित्वं चेति । अणोर्भा

वोऽणिमा सूक्ष्मो भूत्वा जगति विचरतीति। महिमा महान् भूत्वा विच रतीति। लघिमा मृणालीतूलावयवादपि लघुतया पुष्पकेसराग्रेष्वपि तिष्ठति। प्राप्तिरभिमतं वस्तु यत्र तत्रावस्थितः प्राप्नोति। प्राकाम्यं प्रका मतो यदेवेच्छति तदेव विदधाति। ईशित्वं प्रभुतया त्रैलोक्यमपीष्टे। वशित्वं सर्वं वशीभवति। यत्रकामावसायित्वं ब्रह्मादिस्तम्बपर्य्यन्तं यत्र कामस्तत्रैवास्य स्वेच्छया स्थानासनविहारानाचरतीति। चत्वार एतानि बुद्धेः सात्विकानि रूपाणि यदा सत्वेन रजस्तमसी अभिभूते तदा पुमान् बुद्धिगुणान् धर्म्मा दीनाप्नोति। किंचान्यत् तामसमस्माद्विपर्य्यस्तमस्माद्धर्म्मादेर्विपरीतं ता मसं बुद्धिरूपं तत्र धर्म्माद्विपरीतोऽधर्म्म एवमज्ञानमवैराग्यमनैश्वर्य्यमि ति। एवं सात्विकैस्तामसै स्वरूपैरष्टांगा बुद्धिस्त्रिगुणादव्यक्तादुत्पद्यते। एवं बुद्धिलक्षणमुक्तमहंकारलक्षणमुच्यते।

अभिमानोऽहंकारस्तस्माद्द्विविधः प्रवर्त्तते सर्गः
एकादशकश्चगणस्तन्मात्रः पञ्चकश्चैव ।२४।

एकादशकश्चगण एकादशेन्द्रियाणि तथा तन्मात्रो गणः पञ्चकः पञ्चलक्ष णोपेतः शब्दतन्मात्र स्पर्शतन्मात्ररूपतन्मात्ररसतन्मात्रगन्धतन्मात्रलक्षणो पेतः किं लक्षणात् सर्ग इत्येतदाह।

सात्विक एकादशकः प्रवर्त्तते वैकृतादहंकारात्
भूतादेस्तन्मात्रः सतामसस्तैजसादुभयं ।२५।

सत्वेनाभिभूते यदा रजस्तमसी अहंकारे भवतस्तदा सोऽहंकारः सात्विकस्तस्य च पूर्व्वाचार्य्यै संज्ञा कृता वैकृत इति तस्माद्विकृतादहंकारादेकादशक इन्द्रि

गण उत्पद्यते । तस्मात् सात्विकानि विशुद्धानीन्द्रियाणि स्वविषयसमर्थानि तस्मादुच्यते सात्विक एकादशक इति । किंचान्यद्भूतादेस्तन्मात्रः स तामसः तमसाभिभूते सत्वरजसी अहंकारे यदा भवतः सोहंकारस्तामस उच्यते तस्य पूर्वाचार्य्यकृता सञ्ज्ञा भूतादिस्तस्माद्भूतादेरहंकारात्तन्मात्रः पञ्चको गण उत्पद्यते भूतानामादिभूतस्तमोबहुलस्तेनोक्तः स तामस इति । तस्माद्भूतादेः पञ्चतन्मात्रको गणः किंच तैजसादुभयं यदा रजसाभिभूते सत्वतमसी भवतस्तदा तस्मात् सोऽहंकारस्तैजस इति संज्ञां लभते तस्मात्तैजसादुभयमुत्पद्यते । उभयमिति एकादशो गणस्तन्मात्रः पंचकः । योऽयं सात्विकोऽहंकारो वैकृतिकोः वैकृतो भूत्वा एकादशेन्द्रियाण्युत्पादयति स तैजसमहंकारं सहायं गृह्णाति सात्विको निःक्रियः स तैजसयुक्त इन्द्रियोत्पत्तौ समर्थः तथा तामसोऽहंकारो भूतादिः सञ्ज्ञितो निःक्रियत्वात्तैजसेनाहंकारेण क्रियावता युक्तस्तन्मात्राण्युत्पादयति तेनोक्तं तैजसादुभयमिति एवं तैजसेनाहंकारेणेन्द्रियाण्येकादश पञ्चतन्मात्राणि कृतानि भवन्ति सात्विक एकादशक इत्युक्तः यो वैकृतात् सात्विकादहंकारादुत्पद्यते तस्य का सञ्ज्ञेत्याह ।

बुद्धीन्द्रियाणि चक्षुः श्रोत्रघ्राणरसनस्पर्शनकानि
वाक्पाणिपादपायूपस्थान् कर्म्मेन्द्रियाण्याहुः । २६ ।

चक्षुरादीनि स्पर्शनपर्य्यन्तानि बुद्धीन्द्रियाण्युच्यन्ते। स्पृश्यत अनेनेति स्पर्शनं त्वगिन्द्रियं तद्वाची सिद्धः स्पर्शनशब्दोऽस्ति तेनेदं पठ्यते स्पर्शनकानीति शब्दस्पर्शरूपरसगन्धान् पञ्चविषयान् बुध्यन्त अवगच्छन्तीति पञ्च बुद्धीन्द्रियाणि । वाक्पाणिपादपायूपस्थान् कर्म्मेन्द्रियाण्याहुः कर्म्म कुर्वन्तीति कर्म्मेन्द्रियाणि । तत्र वाग्वदति हस्तौ नानाव्यापारं कुरुतः पादौ गमनागमनं पायुरुत्सर्गं करोति उपस्थ आनन्दं प्रजोत्पत्त्या । एवं बुद्धीन्द्रियकर्म्मे

न्द्रियभेदेन दशेन्द्रियाणि व्याख्यातानि मन एकादशकं किमात्मकं किं स्वरूपं चेति तदुच्यते ।

उभयात्मकमत्रमनः संकल्पकमिन्द्रियं च साधर्म्यात्
गुणपरिणामविशेषान्नानात्वं बाह्यभेदाश्च ।२७।

अत्रेन्द्रियवर्गे मन उभयात्मकं बुद्धीन्द्रियेषु बुद्धीन्द्रियवत् कर्म्मेन्द्रियेषु कर्म्मेन्द्रियवत् कस्माद्बुद्धीन्द्रियाणां प्रवृत्तिं कल्पयति कर्म्मेन्द्रियाणां च तस्मादुभयात्मकं मनः संकल्पयतीति संकल्पकं। किंचान्यदिन्द्रियं च साधर्म्यात् समानधर्म्मभावात् सात्विकाहंकाराद्बुद्धीन्द्रियाणि कर्म्मेन्द्रियाणि मनसा सहोत्पद्यमानानि मनसः साधर्म्यं प्रति तस्मात्साधर्म्यान्मनोऽपीन्द्रियमेवमेतान्येकादशेन्द्रियाणि सात्विकाद्वैकृतादहंकारादुत्पन्नानि । तत्र मनसः का वृत्तिरिति। संकल्पो वृत्तिः। बुद्धीन्द्रियाणां शब्दादयो वृत्तयः कर्म्मेन्द्रियाणां वचनादयोऽथैतानीन्द्रियाणि भिन्नानि भिन्नार्थग्राहकाणि किमीश्वरेणोत स्वभावेन कृतानि यतः प्रधानबुद्ध्यहंकारा अचेतना पुरुषोऽप्यकर्त्तेत्यत्राह । इह सांख्यानां स्वभावो नाम कश्चित्कारणमस्ति। अत्रोच्यते गुणपरिणामविशेषान्नानात्वं बाह्यभेदाश्च। इमान्येकादशेन्द्रियाणि शब्दस्पर्शरूपरसगन्धाः पञ्चानां वचनादानविहरणोत्सर्गानन्दाश्च पञ्चानां संकल्पश्च मनस एवमेते भिन्नानामेवेन्द्रियाणामर्थाः गुणपरिणामविशेषात् गुणानां परिणामो गुणपरिणामस्तस्य विशेषादिन्द्रियाणां नानात्वं बाह्यार्थभेदाश्च । अथैतन्नानात्वं नेश्वरेण नाहंकारेण न बुद्ध्या नप्रधानेन नपुरुषेण स्वभावात्कृतगुणपरिणामेनेति। गुणानामचेतनत्वात्प्रवर्त्तते प्रवर्त्तत एव कथं वक्ष्यतीहैवत्सविवृद्धिनिमित्तं क्षीरस्य यथा प्रवृत्तिरज्ञस्य पुरुषस्य विमोक्षार्थं तथा प्रवृत्तिः प्रधानस्य। एवमचेतना गुणा एकादशेन्द्रियभावेन प्रवर्त्तन्ते विशेषाऽपि तत्कृत एव येनोच्चैः प्रदेशे चक्षु रवलोकनायस्थितं तथा घ्राणं तथा श्रोत्रं तथा जिह्वा स्वदेशे स्वार्थग्रहणाय। एवं कर्म्मेन्द्रियाण्यपि यथायथं

स्वार्थसमर्थानि स्वदेशावस्थितानि स्वभावतो गुणपरिणामविशेषादेव न तदर्था अपि यत उक्तं शास्त्रान्तरे। गुणा गुणेषु वर्त्तन्ते गुणानां या वृत्तिः सा गुणविषया एवेति बाह्यार्था विज्ञेया गुणकृता एवेत्यर्थः। प्रधानं यस्य कारणमिति। अथेन्द्रियस्य कस्य का वृत्तिरित्युच्यते।

शब्दादिषु पञ्चानामालोचनमात्रमिष्यते वृत्तिः
वचनादानविहरणोत्सर्गानन्दाश्चपञ्चानाम् ।२८।

मात्रशब्दो विशेषार्थः। अविशेषव्यावृत्यर्थो यथा भिक्षा मात्रं लभ्यते नान्यो विशेष इति। तथा चक्षू रूपमात्रे न रसादिषु एवं शेषाण्यपि तद्यथा चक्षुषो रूपं जिह्वाया रसो घ्राणस्य गन्धः श्रोत्रस्य शब्दः त्वचः स्पर्शः। एव मेषां बुद्धीन्द्रियाणां वृत्तिः कथिता कर्म्मेन्द्रियाणां वृत्तिः कथ्यते वचनादा नविहरणोत्सर्गानन्दाश्चपञ्चानां कर्म्मेन्द्रियाणामित्यर्थः। वाचो वचनं हस्त योरादानं पादयोर्विहरणं पायोर्भुक्तस्याहारस्यपरिणतो मलोत्सर्गः उप स्थस्यानन्दः सुतोत्पत्तिर्विषया वृत्तिरिति सम्बन्धः। अधुना बुद्ध्यहंकारमन सामुच्यते।

स्वालक्षण्यं वृत्तिस्त्रयस्य सैषा भवत्यसामान्या
सामान्यकरणवृत्तिः प्राणाद्या वायवः पञ्च ।२९।

स्वलक्षणस्वभावा स्वालक्षण्या। अध्यवसायो यो बुद्धिरितिलक्षणमुक्तं सैव बुद्धिवृत्तिः। तथाऽभिमानोऽहंकार इत्यभिमानलक्षणोऽभिमानवृत्तिश्च। संकल्पकं मन इति लक्षणमुक्तं तेन संकल्प एव मनसो वृत्तिः। त्रयस्य बुद्ध्यहंकारमनसां स्वालक्षण्या वृत्तिरसामान्या या प्रागभिहिता बुद्धीन्द्रिया णां च वृत्तिः साऽप्यसामान्यैवेति। इदानीं सामान्या वृत्तिराख्यायते। सा

मान्यकरणवृत्तिः सामान्येन करणानां वृत्तिः प्राणाद्या वायवः पंच प्राणापानसमानोदानव्याना इति पञ्च वायवः सर्व्वेन्द्रियाणां सामान्या वृत्तिर्यतः। प्राणो नाम वायुर्मुखनासिकान्तर्गोचरस्तस्य यत् स्यन्दनं कर्म्म तत् त्रयोदशविधस्याऽपि सामान्या वृत्तिः सति प्राणे यस्मात् करणानामात्मलाभ इति। प्राणोऽपि पञ्जरशकुनि वत् सर्व्वस्य चलनं करोतीति। प्राणनात् प्राण इत्युच्यते। तथाऽपनयनादपानस्तत्र यत्स्यन्दनं तदपि सामान्यवृत्तिन्द्रियस्य। तथा समानो मध्यदेशवर्त्ती य आहारादिनयनात्समं नयनात् समानो वायुस्तत्र यत्स्यन्दनं तत् सामान्यकरणवृत्तिः। तथा ऊर्ध्वारोहणादुत्कर्षादुन्नयनाद्वा उदानो नाभिदेशमस्तकान्तर्गोचरस्तत्रोदाने यत्स्यन्दनं तत् सर्व्वेन्द्रियाणां सामान्या वृत्तिः। किंच शरीरव्याप्तिरभ्यन्तरविभागश्च येन क्रियतेऽसौ शरीरव्याप्याकाशवद्व्यानस्तत्र यत् स्यन्दनं तत् करणजालस्य सामान्या वृत्तिरिति। एवमेते पञ्चवायवः सामान्यकरणवृत्तिरिति व्याख्याता त्रयोदशविधस्यापि करणसामान्या वृत्तिरित्यर्थः।

युगपच्चतुष्टयस्य तु वृत्तिः क्रमशश्च तस्य निर्दिष्टा
दृष्टे तथाप्यदृष्टे त्रयस्य तत्पूर्व्विका वृत्तिः ।३०।

युगपच्चतुष्टयस्य बुद्ध्यहंकारमनसामेकैकेन्द्रियसम्बन्धे सति चतुष्टयं भवति चतुष्टयस्य दृष्टे प्रतिविषयाध्यवसाये युगपद्वृत्तिर्बुद्ध्यहंकारमनश्चक्षूंषि युगपदेककालं रूपं पश्यति स्थाणुरयमिति। बुद्ध्यहंकारमनोजिह्वा युगपद्रसं गृह्णन्ति। बुद्ध्यहंकारमनोघ्राणानि युगपद्गन्धं गृह्णन्ति। तथा त्वक्श्रोत्रे अपि। किंच क्रमशश्चतस्य निर्दिष्टा तस्येति चतुष्टयस्य क्रमशश्च वृत्तिर्भवति। यथा कश्चित् पथि गच्छन् दूरादेव दृष्ट्वा स्थाणुरयं पुरुषो वेति संशये सति तत्रोपरूढां तल्लिङ्गं पश्यति शकुनिं वा ततो तस्य मनसा संकल्पिते संशये व्यवच्छेदभूता बुद्धिर्भवति स्थाणुरयमित्यतोऽहंकारश्च निश्चयार्थः स्थाणुरेवेत्येवं

बुद्ध्यहंकारमनश्चक्षुषां क्रमशो वृत्तिर्दृष्टा यथा रूपे तथा शब्दादिष्वपि बो ध्या दृष्टे दृष्टविषये। किंचान्यत्तथाऽप्यदृष्टे त्रयस्य तत्पूर्व्विका वृत्तिरदृष्टेऽना गतेऽतीते च काले बुद्ध्यहंकारमनसां रूपे चक्षुः पूर्व्विका त्रयस्य वृत्तिः स्पर्शे त्वक्पूर्व्विका गन्धे घ्राणपूर्व्विका रसे रसनपूर्व्विका शब्दे श्रवणपूर्व्विका बुद्ध्यहं कारमनसामनागते भविष्यति कालेऽतीते च तत् पूर्व्विका क्रमशो वृत्तिर्व र्त्तमाने युगपत् क्रमशश्चेति। किंच।

स्वां स्वां प्रतिपद्यन्ते परस्पराकूतहेतुकां वृत्तिं
पुरुषार्थ एव हेतुर्न केनचित् कार्य्यते करणं। ३१।

स्वां स्वामिति वीप्सा बुद्ध्यहंकारमनांसि स्वां स्वां वृत्तिं परस्पराकूतहेतुका माकूतकादरसम्भ्रम इति प्रतिपद्यन्ते पुरुषार्थकरणाय। बुद्धेरहंकारादयो बुद्धिरहंकाराकूतं ज्ञात्वा स्वस्वविषयं प्रतिपद्यते किमर्थमिति चेत् पुरुषार्थ एव हेतुः पुरुषार्थः कर्त्तव्य इत्येवमर्थं गुणानां प्रवृत्तिस्तस्मादेतानि करणानि पुरुषार्थं प्रकाशयन्ति कथं स्वयं प्रवर्त्तन्ते न केनचित् कार्य्यते करणं पुरु षार्थ एवैकः कारयतीति वाक्यार्थो न केनचिदीश्वरेण पुरुषेण कार्य्यते प्रबो ध्यते करणं। बुद्ध्यादि कतिविधं तदित्युच्यते।

करणं त्रयोदशविधं तदाहरणधारणप्रकाशकरं
कार्य्यं च तस्य दशधाहार्य्यं धार्य्यं प्रकाश्यं च। ३२।

करणं महदादि त्रयोदशविधं बोद्धव्यं पंचबुद्धीन्द्रियाणि चक्षुरादीनि पंच कर्म्मेन्द्रियाणि वागादीनीति त्रयोदशविधं करणं तत्किं करोतीत्येतदाह तदा हरणधारणप्रकाशकरं। तत्राहरणं धारणं च कर्म्मेन्द्रियाणि कुर्व्वन्ति प्रकाशं

बुद्धीन्द्रियाणि । कतिविधं कार्य्यं तस्येति तदुच्यते । कार्य्यं च तस्य दशधा तस्य करणस्य कार्य्यं कर्त्तव्यमिति दशधा दशप्रकारं शब्दस्पर्शरूपरसगन्धाख्यं वचनादानविहरणोत्सर्गानन्दाख्यमेतद्दशविधं कार्य्यं बुद्धीन्द्रियैः प्रकाशितं कर्म्मेन्द्रियाण्याहरन्ति धारयन्ति चेति ।

अन्तः करणं त्रिविधं दशधा बाह्यं त्रयस्य विषयाख्यं
साम्प्रतकालं बाह्यं त्रिकालमाभ्यन्तरं करणं । ३३ ।

अन्तः करणमिति बुद्ध्यहंकारमनांसि त्रिविधं महदादिभेदात् । दशधा बाह्यं च बुद्धीन्द्रियाणि पञ्च कर्म्मेन्द्रियाणि पञ्च दशविधमेतत्करणं बाह्यं त्रयस्यान्तः करणस्य विषयाख्यं बुद्ध्यहंकारमनसां भोग्यं साम्प्रतकालं श्रोत्रं वर्त्तमानमेव शब्दं शृणोति नातीतं न च भविष्यन्तं चक्षुरपि वर्त्तमानं रूपं पश्यति नातीतं नानागतं त्वग्वर्त्तमानं स्पर्शं जिह्वा वर्त्तमानं रसं नासिका वर्त्तमानं गन्धं नातीतानागतं चेति । एवं कर्म्मेन्द्रियाणि वाग्वर्त्तमानं शब्दमुच्चारयति नातीतम् नानागतं पाणी वर्त्तमानं घटमाददाते नातीतमनागतं च पादौ वर्त्तमानं पन्थानं विहरतो नातीतं नाप्यनागतं पायूपस्थौ च वर्त्तमानावुत्सर्गानन्दौ कुरुतो नातीतौ नानागतौ । एवं बाह्यं करणं साम्प्रतकालमुक्तं त्रिकालमाभ्यन्तरं करणं बुद्ध्यहंकारमनांसि त्रिकालविषयाणि बुद्धिर्वर्त्तमानं घटं बुध्यत अतीतमनागतं चेति । अहंकारो वर्त्तमानेऽभिमानं करोत्यतीतेऽनागते च । तथा मनो वर्त्तमाने संकल्पं कुरुत अतीतेऽनागते च एवं त्रिकालमाभ्यन्तरं करणमिति । इदानीमिन्द्रियाणि कति सविशेषं विषयं गृह्णन्ति कानि निर्विशेषमिति तदुच्यते ।

बुद्धीन्द्रियाणि तेषां पञ्च विशेषाविशेषविषयाणि
वाग्भवति शब्दविषया शेषाणि तु पञ्चविषयाणि ।३४।

बुद्धीन्द्रियाणि तानि सविशेषं विषयं गृह्णन्ति सविशेषविषयं मानुषाणां शब्दस्पर्शरूपरसगन्धान् सुखदुःखमोहविषययुक्तान् बुद्धीन्द्रियाणि प्रकाशयन्ति देवानां निर्विशेषान्विषयान् प्रकाशयन्ति तथा कर्म्मेन्द्रियाणां मध्ये वाग्भवति शब्दविषया देवानां मानुषाणां च वाग्वदति श्लोकादीनुच्चारयति तस्माद्देवानां मानुषाणां च वागिन्द्रियं तुल्यं शेषाण्यपि वाग्व्यतिरिक्तानि पाणिपादपायूपस्थसञ्ज्ञितानि पञ्चविषयाणि पञ्चविषयाः शब्दादयो येषां तानि पञ्चविषयाणि शब्दस्पर्शरूपरसगन्धाः पाणौ सन्ति पञ्चशब्दादिलक्षणायां भुवि पादो विहरति पायिन्द्रियं पंचक्लृप्तमुत्सर्गं करोति तथोपस्थेन्द्रियं पञ्चलक्षणं शुक्रमानन्दयति ।

सान्तःकरणा बुद्धि सर्वं विषयमवगाहते यस्मात्
तस्मात् त्रिविधं करणं द्वारि द्वाराणि शेषाणि ।३५।

सान्तःकरणा बुद्धिरहंकारमनः सहितेत्यर्थः यस्मात् सर्वं विषयमवगाहते गृह्णाति त्रिष्वपि कालेषु शब्दादीन् गृह्णाति तस्मात्त्रिविधं करणं द्वारि द्वाराणि शेषाणि शेषाणि करणानीति वाक्यशेषः । किंचान्यत् ।

एते प्रदीपकल्पाः परस्परविलक्षणा गुणविशेषाः
कृत्स्नं पुरुषस्यार्थं प्रकाश्य बुद्धौ प्रयच्छन्ति ।३६।

यानि करणान्युक्तानि एते गुणविशेषाः किं विशिष्टाः प्रदीपकल्पाः प्रदीप

वद्विषयप्रकाशकाः परस्परविलक्षणा असदृशा भिन्नविषया इत्यर्थः । गुण विषया इत्यर्थः । गुणविशेषा गुणेभ्यो जाताः । कृत्स्नं पुरुषस्यार्थं बुद्धीन्द्रियाणि कर्म्मेन्द्रियाण्यहंकारो मनश्चैतानि स्वं स्वमर्थं पुरुषस्य प्रकाश्य बुद्धौ प्रयच्छन्ति बुद्धिस्थं कुर्वन्तीत्यर्थः । यतो बुद्धिस्थं सर्वं विषयं सुखादिकं पुरुष उपलभ्यते । इदंचान्यत् ।

सर्वं प्रत्युपभोगं यस्मात् पुरुषस्य साधयति बुद्धिः
सैव च विशिनष्टि पुनः प्रधानपुरुषान्तरं सूक्ष्मं । ३७ ।

सर्वेन्द्रियगतं त्रिष्वपि कालेषु सर्वं प्रत्युपभोगमुपभोगं प्रति देवमनुष्य तिर्य्यग् बुद्धीन्द्रियकर्म्मेन्द्रियद्वारेण सान्तः करणा बुद्धिः साधयति सम्पादयति यस्मात् तस्मात् सैव च विशिनष्टि प्रधानपुरुषयोर्विषयविभागं करोति प्रधानपुरुषान्तरं नानात्वमित्यर्थः । सूक्ष्ममित्यनधिकृततपश्चरणैरप्राप्य इयं प्रकृतिः सत्वरजस्तमसां साम्यावस्था इयं बुद्धिरयमहंकार एतानि पंच तन्मात्राण्येकादशेन्द्रियाणि पंचमहाभूतान्ययमन्यः पुरुष एभ्यो व्यतिरिक्त इत्येव वोधयति बुद्धिर्यस्यावापादपवर्गो भवति । पूर्व्वमुक्तं विशेषाविशेषविषयाणि तत् के विषयास्तन्दर्शयति ।

तन्मात्राण्यविशेषास्तेभ्यो भूतानि पञ्च पञ्चभ्यः
एते स्मृता विशेषाः शान्ता घोराश्च मूढाश्च । ३८ ।

यानि पंच तन्मात्राण्यहंकारादुत्पद्यन्ते ते शब्दतन्मात्रं स्पर्शतन्मात्रं रूपतन्मात्रं रसतन्मात्रं गन्धतन्मात्रमेतान्यविशेषा उच्यन्ते देवानामेते सुखलक्षणा विषया दुःखमोहरहितास्तेभ्यः पञ्चभ्यस्तन्मात्रेभ्यः पञ्चमहाभूतानि पृथिव्यप्तेजोवायुाकाशसञ्ज्ञानि यान्युत्पद्यन्ते । एते स्मृता विशेषाः । गन्धतन्मा

त्रात् पृथिवी रसतन्मात्रादापो रूपतन्मात्रात्तेजः स्पर्शतन्मात्राद्वायुः शब्द तन्मात्रादाकाशमित्येवमुत्पन्नान्येतानि महाभूतान्येते विशेषा मानुषाणां वि षयाः शान्ताः सुखलक्षणा घोरा दुःखलक्षणा मूढा मोहजनका यथाकाशं कस्यचिदनवकाशादन्तर्गृहादेर्निर्गतस्य सुखात्मकं शान्तं भवति तदेव शी तोष्णवातवर्षाभिभूतस्य दुःखात्मकं घोरं भवति तदेव पन्थानं गच्छतो वन मार्गाद् भ्रष्टस्य दिङ् मोहान्मूढं भवति।एवं वायुर्घर्म्मार्त्तस्य शान्तो भवति शीतार्त्तस्य घोरो धूलीशर्क्कराविमिश्रोऽतिवान् मूढ इति । एवं तेजः प्रभृ तिषु द्रष्टव्यं । अथाऽन्ये विशेषाः ।

सूक्ष्मा मातापितृजाः सहप्रभूतैस्त्रिधा विशेषाः स्युः
सूक्ष्मास्तेषां नियता मातापितृजा निवर्त्तन्ते ।३९।

सूक्ष्मास्तन्मात्राणि यत्संगृहीतं तन्मात्रिकं सूक्ष्मशरीरं महदादिलिङ्गं सदा तिष्ठति संसरतिच ते सूक्ष्मास्तथामातापितृजा स्थूलशरीरोपचायका ऋतु काले मातापितृसंयोगे शोणितशुक्रमिश्रीभावेनोदरान्तः सूक्ष्मशरीरस्योप चयं कुर्वीत तत् सूक्ष्मशरीरं पुनर्मातुरशितपीतनानाविधरसेन नाभीनि बन्धेनाप्यायते तथाप्यारब्धं शरीरं सूक्ष्मैर्मातापितृजैश्च सहमहाभूतैस्त्रिधावि शेषैः पृष्ठोदरजंघाकट्युरः शिरः प्रभृति षाट् कौशिकं पञ्चभौतिकं रुधिरमांस स्नायुशुक्रास्थिमज्जसंभृतमाकाशोऽवकाशदानाद्वायुर्वर्द्धनात् तेजः पाकादापः संग्रहात्पृथिवी धारणात् समस्तावयवोपेतं मातुरुदराद्बहिर्भवति । एवमेते त्रिविधा विशेषा स्युः । अत्राह के नित्याः के वाऽनित्याः सूक्ष्मास्तेषांनियताः सूक्ष्मास्तन्मात्रसञ्ज्ञकास्तेषांमध्ये नियता नित्यास्तैरारब्धं शरीरं कर्म्मवशात् पशुमृगपक्षिसरीसृपस्थावरजातिषु संसरति धर्म्मवशादिन्द्रकादिलोकेष्वेवमेत न्नियतं सूक्ष्मशरीरं सरति यावत् ज्ञानमुत्पद्यते उत्पन्ने ज्ञाने विद्वांच्छरीरं त्यक्त्वा मोक्षं गच्छति तस्मादेते विशेषा सूक्ष्मा नित्या इति मातापितृजा

निवर्त्तन्ते तत् सूक्ष्मशरीरं परित्यज्येहैव प्राणत्यागवेलायां मातापितृजा नि वर्त्तन्ते मरणकाले मातापितृजं शरीरमिहैवनिवर्त्त्य भूम्यादिषु प्रलीयते यथा तत्वं सूक्ष्मं च कथं संसरति तदाह ।

पूर्वोत्पन्नमसक्तं नियतं महदादिसूक्ष्मपर्य्यन्तं
संसरति निरूपभोगं भावैरधिवासितं लिंगं ।४०।

यदा लोकाऽनुत्पन्नाः प्रधानादिसर्गे तदा सूक्ष्मशरीरमुत्पन्नमिति । किंचान्य दसक्तं न संयुक्तं तिर्य्यग्योनिदेवमानुषस्थानेषु सूक्ष्मत्वात् कुत्रचिदसक्तं पर्व्वता दिष्वप्रतिहतप्रसरं सरति गच्छति । नित्यं यावन्नज्ञानमुत्पद्यते तावत् संसरति तच्च महदादिसूक्ष्मपर्य्यन्तं महानादौ यस्य तन्महदादि बुद्धिरंहकारो मन इति पञ्च तन्मात्राणि सूक्ष्मपर्य्यन्तं तन्मात्रपर्य्यन्तं संसरति भूलग्रहपिपीलि का वत् त्रीनपि लोकान् । निरूपभोगं भोगरहितं तत् सूक्ष्मशरीरं पितृमा तृजेन बाह्येनोपचयेन क्रियाधर्म्मग्रहणाद् भोगेषु समर्थं भवतीत्यर्थः । भावै रधिवासितं पुरस्ताद्भावान् धर्म्मादीन् वक्ष्यामस्तैरधिवासितमुपरञ्जितं लिं गमिति । प्रलयकाले महदासूक्ष्मपर्य्यन्तं करणोपेतं प्रधाने लीयत असंस रयुक्तं सदासर्गकालमत्रवर्त्तते प्रकृतिमोहबन्धनबद्धं सत् संसरणादिक्रियास्वस मर्थमिति पुनः सर्गकाले संसरति तस्माल्लिंगं सूक्ष्मं । किं प्रयोजनेन त्रयो दशविधं करणं संसरतीन्येवं चोदिते सत्याह ।

चित्रं यथाश्रयमृते स्थाण्वादिभ्यो यथा विना छाया
तद्वद्विना विशेषैर्न तिष्ठति निराश्रयं लिंगं ।४१।

चित्रं यथा कुड्याश्रयमृते न तिष्ठति स्थाण्वादिभ्यः कीलकादिभ्यो विना

छाया न तिष्ठति तैर्विना न भवत्यादिग्रहणाद्यथा शैत्यं विना नापो भवन्ति शैत्यं वाऽग्निर्विना । अग्निरुष्णं विना वायुः स्पर्शंविना आकाशमवकाशं विना पृथिवी गन्धं विना तद्वदेतेन दृष्टान्तेन न्यायेन विना विशेषैरविशेषै स्तन्मात्रैर्विना न तिष्ठति । अथ विशेषभूतान्युच्यन्ते शरीरं पंचभूतमयं वैशेषिणा शरीरेण विना क्व लिङ्गस्थानं चेति क एकदेहमुज्झति तदेवान्य माश्रयति निराश्रयमाश्रयरहितं लिङ्गं त्रयोदश विधं करणमित्यर्थः । कि मर्थं तदुच्यते ।

पुरुषार्थहेतुकमिदं निमित्तनैमित्तिकप्रसंगेन
प्रकृतेर्विभुत्वयोगान्नटवद्व्यवतिष्ठते लिंगं ।४२।

पुरुषार्थः कर्त्तव्य इति प्रधानं प्रवर्त्तते स च द्विविधः शब्दाद्युपलब्धिलक्षणो गुणपुरुषान्तरोपलब्धिर्मोक्ष इति तस्मादुक्तं पुरुषार्थहेतुकमिदं सूक्ष्मशरीरं प्रवर्त्तत इति । निमित्तनैमित्तिकप्रसंगेन निमित्तं धर्म्मादि नैमित्तिकमूर्द्धग मनादि पुरस्तादेव वक्ष्यामः प्रसंगेन प्रसक्त्या प्रकृतेः प्रधानस्य विभुत्वयो गाद्यथा राजा स्वराष्ट्रे विभुत्वाद्यद्यदिच्छति तत्तत् करोतीति तथा प्रकृतेः सर्वत्रविभुत्वयोगान्निमित्तनैमित्तिकप्रसंगेन व्यवतिष्ठते पृथक् पृथग्देहधारणे लिङ्गस्य व्यवस्थां करोति । लिंगं सूक्ष्मः परमाणुभिस्तन्मात्रैरुपचितं शरीरं त्रयोदशविधकरणोपेतं मानुषदेवतिर्य्यग्योनिषु व्यवतिष्ठते कथं नटवत् यथा नटः पटान्तरेण प्रविश्य देवो भूत्वा निर्गच्छति पुनर्मानुषः पुनर्विदुषकः । एवं लिंगं निमित्तनैमित्तिकप्रसंगेनोदरान्तः प्रविश्य हस्ती स्त्री पुमान् भव ति । भावैरधिवासितं लिंगं संसरतीत्युक्तं तत् के भावा इत्याह ।

सांसिद्धिकाश्चभावाः प्राकृतिका वैकृतिकाश्चधर्म्माद्याः
दृष्टाः करणाश्रयिणः कार्य्याश्रयिणश्च कललाद्याः । ४३ ।

भावास्त्रिविधाश्चिंत्यन्ते सांसिद्धिकाः प्राकृता वैकृताश्च । तत्र सांसिद्धिका यथा भगवतः कपिलस्यादिसर्गे उत्पद्यमानस्य चत्वारो भावाः सहोत्पन्ना धर्म्मो ज्ञानं वैराग्यमैश्वर्य्यमिति । प्राकृताः कथ्यन्ते ब्रह्मणश्चत्वारः पुत्राः सनकसनंदनसनातनसनत्कुमारा बभूवुः तेषामुत्पन्नकार्य्यकारणानां शरीरिणां षोडशवर्षाणामेते भावाश्चत्वारसमुत्पन्नास्तस्मादेते प्राकृताः । तथा वैकृता यथा आचार्य्यमूर्त्तिनिमित्तं कृत्वाऽस्मदादीनां ज्ञानमुत्पद्यते ज्ञानाद्वैराग्यं वैराग्याद्धर्म्मो धर्म्मादैश्वर्य्यमिति । आचार्य्यमूर्त्तिरपि विकृतिरिति तस्माद्वैकृता एते भावा उच्यन्ते यैरधिवासितं लिंगं संसरत्येते चत्वारो भावाः सात्विकास्तामसाविपरीताः सात्विकमेतद्रूपं तामसमस्माद्विपर्य्यस्तमित्यत्र व्याख्याता एवमष्टौ धर्म्मो ज्ञानं वैराग्यमैश्वर्य्यमधर्म्मोऽज्ञानमवैराग्यमनैश्वर्य्यमित्यष्टौ भावाः । क्व वर्त्तन्ते दृष्टाः करणाश्रयिणो बुद्धिः करणं तदाश्रयिणः । एतदुक्तमध्यवसायो बुद्धिः धर्म्मो ज्ञानमिति कार्य्यं देहस्तदाश्रयाः कललाद्या ये मातृजा इत्युक्ताः शुक्रशोणितसंयोगे विवृद्धिहेतुकाः कललाद्या बुद्बुदमांसपेशीप्रभृतयः तथा कौमारयौवनस्थविरत्वादयो भावा अन्नपानरसनिमित्ता निष्पद्यन्त अतः कार्य्याश्रयिण उच्यन्त अन्नादिविषयभोगनिमित्ता जायन्ते। निमित्तनैमित्तिकप्रसंगेनेति यदुक्तमत्रोच्यते ।

धर्म्मेण गमनमूर्द्ध्वं गमनमधस्ताद्भवत्यधर्म्मेण
ज्ञानेन चापवर्गो विपर्य्ययादिष्यते बन्धः । ४४ ।

धर्म्मेण गमनमूर्द्ध्वं धर्म्मं निमित्तं कृत्वोर्द्ध्वमुपनयति ऊर्द्ध्वमित्यष्टौ स्थानानि

गृह्यन्ते तद्यथा। ब्राह्मं प्राजापत्यं सौम्यमैन्द्रं गान्धर्वं याक्षं राक्षसं पैशाच मिति तत् सूक्ष्मं शरीरं गच्छति पशुमृगपक्षिसरीसृपस्थावरान्तेष्वधर्म्मो निमित्तं। किंच ज्ञानेनचापवर्गश्च पञ्चविंशति तत्वज्ञानं तेन निमित्तेनापवर्गो मोक्षः ततः सूक्ष्मं शरीरं निवर्त्तते परमात्मा उच्यते। विपर्य्ययादिष्यते बन्ध अज्ञानं निमित्तं सचैष नैमित्तिकः प्राकृतो वैकारिको दाक्षिणिकश्च बन्ध इति वक्ष्यति पुरस्ताद्यदिदमुक्तं प्राकृतेन च बन्धेन तथा वैकारिकेण च। दक्षिणाभिस्तृतीयेन बद्धो नान्येन मुच्यते। तथाऽन्यदपि निमित्तं।

वैराग्यात् प्रकृतिलयः संसारो भवति राजसाद्रागात्
ऐश्वर्य्यादविघातो विपर्य्ययात् तद्विपर्य्यासः ।४५।

यथा कस्यचिद्वैराग्यमस्ति न तत्वज्ञानं तस्मादज्ञानपूर्वाद्वैराग्यात् प्रकृतिलयो मृतोऽष्टासु प्रकृतिषु प्रधानबुद्ध्यहंकारतन्मात्रेषु लीयते न मोक्षः ततो भूयोऽपि संसरति तथा योऽयं राजसो रागः यजामि दक्षिणां ददामि येनामुष्मिल्लोकेऽत्र यद्दिव्यं मानुषं सुखमनुभवाम्येतस्माद्राजसाद्रागात् संसारो भवति। तथा ऐश्वर्य्यादविघात एतदैश्वर्य्यमष्टगुणमणिमादियुक्तं तस्मादैश्वर्य्यनिमित्तादविघातो नैमित्तिको भवति ब्रह्मादिषु स्थानेष्वैश्वर्य्यं न विहन्यते। किंचान्यद्विपर्य्ययाद्विपर्य्यासः तस्याविघातस्यविपर्य्यासो विघातो भवत्यनैश्वर्य्यात् सर्वत्र विहन्यते। एष निमित्तैः सह नैमित्तिकः षोडशविधो व्याख्यातः स किमात्मक इत्याह।

एष प्रत्ययसर्गो विपर्य्ययाशक्तितुष्टिसिद्ध्याख्यः
गुण वैषम्यविमर्द्दात् तस्य च भेदास्तु पंचाशत् ।४६।

यथा एष शोडशविधो निमित्तनैमित्तभेदो व्याख्यात एष प्रत्ययसर्ग उच्यते। प्रत्ययो बुद्धिरित्युक्ताऽध्यवसायो बुद्धिर्धर्म्मो ज्ञानमित्यादि स च प्रत्यय सर्गश्चतुर्धा भिद्यते विपर्य्ययाशक्तितुष्टिसिद्ध्याख्यभेदात् । तत्र संशयोऽज्ञानं । यथा कस्यचित् स्थाणुदर्शने स्थाणुरयं पुरुषो वेति संशयः । अश क्तिर्यथा । तमेवस्थाणुं सम्यग्दृष्ट्वा संशयं छेत्तुं न शक्नोतीत्यशक्तिः । एवं तृतीयस्तुष्ट्याख्यो यथा । तमेवस्थाणुं ज्ञातुं संशयितुं वा नेच्छति किमनेना स्माकमित्येषा तुष्टिः । चतुर्थः सिद्ध्याख्यो यथा । आनन्दितेन्द्रियः स्थाणु मारूढां वल्लिं पश्यति शकुनिं वा तस्य सिद्धिर्भवति स्थाणुरयमिति । एव मस्य चतुर्विधस्य प्रत्ययसर्गस्य गुणवैषम्यविमर्द्दे तस्यभेदास्तु पञ्चाशत् योऽयं सत्वरजस्तमोगुणानां वैषम्यो विमर्द्दः तेन तस्य प्रत्ययसर्गस्य पञ्चाशद्भेदा भवन्ति तथा क्वापि सत्वमुत्कटं भवति रजस्तमसी उदासीने क्वापि रजः क्वापि तम इति भेदाः कथ्यन्ते ।

पंच विपर्य्ययभेदा भवन्त्यशक्तिश्चकरणवैकल्यात्
अष्टाविंशतिभेदास्तुष्टिर्नवधाऽष्टधा सिद्धिः ।४७।

पंच विपर्य्ययभेदास्तेयथा तमो मोहो महामोहस्तामिस्रोऽन्धतामिस्र इत्ये षां भेदानां नानात्वं वक्ष्यतेऽनन्तरमेवेति। अशक्तेस्त्वष्टाविंशति भेदा भवन्ति करणवैकल्यात् तानपि वक्ष्यामस्तथा च तुष्टिर्नवधा ऊर्द्धश्रोतसि राजसानि ज्ञानानि। तथाष्टविधा सिद्धिः सात्विकानि ज्ञानानि तत्रैवोर्द्धश्रोतसि। एतत् क्रमेणैव वक्ष्यन्ते तत्रविपर्य्ययभेदा उच्यन्ते ।

भेदस्तमसोऽष्टविधो मोहस्य च दशविधो महामोहः
तामिस्रोऽष्टदशधा तथा भवत्यन्धतामिस्रः । ४८ ।

तमसस्तावदष्टधा भेदः प्रलयोऽज्ञानाद्विभज्यते सोऽष्टासु प्रकृतिषु लीयते प्रधानबुद्ध्यहंकारपंचतन्मात्राख्यासु तत्र लीनमात्मानं मन्यते मुक्तोहमिति तमो भेद एषोऽष्टविधस्य मोहस्य भेदोऽष्टविध एवेत्यर्थः । यथाष्टगुणमणि माद्यैश्वर्य्यं तत्र संगादिन्द्रादयो देवा न मोक्षं प्राप्नुवन्ति पुनश्चतत् क्षये संस रंत्येषोऽष्टविधो मोह इति । दशविधो महामोहः शब्दस्पर्शरूपरसगन्धा देवानामेते पंचविषयाः सुखलक्षणाः मानुषाणामप्येते एव शब्दादयः पञ्च विषया एवमेतेषु दशसु महामोह इति । तामिस्रोऽष्टदशधाऽष्टविधमैश्वर्य्यं दृष्टानुश्रविका विषया दश एतेषामष्टादशानां सम्पदमनुनन्दन्ति विपदं ना नुमोदन्त्येषोऽष्टादशविधो विकल्पस्तामिस्रो । यथा तामिस्रमष्टगुणमैश्वर्य्यं दृष्टानुश्रविका दशविषयास्तथान्धतामिस्रोऽप्यष्टादशभेद एवं किंतु विषयस म्पत्तौ सम्भोगकाले य एव म्रियतेऽष्टगुणैश्वर्य्याद्वा भ्रश्यते ततस्तस्य महद्दुः खमुत्पद्यते सोऽन्धतामिस्र इति । एवं विपर्य्ययभेदास्तमः प्रभृतयः पंच प्रत्येकं भिद्यमाना द्विषष्टिभेदाः संवृत्ता इति । अशक्तिभेदाः कथ्यन्ते ।

एकादशेन्द्रियवधा सह बुद्धिवधैरशक्तिरुद्दिष्टा
सप्तदशवधा बुद्धेर्विपर्य्ययात् तुष्टिसिद्धीनाम् । ४९ ।

भवंत्यशक्तेश्च करणवैकल्यादष्टाविंशतिभेदा इत्युद्दिष्टं तत्रैकादशेन्द्रियवधाः बाधिर्य्यमन्धताप्रसुप्तिरुपजिह्विकाघ्राणपाको मूकता कुणित्वं खाञ्ज्यं गुदा वर्तः क्लैब्यमुन्माद इति । सह बुद्धिवधैरशक्तिरुद्दिष्टा ये बुद्धिवधास्तैः सहाश क्तेरष्टाविंशतिभेदा भवन्ति सप्तदशवधा बुद्धेः सप्तदशवधास्ते तुष्टिभेदसिद्धि भेदवैपरीत्येन तुष्टिभेदा नव सिद्धिभेदा अष्टौ ये ते विपरीतैः सह एकादश

विधा एवमष्टाविंशतिविकल्या अशक्तिरिति विपर्य्ययात् सिद्धितुष्टीनामेव भेदक्रमो द्रष्टव्यः। तत्र तुष्टिर्नवधा कथ्यते।

आध्यात्मिकाश्चतस्रः प्रकृत्युपादानकालभाग्याख्याः
बाह्या विषयोपरमात् पंच नव तुष्टयोऽभिमताः ।५०।

आध्यात्मिकाश्चतस्र तुष्टयोऽध्यात्मनि भवा आध्यात्मिका ताश्च प्रकृत्युपादानकालभाग्याख्याः। तत्र प्रकृत्याख्या यथा कश्चित् प्रकृतिं वेत्ति तस्याः सगुणनिर्गुणत्वं च तेन तत्वं तत् कार्य्यं विज्ञायैव केवलं तुष्टस्तस्य नास्ति मोक्ष एषा प्रकृत्याख्या। उपादानाख्या यथा कश्चिदविज्ञायैव तत्वान्युपादान ग्रहणं करोति त्रिदण्डकमण्डलुविविदिकाभ्यो मोक्ष इति तस्यापि नास्त्येषा उपादानाख्या। तथा कालाख्या कालेन मोक्षो भविष्यतीति किं तत्वाभ्यासेनेत्येष कालाख्या तुष्टिस्तस्य नास्ति मोक्ष इति। तथा भाग्याख्या भाग्येनैव मोक्षो भविष्यतीति भाग्याख्या। चतुर्थी तुष्टिरिति। बाह्याविषयोपरमाश्च पंच। बाह्यास्तुष्टयः पञ्च विषयोपरमात् शब्दस्पर्शरूपरसगन्धेभ्य उपरतोऽर्जनरक्षणक्षयसंगहिंसादर्शनात्। वृद्धिनिमित्तं पाशुपाल्यवाणिज्यप्रतिग्रहसेवाः कार्य्या एतदर्जनं दुःखमर्जितानां रक्षणे दुःखमुपभोगात् क्षीयत इति क्षयदुःखं। तथा विषयोपभोगसंगे कृते नास्तीन्द्रियाणामुपशम इति संगदोषः। तथा न अनुपहत्य भूतान्युपभोग इत्येषहिंसादोषः। एवमर्ज्जनादिदोषदर्शनात् पंचविषयोपरमात् पंच तुष्टयः। एवमाध्यात्मिकबाह्यभेदान्नव तुष्टयस्तासां नामानि शास्त्रान्तरे प्रोक्तानि। अम्भः सलिलमोघो वृष्टिः सुतमो पारं सुनेत्रं नारीकमनुत्तमांभसिकमिति। आसां तुष्टीनां विपरीताशक्तिभेदाद्बुद्धिवधा भवन्ति। तद्यथा अनम्भोऽसलिलमनोघ इत्यादिवैपरीत्याद्बुद्धिवधा इति। सिद्धिरुच्यते।

ऊहः शब्दोऽध्ययनं दुःखविघातास्त्रयः सुहृत्प्राप्तिः
दानं च सिद्धयोऽष्टौ सिद्धेः पूर्वोऽङ्कुशस्त्रिविधः । ५१ ।

ऊहो यथा कश्चिन्नित्यमूहते किमिह सत्यं किं परं किं नैश्रेयसं किं कृतार्थः स्यामिति चिंतयतो ज्ञानमुत्पद्यते प्रधानादन्य एव पुरुष इत्यन्या बुद्धिरन्यो ऽहंकारोऽन्यानि तन्मात्राणीन्द्रियाणिपंचमहाभूतानीत्येवं तत्त्वज्ञानमुत्पद्यते येन मोक्षो भवति एषा ऊहाख्या प्रथमा सिद्धिः । तथा शब्दज्ञानात् प्रधानपुरुषबुद्ध्यहंकारतन्मात्रेन्द्रियपञ्चमहाभूतविषयं ज्ञानं भवति ततो मोक्ष इत्येषा शब्दाख्या सिद्धिः । अध्ययनाद्वेदादिशास्त्राध्ययनात् पंचविंशतितत्त्व ज्ञानं प्राप्य इत्येषा तृतीया सिद्धिः । दुःखविघातत्रयमाध्यात्मिक आधिभौतिक आधिदैविक दुःखत्रयविघाताय गुरुं समुपगम्य तत उपदेशान्मोक्षं यात्येषा चतुर्थी सिद्धिः । एषैवदुःखत्रयभेदात् त्रिधा कल्पनीया इति षट् सिद्धयः । तथासुहृत्प्राप्तिर्यथा कश्चित् सुहृत् ज्ञानमधिगम्य मोक्षं गच्छति एषा सप्तमी सिद्धिः । दानं यथा कश्चिद्भगवतां प्रत्याश्रयौषधित्रिदण्डकुण्डि कादीनां ग्रासाच्छादनादीनां च दानेनोपकृत्य तेभ्यो ज्ञानमवाप्य मोक्षंयात्ये षाष्टमी सिद्धिः । आसामष्टानां सिद्धीनां शास्त्रान्तरे संज्ञाःकृतास्तारं सुतारं तारतारं प्रमोदं प्रमुदितं प्रमोदमानं रम्यकं सदाप्रमुदितमिति । आसां विपर्य्ययाद्बुद्धेर्बधा ये विपरीतास्त अशक्तौ निक्षिप्ता यथाऽतारमसुतारम तारतारमित्यादिद्रष्टव्यमशक्तिभेदा अष्टाविंशतिरुक्तास्ते सहबुद्धिबधैरेकादशे न्द्रियबधा इति । तत्र तुष्टिविपर्य्यया नव सिद्धीनां विपर्य्यया अष्टौ एव मेते सप्तदशबुद्धिबधा एतैः सहेन्द्रियबधा अष्टाविंशतिरशक्तिभेदाः प्रत्यात् कथिता इति विपर्य्ययाशक्तितुष्टिसिद्धीनामेवोद्देशो निर्देशश्चकृता इति । किं चान्यत् सिद्धेः पूर्वोऽङ्कुशस्त्रिविधः सिद्धेः पूर्वा या विपर्य्ययाशक्तितुष्टयस्ता एव सिद्धेरंकुशस्तद्भेदादेवं त्रिविधो यथा हस्ती गृहीतांकुशेन वशो भवत्येव विपर्य्ययाशक्तितुष्टिभिर्गृहीतो लोकोऽज्ञानमाप्नोति तस्मादेताः परित्यज्य

सिद्धिः सेव्या स सिद्धेस्तत्वज्ञानमुत्पद्यते तन्मोक्ष इति। अथ यदुक्तं भावैरधि वासितं लिंगं तत्र भावा धर्म्मादयोऽष्टावुक्ता बुद्धिपरिणामा विपर्य्ययाश क्तितुष्टिसिद्धिपरिणताः स भावाख्यः प्रत्ययसर्गः लिंगंच तन्मात्रसर्गश्चतु र्दशभूतपर्य्यन्त उक्तस्तत्रैकेनैवसर्गेण पुरुषार्थसिद्धौ किमुभयविधसर्गेणेत्यत आह।

न विना भावैर्लिंगं न निवा लिंगेन भावनिर्वृत्तिः
लिंगाख्यो भावाख्यस्तस्माद्द्विविधः प्रवर्त्तते सर्गः ।५२।

भावैः प्रत्ययसर्गैर्विना लिंगं न तन्मात्रसर्गो न पूर्वपूर्वसंस्काराहष्टकारित त्वादुत्तरोत्तरदेहलम्भस्य लिंगेन तन्मात्रसर्गेण च विना भावनिर्वृत्तिर्न स्थूल सूक्ष्मदेहसाध्यत्वाद्धर्म्मादेरनादित्वाच्च सर्गस्य वीजांकुरावन्योन्याश्रयो न दो षाय तत्तज्जातीयापेक्षित्वेऽपि तत्तद्व्यक्तीनां परस्परानपेक्षित्वात्तस्माद्भावाख्यो लिंगाख्यश्चद्विविधः प्रवर्त्तते सर्ग इति किंचान्यत्।

अष्टविकल्पो दैवस्तैर्य्यग्योनश्च पंचधा भवति
मानुष्यश्चैकविधः समासतो भौतिकः सर्गः ।५३।

तत्र दैवमष्टप्रकारं ब्राह्मं प्राजापत्यं सौम्यमैन्द्रं गान्धर्वं याक्षं राक्षसं पैशाच मिति। पशुमृगपक्षिसरीसृपस्थावराणि भूतान्येव पंचविधस्तैरश्चः। मानुष योनिरेकैव इति चतुर्द्दशभूतानि त्रिष्वपि लोकेषु गुणत्रयमस्ति तत्र कस्मिन् किमधिकमुच्यते।

ऊर्द्ध्वं सत्वविशालस्तमोविशालश्च मूलतःसर्गः
मध्ये रजोविशालो ब्रह्मादिस्तम्बपर्य्यन्तं । ५४ ।

ऊर्द्ध्वमित्यष्टसु देवस्थानेषु सत्वविशालः सत्वविस्तारः सत्वोत्कट ऊर्द्ध्वसत्व इति । तत्रापि रजस्तमसी स्तः । तमोविशालो मूलतः पश्वादिषुस्थावरान्तेषु सर्वःसर्गस्तमसाधिक्येन व्याप्तस्तत्रापि सत्वरजसी स्तः । मध्ये मानुष्ये रज उत्कटं तत्रापि सत्वतमसी विद्येते तस्माद्दुःखप्राया मनुष्याः । एवं ब्रह्मादिस्तम्बपर्य्यन्तः ब्रह्मादिस्थावरान्त इत्यर्थः । एवमभौतिकः सर्गो लिंगसर्गो भावसर्गो भूतसर्गो दैवमानुषतैर्य्यग्योनय इत्येषः प्रधानकृतः षोडशसर्गः ।

तत्र जरामरणकृतं दुःखं प्राप्नोति चेतनः पुरुषः
लिंगस्याविनिवृत्तेस्तस्माद्दुःखं स्वभावेन । ५५ ।

तत्रेति तेषु देवमानुषतिर्य्यग्योनिषु जराकृतं मरणकृतं चैव दुःखं चेतनः चैतन्यवान् पुरुषः प्राप्नोति न प्रधानं न बुद्धिर्नाहंकारो न तन्मात्राणीन्द्रियाणिमहाभूतानि च । कियन्तकालं पुरुषो दुःखं प्राप्नोतीति तद्विविनक्ति । लिंगस्याविनिवृत्तेर्यत्तन्महदादि लिंगशरीरेणाविश्य तत्र व्यक्तीभवति तद्यावन्निवर्त्तते संसारशरीरमिति संक्षेपेण त्रिषु स्थानेषु पुरुषो जरामरणकृतं दुःखं प्राप्नोति लिंगस्याविनिवृत्तेः लिंगस्य विनिवृत्तिं यावत् । लिंगनिवृत्तौ मोक्षो मोक्षप्राप्तौ नास्तिदुःखमिति । तत्पुनः केन निवर्त्तते यदा पंचविंशतितत्वज्ञानं स्यात् सत्वपुरुषान्यथाख्यातिलक्षणमिदं प्रधानमियं बुद्धिरयमहंकार इमानि पंचतन्मात्राण्येकादशेन्द्रियाणि पंच महाभूतानि येभ्योन्यः पुरुषो विसदृश इत्येवं ज्ञानाल्लिंगनिवृत्तिस्ततो मोक्ष इति । प्रवृत्तेः किं निमित्तमारम्भ इत्युच्यते ।

इत्येष प्रकृतिकृतो महदादिविशेषभूतपर्य्यन्तः
प्रतिपुरुषविमोक्षार्थं स्वार्थ इव परार्थ आरम्भः । ५६ ।

इत्येष परिसमाप्तौ निर्द्देशे च प्रकृतिकृतौ प्रकृतिकरणे प्रकृतिक्रियायां य आरम्भो महदादिविशेषभूतपर्य्यन्तः प्रकृतेर्महान् महतोऽहंकारस्तस्मात्तन्मात्राण्येकादशेन्द्रियाणि तन्मात्रेभ्यः पंचमहाभूतानीत्येषः प्रतिपुरुषविमोक्षार्थं पुरुषं प्रति देवमनुष्यतिर्य्यग्भावं गतानां विमोक्षार्थमारम्भः कथं स्वार्थ इव परार्थमारम्भः यथा कश्चित् स्वार्थं त्यक्त्वा मित्रकार्य्याणि करोति एवं प्रधानं । पुरुषोऽत्रप्रधानस्य न किञ्चित् प्रत्युपकारं करोति । स्वार्थ इव न च स्वार्थः परार्थ एवार्थः शब्दादिविषयोपलब्धिर्गुणपुरुषान्तरोपलब्धिश्च त्रिषु लोकेषु शब्दादिविषयैः पुरुषा योजयितव्या अन्तेच मोक्षेणेति प्रधानस्य प्रवृत्तिस्तथा चोक्तं । कुम्भवत् प्रधानं पुरुषार्थं कृत्वा निवर्त्तत इति । अत्रोच्यतेऽचेतनं प्रधानं चेतनः पुरुष इति मया त्रिषु लोकेषु शब्दादिभिर्विषयैः पुरुषो योज्योऽन्ते मोक्षः कर्त्तव्य इति कथं चेतनवत् प्रवृत्तिः । सत्यं किंत्वचेतनानामपि प्रवृत्तिर्दृष्टा निवृत्तिश्चयस्मादित्याह ।

वत्सविवृद्धिनिमित्तं क्षीरस्य यथा प्रवृत्तिरज्ञस्य
पुरुषविमोक्षनिमित्तं तथा प्रवृत्तिः प्रधानस्य । ५७ ।

यथा तृणोदकं गवा भक्षितं क्षीरभावेन परिणम्य वत्सविवृद्धिं करोति पुष्टे च वत्से निवर्त्तत एव पुरुषविमोक्षनिमित्तं प्रधानं । अज्ञस्यप्रवृत्तिरिति । किंच ।

औत्सुक्यनिवृत्त्यर्थं यथा क्रियासु प्रवर्त्तते लोकः
पुरुषस्य विमोक्षार्थं प्रवर्त्तते तद्वदव्यक्तं । ५८ ।

यथा लोक इष्टौत्सुक्ये सति तस्य निवृत्त्यर्थं क्रियासु प्रवर्त्तते गमनागमन क्रियासु कृतकार्य्यो निवर्त्तते तथा पुरुषस्य विमोक्षार्थं शब्दादिविषयोपभो गोपलब्धिलक्षणं गुणपुरुषान्तरोपलब्धिलक्षणं च द्विविधमपि पुरुषार्थं कृत्वा प्रधानं निवर्त्तते । किंचान्यत् ।

रङ्गस्य दर्शयित्वा निवर्त्तते नर्त्तकी यथा नृत्यात्
पुरुषस्य तथात्मानं प्रकाश्य निवर्त्तते प्रकृतिः । ५९ ।

यथा नर्त्तकी शृङ्गारादिरसैरितिहासादिभावैश्च निबद्धगीतवादित्रवृत्तानि रङ्गस्य दर्शयित्वा कृतकार्य्या नृत्यान्निवर्त्तते तथा प्रकृतेरपि पुरुषस्यात्मानं प्रकाश्य बुद्ध्यहंकारतन्मात्रेन्द्रियमहाभूतभेदेन निवर्त्तते । कथं को वा स्यान्नि वर्त्तको हेतुस्तदाह ।

नानाविधैरुपायैरुपकारिण्यनुपकारिणः पुंसः
गुणवत्यगुणस्य सतस्तस्यार्थमपार्थकं चरति । ६० ।

नानाविधैरुपायैः प्रकृतिः पुरुषस्योपकारिण्यनुपकारिणः पुंसः कथं देवमा नुषतिर्य्यग्भावेन सुखदुःखमोहात्मकभावेन शब्दादिविषयभावेन एवं नाना विधैरुपायैरात्मानं प्रकाश्याहमन्या त्वमन्य इति निवर्त्तत अतो नित्यस्य तस्यार्थमपार्थं कुरुते चरति च यथा कश्चित् परोपकारी सर्व्वस्योपकुरुते नात्मनः प्रत्युपकारमीहत एव प्रकृतिः पुरुषार्थं चरति करोत्यपार्थकं। पश्चा दुक्तमात्मानं प्रकाश्य निवर्त्तते निवृत्ता च किं करोतीत्याह ।

प्रकृतेः सुकुमारतरं न किंचिदस्तीति मे मतिर्भवति
या दृष्टास्मीति पुनर्न दर्शनमुपैति पुरुषस्य ।६१।

लोके प्रकृतेः सुकुमारतरं न किञ्चिदस्तीत्येवं मे मतिर्भवति येन परार्थं एवं मतिरुत्पन्ना कस्मादहमनेन पुरुषेण दृष्टास्मीत्यस्य पुंसो पुनर्दर्शनं नो पैति पुरुषस्यादर्शनमुपयातीत्यर्थः । तत्र सुकुमारतरं वर्णयति । ईश्वरं कारणं ब्रुवते। अजो जन्तुरनीशोयमात्मा नः सुखदुःखयोरीश्वरप्रेरितोगच्छेत् स्वर्गं नरकमेव वा। अपरे स्वभावकारणिकां ब्रुवते। केन शुक्लीकृता हंसा मयूराः केन चित्रिताः । स्वभावेनैवेति । अत्रसांख्याचार्य्या आहुः निर्गुणत्वादीश्वरस्य कथं सगुणतः प्रजा जायेरन् कथं वा पुरुषान्निर्गुणादेव तस्मात् प्रकृते युंज्यते तथा शुक्लेभ्यस्तन्तुभ्यः शुक्ल एव पटो भवति कृष्णेभ्यः कृष्ण एवेति। एवं त्रिगुणात् प्रधानात् त्रयो लोकास्त्रिगुणाः समुत्पन्ना इति गम्यते। निर्गुण ईश्वरः सगुणानां लोकानां तस्मादुत्पत्तिरयुक्तेति। अनेन पुरुषो व्याख्यातः। तथा केषांचित् कालः कारणमित्युक्तं च। कालः पञ्चास्ति भूतानि कालः संहरते जगत् । कालः सुप्तेषु जागर्त्ति कालो हि दुरतिक्रमः । व्यक्तमव्यक्तपुरुषास्त्रयः पदार्थास्तेन कालोऽन्तर्भूतोस्ति स व्यक्तः सर्वकर्तृत्वात् कालस्यापि प्रधानमेवकारणं स्वाभावोप्यत्रैवलीनः तस्मात् कालो न कारणं। नापि स्वभाव इति । तस्मात् प्रकृतिरेव कारणं न प्रकृतेः कारणान्तरमस्तीति । न पुनर्दशनमुपयाति पुरुषस्य । अतः प्रकृतेः सुकुमारतरं सुभोग्यतरं न किंचिदीश्वरादिकारणमस्तीति मे मतिर्भवति । तथा च श्लोके रूढं । पुरुषो मुक्तः पुरुषः संसारीति चोदितेत्याह ।

तस्मान्नबध्यते नापि मुच्यते नापि संसरति कश्चित्
संसरति बध्यते मुच्यते च नानाश्रया प्रकृतिः ।६२।

तस्मात् कारणात् पुरुषो न बध्यते नापि मुच्यते नापि संसरति यस्मात्

कारणात् प्रकृतिरेव नानाश्रया दैवमानुषतिर्य्यग्योन्याश्रया बुद्ध्यहंकारतन्मात्रेन्द्रियभूतस्वरूपेण बध्यते मुच्यते संसरति चेति। अथ मुक्त एव स्वभावात् सस र्वगतश्चकथं संसरत्यप्राप्तप्रापणार्थं संसरणमिति तेन पुरुषो बध्यते पुरुषो मुच्यते संसरति व्यपदिश्यते येन संसारित्वं न विद्यते सत्वपुरुषान्तज्ञानात् तत्वं पुरुषस्याभिष्वज्यते। तदभिव्यक्तौ केवलः शुद्धो मुक्तः स्वरूपप्रतिष्ठः पुरुष इति। अथ यदि पुरुषस्य बन्धो नास्ति ततो मोक्षोऽपि नास्ति। अथोच्यते प्रकृतिरेवात्मानं बध्नाति मोचयति च यत्र सूक्ष्मशरीरं तन्मात्रकं त्रिविधकरणोपेतं तत् त्रिविधेन बन्धेन बध्यते। उक्तं च। प्राकृतेन च बन्धेन तथा वैकारिकेण च। दाक्षिणेन तृतीयेन बद्धो नान्येन मुच्यते। तत् सूक्ष्मं शरीरं धर्म्माधर्म्म संयुक्तं। प्रकृतिश्च बध्यते प्रकृतिश्च मुच्यते संसरतीति कथं तदुच्यते।

रूपैः सप्तभिरेवबध्नात्यात्मानमात्मना प्रकृतिः
सैव च परुषार्थं प्रति विमोचयत्येकरूपेण। ६३।

रूपैः सप्तभिरेवैतानि सप्त प्रोच्यन्ते धर्म्मो वैराग्यमैश्वर्य्यमधर्म्मोऽज्ञानमवैराग्यमनैश्वर्य्यमेतानि प्रकृतेः सप्तरूपाणि तैरात्मानं स्वं बध्नाति प्रकृतिरात्मानं स्वमेव सैव प्रकृतिः पुरुषस्यार्थः पुरुषार्थः कर्त्तव्य इति विमोचयत्यात्मानमेकरूपेण ज्ञानेन। कथं तज्ज्ञानमुत्पद्यते।

एवं तत्वाभ्यासान्नास्ति न मे नाहमित्यपरिशेषं
अविपर्य्ययाद्विशुद्धं केवलमुत्पद्यते ज्ञानं। ६४।

एवमुक्तेन क्रमेण पञ्चविंशतितत्वालोचनाभ्यासादियं प्रकृतिरयं पुरुष एतानि पंचतन्मात्रेन्द्रियमहाभूतानीति पुरुषस्य ज्ञानमुत्पद्यते नास्ति नाहमेव

भवामि न मे मम शरीरं तद्यतोऽहमन्यः शरीरमन्यन्नाहमित्यपरिशेषमहं काररहितमपरिशेषमविपर्य्ययाद्विशुद्धं विपर्य्ययः संशयोऽविपर्य्ययादसंशया द्विशुद्धं केवलं तदेवनान्यदस्तीति मोक्षकारणमुत्पद्यतेऽभिव्यज्यते ज्ञानं पंच विंशतितत्वज्ञानं पुरुषस्येति । ज्ञाने पुरुषः किं करोति ।

तेन निवृत्तप्रसवामर्थवशात् सप्तरूपविनिवृत्तां
प्रकृतिं पश्यति पुरुषः प्रेक्षकवदवस्थितः सुस्थः । ६५ ।

तेन विशुद्धेन केवलज्ञानेन पुरुषः प्रकृतिं पश्यति प्रेक्षकवत् प्रेक्षकेण तुल्यम वस्थितः स्वस्थो यथा रंगप्रेक्षकोऽवस्थितो नर्त्तकीं पश्यति स्वस्थः स्वस्मि न्स्तिष्ठति स्वस्थः स्वस्थानस्थितः । कथं भूतां प्रकृतिं निवृत्तप्रसवां निवृत्त बुद्ध्यहंकारकार्य्यानर्थवशात् सप्तरूपविनिवृत्तां निवर्त्तितोभयपुरुषप्रयोजन वशाद्यैः सप्तभीरूपैर्धर्म्मादिभिरात्मानं बध्नाति तेभ्यः सप्तभ्यो रूपेभ्यो विनि वृत्तिं प्रकृतिं पश्यति । किंच ।

दृष्टा मयेत्युपेक्षक एको दृष्टाहमित्युपरमत्यन्या
सति संयोगेऽपि तयोः प्रयोजनं नास्ति सर्गस्य । ६६ ।

रंगस्थ इति यथा रंगस्थ इत्येवमुपेक्षक एकः केवलः शुद्धः पुरुषस्तेनाहंदृष्टेति कृत्वा उपरता निवृत्ता एका एकैव प्रकृतिः त्रैलोक्यस्यापि प्रधानकारणं भूता न द्वितीया प्रकृतिरस्ति मूर्त्तिवधे जातिभेदादेवं प्रकृतिपुरुषयो निर्वृत्ता वपि व्यापकत्वात् संयोगोऽस्ति न तु संयोयात् कुतः सर्गो भवति । संति संयोगेऽपि तयोः प्रकृतिपुरुषयोः सर्वगतत्वात् सत्यपि संयोगे प्रयोजनं ना स्ति सर्गस्य सृष्टेश्चरितार्थत्वात् प्रकृतेर्द्विविधप्रयोजनं शब्दविषयोपलब्धिर्गु

णपुरुषान्तरोपलब्धिश्च। उभयथापि चरितार्थत्वात् सर्गस्य नास्ति प्रयोजनं यः पुनः सर्ग इति। यथा दानग्रहणनिमित्त उत्तमर्णाधमर्णयोर्द्रव्यविशुद्धौ सत्यपि संयोगे न कश्चिदर्थसम्बन्धी भवति। एवं प्रकृति पुरुषयोरपि नास्ति प्रयोजनमिति। यदि पुरुस्योत्पन्ने ज्ञाने मोक्षो भवति ततो मम कस्मान्न भव तीति। अत उच्यते।

सम्यग्ज्ञानाधिगमाद्धर्म्मादीनामकारणप्राप्तौ
तिष्ठति संस्कारवशाच्चक्रभ्रमवद्धृतशरीरः ।६७।

यद्यपि पंचविंशतितत्वज्ञानं सम्यक् ज्ञानं भवति तथाऽपि संस्कारवशाद्धृत शरीरो योगी तिष्ठति कथं चक्रभ्रमवच्चक्रभ्रमेण तुल्यं यथा कुलालश्चक्रं भ्रमयित्वा घटं करोति मृत्पिण्डं चक्रमारोप्य पुनः कृत्वा घटं पर्यामुंचति चक्रं भ्रमत्येव संस्कारवशादेवं सम्यग्ज्ञानाधिगमादुत्पन्नसम्यग्ज्ञानस्य धर्म्मा दीनामकारणप्राप्तौ एतानि सप्तरूपाणि बन्धनभूतानि सम्यग्ज्ञानेन दग्धा नि यथा नाग्निना दग्धानि वीजानि प्ररोहणसमर्थान्येवमेतानि धर्म्मा दीनि बन्धनानि न समर्थानि। धर्म्मादीनामकारणप्राप्तौ संस्कारवशाद्धृत शरीरस्तिष्ठति ज्ञानाद्वर्त्तमानधर्म्माधर्म्मक्षयः कस्मान्नभवति वर्त्तमानत्वादेव क्षणान्तरे क्षयमप्येति ज्ञानं त्वनागतकर्म्म दहति वर्त्तमानशरीरेण च यत् करोति तदपीति विविहितानुष्ठानकरणादिति संस्कारक्षयाच्छरीरपाते मोक्षः। स किं विशिष्टो भवतीत्युच्यते।

प्राप्ते शरीरभेदे चरितार्थत्वात् प्रधानविनिवृत्तौ
ऐकान्तिकमात्यन्तिकमुभयं कैवल्यमाप्नोति ।६८।

धर्म्माधर्म्मजनितसंस्कारक्षयात् प्राप्ते शरीरभेदे चरितार्थत्वात् प्रधानस्यनि

वृत्तौ ऐकान्तिकमवश्यमात्यन्तिकमनंतर्हितं कैवल्यं केवलभावान्मोक्ष उभय मैकान्तिकात्यन्तिकमित्येवविशिष्टकैवल्यमाप्नोति ।

पुरुषार्थज्ञानमिदं गुह्यं परमर्षिणा समाख्यातं
स्थित्युत्पत्तिप्रलयाश्चिन्त्यन्ते यत्र भूतानां । ६९ ।

पुरुषार्थो मोक्षस्तदर्थं ज्ञानमिदं गुह्यं रहस्यं परमर्षिणा श्रीकपिलर्षिणा समाख्यातं सम्यगुक्तं यत्र ज्ञाने भूतानां वैकारिणां स्थित्युत्पत्तिप्रलया अव स्थानाविर्भावतिरोभावाश्चिन्त्यन्ते विचार्य्यन्ते येषां विचारात् सम्यक् पंच विंशतितत्वविवेचनात्मिका सम्पद्यते संवित्तिरिति

सांख्यं कपिलमुनिना प्रोक्तं संसारविमुक्तिकारणं हि
यत्रैताः सप्ततिरार्य्या भाष्यं चात्रगौडपादकृतं ।

एतत् पवित्रमग्र्यं मुनिरासुरयेऽनुकम्पया प्रददौ
आसुरिरपि पंचशिखाय तेन च बहुधा कृतं तन्त्रं । ७० ।
शिष्यपरम्परयागतमीश्वरकृष्णेन चैतदार्य्याभिः
संक्षिप्तमार्य्यमतिना सम्यग्विज्ञाय सिद्धान्तं । ७१ ।
सप्तत्यां किल येऽर्थास्तेऽर्थाः कृत्स्नस्यषष्टितन्त्रस्य
आख्यायिकाविरहिताः परवादविवर्ज्जिताश्चापि । ७२ ।

VARIATIONS AND CORRECTIONS.

THE text of the *Káriká* has been in the first instance derived from a copy in the handwriting of Mr. Colebrooke, which he had prepared for the press. I have collated this with Professor Lassen's edition and with a very good manuscript in my own possession. Besides these, the different commentaries include the text, and the *Sánkhya Pravachana Bháshya* cites many verses of the *Káriká*. Altogether, therefore, the text may be considered as printed upon a collation of eight copies, which may be thus referred to: A. Mr. Colebrooke's transcript; B. my MS. copy; C. Professor Lassen's edition; D. the text in Gaurapáda's commentary; E. that in the *Sánkhya Tatwa Kaumudí;* F. that in the *Sánkhya Chandriká;* G. that in the *Sánkhya Kaumudí;* and H. the passages of it in the *Sánkhya Pravachana Bháshya*. Of the *Sánkhya Tatwa Kaumudí* I had three copies, and two copies of the *Sánkhya Chandriká*. I had but one copy of the *Bháshya* of Gaurapáda.

P. 1. l. 1. तदभिघातके A. D. G. तदपघातके B. C. E. F.

P. 2. l. 14. हेतुः दुःख would be more correctly हेतुर्दुःखः Wilkins, r. 53. In noticing this deviation from rule, however, my chief object is to observe, that such deviations are frequent in the MSS., and that, although I have corrected some of them, I do not regard them in all cases as errors or inadvertencies: they seem in general to be intentional, and to be designed for the sake of greater perspicuity.

P. 3. l. 9. For विशुद्दि read विशुद्धि

P. 5. l. 17. For तस्भिन् read तस्मिन्

P. 5. l. 18. प्रतिजान्वाससज्ञानं. As intimated in the translation (p. 21), these words are of questionable import, and possibly erroneous. The want of another copy renders their correction hazardous, but in all probability the first term should be प्रतिभा or प्रतिभान् ordinarily 'light' or 'shining,' but perhaps here said to denote वास 'abode, place;' or the construction may be प्रतिभा — अन्वाससंज्ञानं implying 'conformity, adaptation,' from अनु 'according to,' and आस 'to sit.'

P. 6. v. 6. प्रतीति—प्रसिद्धि D.

P. 8. v. 8. सरूपं—स्वरूपं G. which Professor Lassen has followed. All the other copies concur in the first reading, which the sense of the verse, as explained by the scholiasts, requires.

P. 10. l. 11. For रुपं read रूपं

P. 11. l. 4, 5, 7. Some blanks occur in this part of the MSS. of the *Bháshya,* which have been conjecturally supplied; as, कृष्णतन्तु - - कृष्ण and प्रधानमेव - - वेक्तुं न या - - दविवेकि and तथा सामान्या - - प्रधानं How these have been supplied may be seen in the respective passages.

P. 11. l. 11. For पुरुश read पुरुष

P. 12. l. 10. For अभिवा and अभिमवा read अभिभवा

P. 13. l. 2. For सत्वमसो read सत्वतमसो

P. 13. v. 13. Professor Lassen changes उपष्टम्भकं to उपस्तम्भकं which he derives from ष्टभ 'stabilire, firmare.' All the MSS., however, read the word with the cerebral, not the dental sibilant, and there is no doubt of their accuracy. The rule of Panini by which a radical ष is changed in inflexion to स, धात्वादेः षः सः not applying to this word, which is derived from स्तम्भु cl. 5 and 9. This root is the subject of a special rule, by which it is provided that after a preposition containing the vowel इ or उ the radical स shall be changed to ष. Of course after ष, त is changed to ट, making उपष्टम्भ. The original rule is Panini, 8. 3. 67. स्तम्भेः। स्तम्भु। इत्येतस्य धातोरवयवस्यस्॥ इत्येतस्योपसर्गस्यादिण उत्तरस्य मूर्द्धन्य आदेशः स्यात्। अभिष्टभ्नोति परिष्टभ्नाति; to which we may add उपष्टभ्नाति, whence उपष्टम्भक

P. 16. l. 14. आर्य्योद्वयेन has been substituted for the आदावद्वयेन of the MSS., which is evidently incorrect.

P. 16. l. 15. For मयमुपगम्यते read मभ्युपगम्यते

P. 16. v. 17. H. reads संहत for संघात. The sense is the same.

P. 16. l. 18. For माक्ष read मोक्ष

P. 17. l. 7. For अस्यात्मा read अस्त्यात्मा

P. 17. v. 18. For जनन—जन्म B. D. Either word is correct.

P. 19. v. 20. भवत्युदासीन B. D. omitting इति. The sense is unaffected, and the metre is preserved by reading the final syllable long.

P. 19. l. 8. The third word should be उदासीनो

P. 19. l. 19. For वचसो विश्वस्त read वचसोर्विश्वस्त

P. 20. l. 9. For अलिंगस्य read अलिंगस्याः

P. 21. l. 1. For यमोक्तं read यथोक्तं

P. 22. v. 24. The second line is read ऐन्द्रिय एकादशकस्तन्मात्रः पञ्चकश्चैव B. and एकादशकश्चगणस्तन्मात्रः पंचलक्षणोपेतः D. The sense is much the same, but the last is wrong as to metre. It is evident also from the comment that follows that it is a mistake, and that the final words should be पंचकश्चैव—पंचलक्षणोपेत being the explanation of पंचक

P. 23. v. 26. पायूपस्थानि B. पायूपस्थाः E. In the first line, रसनत्व गाख्यानि is the reading of B. C. E. F. but D. confirms the text, not only by the same terms, रसनस्पर्शनकानि, but by explaining the term स्पर्शनक

P. 24. v. 27. बाह्यभेदाश्च A. E. F. बाह्यभेदाच्च B.C.D. The difference involves a difference of interpretation, as noticed in the Comment (p. 99). The explanation of the *Bháshya*, D, is so clearly incompatible with the reading बाह्यभेदात् that in the first instance I corrected it to बाह्यभेदाः as in the same page, l. 15, 18, which should be read, agreeably to the MSS., बाह्यभेदाच्च

P. 24. l. 23. For तत् कृत read तत् कृता, and for चक्षु स read चक्षुः स

P. 25. v. 28. रूपादिषु B.D. विहार C.D. The variations are immaterial.

P. 25. l. 12. For परिणतो मलोत्सर्गः read परिणतमलोत्सर्गः

P. 26. l. 6, 7. For वृत्तिन्द्रियस्य read वृत्तिरिन्द्रियस्य

P. 26. l. 3, &c. स्यन्दनं ought perhaps to be स्पन्दनं. See Translation, p. 105.

P. 26. l. 22. After तत्रोपरूढां some such word as वह्निं should be inserted, although it is not in the MS.: it occurs in the passage when repeated in p. ३६

P. 27. l. 8. For ३२ read ३१

P. 29. l. 3 and 15. For गृह्णन्ति—गृह्णाति read गृह्णन्ति—गृह्णाति

P. 29. l. 4. For प्रकाशायन्ति read प्रकाशयन्ति

P. 30. l. 11. For प्राप्य इयं read प्राप्यमियं

P. 30. l. 14. अवापात्, which is the reading of the copy, should probably be अवायात् 'after departure' or 'death.'

P. 30. l. 21. For प्रतजो read प्रजो

P. 31. l. 6. भ्रष्टस्य has been conjecturally supplied, the writing of the copy being very indistinct.

P. 31. l. 16. The MS. has पुष्ट्युदर which has no meaning, and has been therefore conjecturally changed to पृष्ठोदर

P. 31. l. 20. Instead of शरीरं कर्म्मवशात् it is possible that the phrase should be शरीरमधर्म्मवशात् 'from the influence of iniquity.'

P. 33. l. 11. A passage has been here omitted: it should run, गुणपुरुषान्तरोपलब्धिलक्षणश्च। शब्दाद्युपलब्धिर्ब्रह्मादिषु लोकेषु गन्धादिभोगावाप्तिः। गुणपुरुषान्तरोपलब्धिर्मोक्ष इति. It has been given in the Translation, p. 137.

P. 33. l. 18. For विदुषक read विदूषक

P. 36. v. 47. शक्तेश्च D. which is allowable.

P. 37. l. 4. तन्मात्राशासु was read in the MSS. तन्मात्राद्यासु which was evidently an error.

P. 37. l. 18. For तत्रैकादश read तत्रैकादश

P. 38. l. 1. The MS. has विपर्य्ययाच्छक्तितुष्टिनामेव which the sense shews to be erroneous.

P. 38. l. 11. For इत्येष read इत्येषा

P. 38. v. 50. आध्यात्मिकयश्चतस्र E. The difference is unimportant. F. has भागाख्या which is incorrect; विषयोपरमाश्च D; and D. F. read अभिहिता for अभिमता

P. 39. l. 9. After प्राप्य insert मोक्षं याति

P. 40. l. 9. For आश्रयो read आश्रयौ

P. 40. v. 53. The reading of this verse is materially varied in D, although the sense is substantially the same:

अष्टविकल्पं दैवं तैर्य्यग्योनं पंचधा भवति
मानुष्यं त्वेकविधं समासतोऽयं त्रिधा सर्गः ।

Professor Lassen has तैर्य्यग्योन्य, which is not warranted by any MS. and although perhaps a defensible, is an unusual form of the derivative. G. has तैर्य्यग्यौन

P. 42. v. 56. प्रकृतिकृतौ D; and the variation is advisedly, as appears by the comment.

P. 43. v. 59. आत्मानं प्रकाश्य—प्रविश्य D. But the term of our text is used in the following comment.

P. 43. v. 60. For चरति—कुरुते D.

P. 44. v. 61. प्रकृतिः सुकुमारतरं C; which is manifestly wrong.

P. 44. l. 6. Although suspecting some error in this citation, I had no means of correcting it. Before printing the translation, however, I met with the passage correctly given in the commentary of Madhusúdana Gupta upon the *Bhagavad Gita*, and have rendered it accordingly in p. 172. It should be, अज्ञो जन्तुरनीशोऽयमात्मनः सुखदुःखयोः

P. 44. v. 62. तस्मान्नबध्यतेऽद्धा E; and अद्धा is explained स्फुटावधारणयोः The particle is not inserted in any other copy. C. is singular in the order of the words, and transposing मुच्यते and बध्यते

P. 45. l. 5. Instead of अभिष्वज्यते read अभिव्यज्यते

P. 46. v. 66. A. B. E. F. G. agree in reading उपरमत्यन्या, although, as Professor Lassen justly objects, "metro refragatur." D. gives the correcter reading उपरतैका, explaining it उपरता निवृत्ता एका एकैव प्रकृतिः

VARIATIONS AND CORRECTIONS.

This copy also varies in the beginning of the hemistich: रंगस्य इत्युपेक्षक एको द्दष्टाहमित्युपरतैका

P. 47. l. 4. For पुरुस्य read पुरुषस्य

Other variations than those specified above may no doubt be discovered in different manuscripts, and even in those which have been consulted; but they are in general palpable blunders of transcription, unworthy of the honour of being perpetuated in print.